THE REMARKABLE KINSHIP OF
MARJORIE KINNAN RAWLINGS AND ELLEN GLASGOW

UNIVERSITY PRESS OF FLORIDA

Florida A&M University, Tallahassee
Florida Atlantic University, Boca Raton
Florida Gulf Coast University, Ft. Myers
Florida International University, Miami
Florida State University, Tallahassee
New College of Florida, Sarasota
University of Central Florida, Orlando
University of Florida, Gainesville
University of North Florida, Jacksonville
University of South Florida, Tampa
University of West Florida, Pensacola

The Remarkable Kinship of
Marjorie Kinnan Rawlings
and
Ellen Glasgow

ASHLEY ANDREWS LEAR

University Press of Florida
Gainesville · Tallahassee · Tampa · Boca Raton
Pensacola · Orlando · Miami · Jacksonville · Ft. Myers · Sarasota

Images and quotes from the Marjorie Kinnan Rawlings Papers courtesy of Marjorie Kinnin Rawlings, Special and Area Studies Collections, George A. Smathers Libraries, University of Florida, Gainesville, Florida. | "The Little Things" by James Stephens courtesy of the Society of Authors as the Literary Representative of the Estate of James Stephens. | "Having left Cities Behind Me" by Marjorie Kinnan Rawling, copyright © by Marjorie Kinnan Rawlings, copyright renewed © 1963 by Norton Baskin. First appeared in Scribner's Magazine. Used by permission of Brandt & Hochman Literary Agents, Inc. Any copying or distribution of this text is expressly forbidden.
All rights reserved.

Copyright 2018 by Ashley Andrews Lear
All rights reserved
Printed in the United States of America on acid-free paper

This book may be available in an electronic edition.

23 22 21 20 19 18   6 5 4 3 2 1

Library of Congress Cataloging-in-Publication Data
Names: Lear, Ashley Andrews, author.
Title: The remarkable kinship of Marjorie Kinnan Rawlings and Ellen Glasgow / Ashley Andrews Lear.
Description: Gainesville : University Press of Florida, 2018. | Includes bibliographical references and index.
Identifiers: LCCN 2017049135 | ISBN 9780813056968 (cloth : alk. paper)
Subjects: LCSH: Rawlings, Marjorie Kinnan, 1896–1953—Biography. | Glasgow, Ellen Anderson Gholson, 1873–1945—Biography. | American literature—Women authors—Biography.
Classification: LCC PS3535.A845 .Z73 2018 | DDC 813/.52 [B] —dc23
LC record available at https://lccn.loc.gov/2017049135

The University Press of Florida is the scholarly publishing agency for the State University System of Florida, comprising Florida A&M University, Florida Atlantic University, Florida Gulf Coast University, Florida International University, Florida State University, New College of Florida, University of Central Florida, University of Florida, University of North Florida, University of South Florida, and University of West Florida.

University Press of Florida
15 Northwest 15th Street
Gainesville, FL 32611-2079
http://upress.ufl.edu

For Scott and Alice

Contents

List of Figures *ix*

Acknowledgments *xi*

Abbreviations *xiii*

Introduction: Friendship and Sympathy *1*

1. A Letter and a Dream *11*

2. A Certain Measure of Achievement *44*

3. Blood of My Blood *70*

4. Women Who Will—Do *106*

5. In Search of Truth, Not Sensation *132*

6. The Sheltered Life *166*

7. "A Woman of To-Morrow" *197*

Afterword: "Beyond Defeat" *226*

Notes *231*

Works Cited *241*

Index *245*

Figures

Figures follow page 100.

1. Ellen Glasgow's house
2. Ellen Glasgow
3. Col. Henry W. Anderson
4. Cross Creek, 1939
5. Marjorie Kinnan Rawlings at her typewriter
6. Norton Baskin

Acknowledgments

I have been fortunate to have had the support of many people throughout the completion of this manuscript. I would like to thank the following individuals and organizations, without whom this project would not have been possible.

Much of the work for this book was completed using materials from archives. The majority came from the University of Florida's George A. Smathers Libraries, which houses the Marjorie Kinnan Rawlings Papers. Those papers include all the material collected by Rawlings on Ellen Glasgow. I would especially like to thank Flo Turcotte, whose extensive knowledge of Marjorie Kinnan Rawlings and willingness to assist me on my many trips to Gainesville were invaluable. The staff at the University of Virginia's Albert and Shirley Small Special Collections Library also gave tremendous assistance during my visit, and in the collection of digital materials leading up to that visit. The Virginia Historical Society, especially Heather Beattie and Jamison Davis, were instrumental in locating photographs of Henry Anderson and Queen Marie of Romania, one of which was used in this manuscript. And, last but not least, Robin Starr with the Richmond Society for the Prevention of Cruelty to Animals, Ellen Glasgow's most beloved organization, to which she left the bulk of her estate, graciously permitted the use of images of Glasgow in this manuscript. I look forward to visiting that society on future trips to Richmond.

My colleagues at Embry-Riddle Aeronautical University have also been tremendously supportive of my endeavor. My department chair, Donna Barbie, was able to secure course releases for me as I completed the manuscript. Lynnette Porter, my mentor and friend, aided me in the preparation of the prospectus and structure of the project. The university itself has generously funded my participation in several conferences and archival trips that helped make this manuscript come together.

Finally, I would like to dedicate this book to my husband, Scott Lear, and to my daughter, Alice. Their constant love and encouragement make my work much more enjoyable.

Abbreviations

BB   *Blood of My Blood* (Rawlings)

CC   *Cross Creek* (Rawlings)

CM   *A Certain Measure: An Interpretation of Prose Fiction* (Glasgow)

EGWT   *Ellen Glasgow and a Woman's Traditions* (Matthews)

MKRP   Marjorie Kinnan Rawlings Papers, Special and Area Studies Collections, George A. Smathers Libraries, University of Florida

MM   *Max and Marjorie: The Correspondence between Maxwell E. Perkins and Marjorie Kinnan Rawlings* (Tarr, ed.)

PC   *Perfect Companionship: Ellen Glasgow's Selected Correspondence with Women* (Matthews, ed.)

PEG   Papers of Ellen Glasgow, Accession #5060, Special Collections, University of Virginia Library

PM   *The Private Marjorie: The Love Letters of Marjorie Kinnan Rawlings to Norton Baskin* (Tarr, ed.)

TD   *The Descendant* (Glasgow)

TS   *The Sojourner* (Rawlings)

WW   *The Woman Within* (Glasgow)

Introduction

Friendship and Sympathy

FROM THE COMFORT OF HER STUDY at One West Main in Richmond, Virginia, Ellen Glasgow composed the first of many letters regarding the up-and-coming author Marjorie Kinnan Rawlings. The year was 1933. The letter, which does not mince words, explained how Glasgow found herself struggling to assist her friend Irita Van Doren, editor of the *New York Herald Tribune Book Review*, with a list of great forthcoming works in American literature. Lumping *South Moon Under* together with Bromfield's *The Farm* and Carroll's *As the Earth Turns*, Glasgow lamented that she had already passed the stage of writing about peasants and could no longer become excited by books that she felt were being written to capitalize on the popularity of that theme (*PC* 139). At the time, Rawlings and Glasgow could not have been farther divided in terms of their profession or personalities. Glasgow was nearing the end of a prolific career, having published all but the last two of her 19 novels, not to mention her various reviews and editorials, short fiction, and poetry.[1] Rawlings, on the other hand, was just beginning to feel successful as a writer, with *South Moon Under* as her first published novel. The two authors seem to have been cut from different cloth. Glasgow, a fashion-forward urban dweller of the New South, lived in the large downtown Richmond home she had inherited from her father, though she spent some time in a New York apartment, vacationed in Maine, and traveled throughout Europe, and once to Egypt. She experienced financial difficulties during the Depression, but was never destitute. She certainly never experienced the harder living to which Rawlings subjected herself by moving to a remote area of central Florida and attempting to manage her own small orange

· 1

grove, constructing a Cracker-style home that eventually supported indoor plumbing. A cursory glance at these women's experiences would not predict that their paths would ever cross, much less that they would become kindred spirits.

All the same, Rawlings explains perfectly what drew her to Glasgow after she had already made an impression on the older writer through her 1938 publication of *The Yearling*. In a letter to Glasgow following Glasgow's praise of *The Yearling* and invitation to visit her in Richmond, Rawlings wrote,

> Superficially, our aims and our material would seem so divergent that one could not conceive of common ground. Yet after reading your Prefaces and your Inscription for the delightful cameo that comes to me with your signature and that of Mr. Cabell, it seems to me possible that our object has been more or less identical: to present human beings, as you know one type and I another, struggling against whatever is inimical within themselves or in their background. The enemy may be a complicated social fabric, or the "ironic perversity" within, or the more explicit natural forces. I happen to be more concerned with man in relation to a natural background, than with man in relation to man against a sophisticated background. And there is much of cowardice in my choice of subject matter.[2]

Rawlings was referencing, in particular, Glasgow's repeated description in her prefaces of the time between novels when she would wait for the springs of her subconscious, what Rawlings refers to as "wells," to fill back up with the creative energy required for a new story to emerge. While both women struggled to keep away from their writing for any substantial period of time, they each toiled over manuscripts with no small measure of frustration, revising and rewriting, and scrapping large sections until their vision was as close to perfect as they felt they could make it.

The catalyst for the convergence of these two writers' lives was the publication of *The Yearling*. Glasgow, who had already stolidly fought to inhabit the more erudite circles of American fiction, made her first overtures of friendship to the younger writer after reading this remarkable book. Unintentionally, Rawlings had written a novel that was most certain to tug on the heartstrings of the older Glasgow by centering her narrative of the disillusionment of Jody Baxter on the boy's relationship with his pet deer, Flag. It is no great secret that Glasgow's deep passion for animals led her not only to establish the Richmond SPCA, but also to bequeath rights to her publications and a large portion of her estate to that establishment when she died. Moreover, Glasgow believed that *The Yearling* showed true genius in its compelling story of the sacrifice in the choice that Jody must make between his own survival and that of Flag, a pet as dear to him as a family member. Glasgow's literature consistently describes the disillusionment of characters coming to terms with impossible situations, but her novels focus on the challenges of characters' relationships with one another and their communities, not on survival. The critics agreed with Glasgow's praise, honoring *The Yearling* with a Pulitzer in 1939, two years before Glasgow was able to earn the same prize with *In This Our Life*, the last of her nineteen books, save for her posthumous autobiography, *The Woman Within*, and the posthumously published sequel to *In This Our Life*, titled *Beyond Defeat*.

Glasgow personally congratulated Rawlings on her success with *The Yearling*, and encouraged her to visit whenever she found herself traveling near or through Richmond. Prior to the receipt of this letter, Rawlings had only once mentioned Glasgow in her correspondences, telling Max Perkins that Glasgow was the one writer who, she had heard, did not struggle with writing the way most writers did—a sentiment she expressed before reading Glasgow's prefaces. She followed this supposition with, "but I was never one of her admirers and have not read her for a long time" (*MM* 235). In spite of this lackluster review, Rawlings was clearly flattered by the attentions of the renowned author, and visited her in 1941, two years after receiving Glasgow's invitation. Her appreciation for Glasgow's writing may be seen in various pontifications, both publicly in her addresses to organizations like the National Council of Teachers of English, and privately in her personal correspondences with family members.[3] The most notable of these were letters Rawlings wrote to her husband, Norton Baskin, while she was working on her biography of Glasgow.

While no one can tell for certain what occurred during that first visit, it clearly had a significant impact on Rawlings, who wrote to Glasgow shortly after the visit to describe a vivid dream in which she found herself taking care of Glasgow's physical needs while Glasgow imparted her advice and wisdom to the younger writer. In the dream, Rawlings helped Glasgow by convincing her to stop cutting ice into geometric patterns in front of a mansion, taking her inside to warm her hands, and offering her a drink, as Glasgow recommended a valence to go with the drapes in the room. Glasgow's response to the dream described in Rawlings's letter was equally personal in nature, as she claimed that Rawlings held a chosen place in her life, described her feelings of emptiness after finishing *In This Our Life*, and then emphatically encouraged Rawlings to complete *Cross Creek*, a book that Glasgow later reviewed favorably. The relationship between the two women continued through a correspondence that reveals their shared values for conservationism and animal rights, similar struggles to complete manuscripts, and bouts with health-related issues. They continued writing to one another until Glasgow's death in 1945. In fact, Glasgow's last letter to Rawlings was sent days before she passed away. In that final letter, she thanked Rawlings for a delivery of mangoes, encouraged her to complete *The Sojourner*, and lamented that she was not well enough to visit Rawlings in St. Augustine, Florida.

The respect and admiration Glasgow and Rawlings had for one another are revealed time and again in their correspondence with both one another and their respective friends and acquaintances. These poignant letters inspired Rosemary M. Magee's *Friendship and Sympathy: Communities of Southern Women Writers*, an anthology of essays, book reviews, and accolades composed by women writers in the South, and, along with other correspondence shared between Glasgow and the women in her life, *Perfect Companionship: Ellen Glasgow's Selected Correspondence with Women* by Pamela Matthews. The very title of Magee's collection is taken from one of Glasgow's letters to Rawlings, in which she thanks her for a letter received that left her with "a thrilling sense of friendship and sympathy." In explaining why such communities have historical significance for women, Magee writes that women often had little to no access to the types of university, social, or private clubs that educated men frequented, and relied heavily upon makeshift communities of fellow writers with whom they could correspond and commiserate about their careers. Even though Glasgow earned a great deal of respect from literary peers during her lifetime, she was excluded from a university education because of her gender, and she would not have been permitted in many of the all-male intellectual clubs and gatherings of Richmond or New York.

Rawlings had more direct exposure to the public literary world through her education at the University of Wisconsin in Madison and her various positions as a journalist, but, by and large, her paid articles focused on topics such as homemaking or important women in the community. Magee pointed out that even relationships like the one Glasgow had with Allen Tate had to bow to women's exclusion from literary societies. The Vanderbilt Fugitives, for example, "referred to one another as 'Brother'" and permitted no women attendees when they met as a group in Greenwich Village (Magee xix). Glasgow may have shared a lifelong friendship with James Branch Cabell, but she was often annoyed by his prejudicial views of women in general and of her as a woman writer. In the lengthy dream described by Rawlings early in her friendship with Glasgow, she depicts Cabell as interrupting the two of them, and then adds in parentheses, "(As of course he would!)" (*PC* 210).

Glasgow and Rawlings also shared personal experiences as women, such as their decisions not to have children and their difficulties with romantic relationships. These experiences beg a sympathetic listener, yet their struggles were unique to their lives as professional novelists who happened to be women, making it difficult to find peers who could understand what they were going through. Glasgow's desire for such connections came across in her first letter to Rawlings and in a series of other letters to women writers with whom she shared a friendship during the latter part of her life.

Glasgow's extension of friendship to Rawlings illustrates the compassion and admiration that women writers of their era often felt for one another, in a sense developing relationships for which the tag of "friendship" is plainly inadequate. In her introduction to the collection of Glasgow's correspondence with women, *Perfect Companionship*, Pamela Matthews describes what she calls "Glasgow's lifelong preference for and dependence on the company of women" (xiii). Glasgow did attempt and establish a great deal of correspondence with other women writers, especially later in her career when she sought solace from companions with whom she could share her history. Matthews locates these desires for friendship "in a time of transition between the nineteenth century's acceptance (even admiration) of 'romantic friendships' between women and the twentieth century's more complicated awareness that such friendships might be sexual" (*PC* xiii). She points to examples of Glasgow's awareness of this shift, but it is important to note that Glasgow, as her writing suggests, maintained a reverence for certain Victorian ideals of the old South. Her novels often depict a struggle between the desire to preserve a tradition and the necessary disruption to tradition that must occur for social justice and personal liberties to thrive. Sadly, Matthews had to contend with the destruction of much of Glasgow's correspondence by friends and relatives because of those same Victorian ideals. Her survivors felt an imperative to preserve Glasgow's modesty and decorum before and after her death by not allowing her more emotional letters to be read by strangers.

In the span of a generation, this concept of preserving modesty by destroying letters had all but disappeared. No one considered destroying any of Rawlings's correspondence, even though she occasionally asked for confidences to be kept. Rawlings's letters are highly informal, at times even lewd. In her letters to Perkins, she went so far as to admit directly to breaking various laws, from moonshining to hunting in restricted areas. One letter to F. Scott Fitzgerald detailed her amusement when a telegraph operator asked her whether "menopause" were all one word (Bigelow and Monti 137). Not only were her letters more informal than Glasgow's, but they also indicated a stronger emotional connection with the men in her life. Rawlings expressed a vulnerability and intimacy in her correspondence with both Norton Baskin, her second husband, and Max Perkins, her editor. These connections meant that for Rawlings, Glasgow signified something more than simply a woman with whom she could share an emotional and professional connection; Rawlings already had those kinds of connections. Instead, Glasgow was a kind of literary matriarch to an up-and-coming writer whose reputation was just beginning to exceed her own expectations. Glasgow had broken through many barriers to excel as a writer, from her gender to her lack of formal education to her Southern heritage. Because of Glasgow and other female literary pioneers, writers like Rawlings were able to succeed based on the merits of their writing alone, without having to prove themselves otherwise worthy of consideration first.

In the time between Glasgow's and Rawlings's first respective published works, there was a massive shift in public acceptance of women writers. This gap is easily measured by their increased acceptance by major publishing houses. To imagine the difference between the careers of Ellen Glasgow and Marjorie Kinnan Rawlings, one need not look any farther than their disparate career trajectories, beginning with the way Ellen Glasgow described her harrowing first attempt to meet with a literary advisor about her first novel. After finding the manuscript unopened on his desk, Glasgow was lewdly propositioned and sexually assaulted. Her response was to send a messenger for the manuscript, burn it, and resolve never to write again. Fortunately for the literary world, her resolve weakened, and she began work within the year on a second novel, *The Descendant*. This work proved equally challenging to publish. Glasgow finally resorted to using her own connections, beginning with Dr. Holmes, a professor of economics from the University of Virginia, to try to gain entry to the publishing world. Eventually, she obtained a letter of introduction from a friend, Louise Collier Willcox, to Willcox's brother at Macmillan's. These advantages were still not sufficient to get Glasgow's manuscript published, however, and one representative even chided her, after not even having read the work, to stop writing and go back to the South and have some babies. When Glasgow was finally paired with a representative from a textbook company with which Dr. Holmes was familiar, her manuscript received its first full read-through. Mr. Patton, the reader, proclaimed that it would be published even if he had to build his own publishing house to do it. Patton clearly appreciated Glasgow's work, but he was also aware of the ways in which she would be received as a woman writing a book as controversial as *The Descendant*, which deals with the rise and fall of a young socialist after he moves from Virginia to New York. Like so much women's literature of the time, the book ended up being published anonymously, and it was re-released with her name included only after it received enough favorable reviews to be considered on its own merits. The struggles faced by Glasgow to gain entry to the literary world were momentous. However, her acceptance by the critical reviewers of that first novel was universal. After clearing that first massive hurdle, she never again struggled with publication.

Thanks, in part, to pioneers like Glasgow, Marjorie Kinnan Rawlings entered a different literary culture when she began writing a generation later. She published articles in the local newspaper while still a high school student, was able to attend university, at Wisconsin (a feat Glasgow could not have achieved because, when she came of age, the institution she wished to attend, the University of Virginia, did not permit women), and then made a career for herself as a journalist before switching to fiction with the publication of her first short stories on the Florida Cracker community. The fact that Rawlings was able to subsist through writing before she could publish her fictional works on Florida marks a dramatic turn in the literary culture of America compared to the late 19th century, when Glasgow's career began. While Glasgow wrote in private and hid her work from her family to keep from being mocked, Rawlings was known to all around her as a writer. According to her pseudo-autobiographical work, *Blood of My Blood*, Rawlings's mother was especially happy to have finally identified a talent in her daughter after it became clear that Rawlings could neither sing nor dance. In contrast to Glasgow's experiences, Rawlings's challenges were much more merit-based. She had to write literature of sufficient quality to be published, and she struggled to find her niche until she finally moved to Florida and began successfully sketching the lives of the Cracker community for *Scribner's Magazine*. Whereas Glasgow had to find an audience for her literature, Rawlings merely had to find the right kind of literature for her audience. The readers with whom she connected had a fascination with regional writing about locations that seemed exotic and people who inhabited the fringes of the civilized world. Rawlings's greatest challenge was accurately representing Florida and its people to an audience that was, at times, scintillated more by the spectacle of Cracker culture than by the universality of the human experiences described in her stories. She occasionally experienced guilt over setting up the people of Florida to be further stereotyped, despite her best intentions.

Rawlings's respect for Glasgow as a writer and friend had grown strong enough for her to consider seriously and eventually accept a proposition from one of Glasgow's literary executors that she write a biography of

Glasgow after Glasgow's death. From their humble beginnings to their literary successes, Rawlings and Glasgow shared similar experiences relating to family members, romantic interests, and professional connections. These connections became the basis for their extraordinary friendship, and made Rawlings want to learn more details about her friend after Glasgow's death. Each struggled to balance her writing life with her desire for personal fulfillment outside her profession, and each faced gendered discrimination that seemed to be dissipating from the time of Glasgow's first publication to that of Rawlings's. While Rawlings's initial work in journalism exclusively focused on women's issues in Louisville and New York, her approach was always to highlight the increasingly diverse personal and professional opportunities available to women in a shifting cultural landscape. They shared a unique affinity for the issues of conservation, animal rights, and social justice. Both writers seemed torn between the progressive modern world, which permitted them the opportunity to make a living from their writing, and the traditional rural lifestyle, which seemed liberated from certain artificial conceits of modern society. Their connections and diversions can tell us much about the evolution of women's literature in America, and about the importance of literary communities among women.

The focus of this book is the intersections between Rawlings's and Glasgow's lives and careers through their correspondence and writing, specifically those materials collected by Rawlings during her attempted Glasgow biography. Sadly, Rawlings passed away before she could begin the manuscript, leaving only collected materials and detailed notes from interviews and reviews. These crafted, preserved moments shed light on what Glasgow and Rawlings meant to each other. The materials and interviews collected by Rawlings toward her biography of Glasgow are housed at the University of Florida's George A. Smathers Libraries in the Special and Area Studies archive, including certain materials that are duplicated from Glasgow's fonds, which are housed at the University of Virginia's Albert and Shirley Small Special Collections. While Rawlings's biography of Glasgow was never written, the materials she gathered and the notes she included with those documents shed light on the values shared by the two authors, and they directed my own study of their relationship. When possible, I have included references to those materials in other publications that may be more accessible to the reader. I have organized the materials from those archives to highlight the areas that Rawlings appeared to find most intriguing in her research, supplementing the narrative with explanations of Rawlings's own experiences that correspond with her notes on Glasgow.

On the surface, the connections between the former Southern debutante, Ellen Glasgow, and the raucous pioneer of the Florida scrub, Marjorie Kinnan Rawlings, may seem a bit stretched. After all, they only exchanged a handful of letters, and met only near the ends of their lives. However, they felt for one another a remarkable kinship that resulted in Rawlings spending her last year researching the life of Ellen Glasgow with the intent of writing a biography that would sustain her legacy. Glasgow returned the sentiment by reprinting in its entirety the letter Rawlings sent her at the beginning of their friendship in the epilogue to her posthumously published autobiography, *The Woman Within*, having realized at the end of her life the significance of faithful friends who could understand, love, and support her through her most trying times. This book will attempt to understand what drew these two remarkable women to each other, and what experiences bound them together in friendship. While theirs was not the only relationship of its kind, it was one of the great literary friendships of the South, and should be studied for the impact that such friendships may have on the lives and experiences of women writers.

1

A Letter and a Dream

*I cannot tell you how much your letter meant to me—
and still means. It came last night after a trying day, and
it brought a thrilling sense of friendship and sympathy.*

Ellen Glasgow to Marjorie Kinnan Rawlings (1941)

PERHAPS THE MOST POWERFUL SENTIMENT expressed in the countless note cards created by Rawlings while working on her biography of Glasgow is one on which she has handwritten across the top of the card, "If I didn't think her work was going to live, I wouldn't be wasting my time on a biography."[1] A dream that Rawlings shared with Glasgow, their correspondence, and later the countless interviews, collected letters and articles, and notes that Rawlings compiled when trying to reconstruct the life of Ellen Glasgow to her own satisfaction illustrate a bond between the two women that transcended any ordinary definition of friendship. In Glasgow, Rawlings saw pieces of herself and experiences she had overcome, struggles with loved ones, insecurities about her writing, and a desire to have herself and her work understood more completely by her audience. While Glasgow and Rawlings were by no means identical in their approaches to life or writing, they shared a common sympathy with one another, a feeling of being displaced in an overly constructed, materialistic world that they both, somewhat guiltily, at times, desired, and a need to locate the authentic in the midst of so many performances by the literary community and the individuals in their lives. Through their shared letters and dreams, they found in one another commiseration and hope.

The relationship between Glasgow and Rawlings occurred, for the most part, through written communication, and only a handful of letters was exchanged.[2] Their dialogue began with Glasgow's praise of *The Yearling* and ended in November of 1945, four days prior to Glasgow's death at her home in Richmond after a lengthy illness. While the two women distinguished themselves as regional writers in the American South, Glasgow lived in downtown Richmond, Virginia, for most of her life, with the exception of several years spent in New York. Rawlings grew up in Washington, D.C., attended the University of Wisconsin in Madison, and lived in New York City, Rochester, and Louisville. After receiving a small inheritance from her mother, Rawlings purchased an orange grove in Cross Creek, Florida, where she developed her career as a novelist, eventually dividing her time among the grove, her second husband Norton Baskin's St. Augustine hotel, her Crescent Beach house, and a property in Van Hornesville, New York. By the time they became correspondents, Glasgow was too ill to travel, and never made it to Florida, so their brief in-person interactions were at Glasgow's home in Richmond. The fact that the two women writers established their friendship predominantly through letters and their study of one another's work adds fitting emphasis to the role that writing played in each of their lives, both as their main livelihoods and as their principal source of self-identification. Their initial exchanges of correspondence have been noted in several publications on each writer's life, and were initially published the year after Glasgow died as "An Exchange of Letters" in *The Atlanta Journal* (1946).[3] The overarching theme through all of the correspondence is that of an emerging author, Marjorie Kinnan Rawlings, paying homage to her predecessor, Ellen Glasgow. Simultaneously, the senior writer attempted to give advice, comfort, and encouragement to Rawlings.

The letter that speaks most profoundly to the nature of their friendship—and what it meant for each woman to have found another writer struggling through the same mire of deadlines, frustrations over perfecting their craft, and challenging relationships with friends and family members who could not understand the writing life as they did—was penned by Marjorie Kinnan Rawlings on July 19, 1941, a few months after their initial face-to-face meeting in Richmond. She wrote the letter from her Crescent Beach house, to which she often escaped to complete work when her Cross Creek home became filled with distractions from neighbors and tourists:

My very dear Ellen Glasgow:

I had such a vivid dream about you last night, that I must write you—which I have been meaning to do ever since our delightful brief visit together. The reality of a dream can never be conveyed to another, but you came to live with me. I was away when you came, and on my return, to one of those strange mansions that are part of the substance of dreams, you were outside in the bitter cold, cutting away ice from the roadway and piling it in geometric pattern. I was alarmed, remembering your heart trouble, and led you inside the mansion and brought you a cup of hot coffee. You had on blue silk gloves, and I laid my hand over yours, and was amazed, for my own hand is small, to have yours fit inside mine, much smaller. You chose your room and suggested draperies to supplement a valance. The valance was red chintz and you showed me a sample of a heavy red brocade of the same shade. I told you that from now on I should take care of you, and you must not do strenuous things, such as cutting the ice in the roadway. James Cabell came into the room and asked what the two of us were up to. (As of course he would!)

My memory of my time with you is quite as vivid as the night's dream. I have thought of you oftener than I can tell you. So often a personality is detached from writings, and the two in fact seem to have nothing to do with each other. You as a person have the vitality, the wit and the irony of your work, but I was not prepared to find you so warm and so beautiful, in spite of the devotion of your friends, which would indicate those things in you.

I am at my cottage on the ocean, and have been working very hard on my book, so hard that I put myself in the hospital for a week. It wouldn't seem necessary to tie oneself into knots to get out a few ideas, but while I *feel* at the drop of a hat, thinking is terribly hard work for me! The first draft of the book is nearly done. Much of it is very bad indeed, and after Max Perkins has seen it and given me, I hope, some of his marvelous suggestions, I shall go at it again.

I am wondering if you went to Maine, and if there is any chance of your visiting Florida this winter. I do hope you are strong again and that I shall see you here.

With much affection, Marjorie (PC 210)

To those familiar with the careers of these writers, this initial letter reveals much about the nature of their friendship and the reasons why the two women bonded quickly. It also serves as the cornerstone for the work that Rawlings would later complete toward her biography of Glasgow.

From the beginning of the letter, Rawlings intuits with her dream the mysticism that Glasgow frequently felt drew her to people and situations. The "strange mansion" and "substance of dreams" that make up the setting for the dream bring to mind so much of Glasgow's own correspondence with friends and family members over the years. She once wrote to a friend, "Don't think me too great a mystic and yet when one meets constantly with wonderful ways of the spirit what else can one be but a believer in and a lover of the unseen" (PC 24). Frequently, Glasgow wrote of spiritual connections between people, and she was a student of Eastern religious philosophies, especially the *Bhagavad Gita*. The mysticism that she employed was a sign of both her emergence from a Victorian period in which women frequently included mysticism in their detailed letters and of the import that she placed on her relationships with women, which nearly always superseded any relationships with men, romantic or otherwise. Pamela Matthews notes that the "spirituality attached to women and to the connections among them can be contextualized historically . . . with particular significance in nineteenth-century female relationships" (Scura 115). Matthews goes on to argue *against* an "unquestionable" view of Glasgow as "heterosexual in the plots of both her personal and fictional lives," and to point out that Glasgow "channeled more of her emotional energy into her relationships with other women than into her much-discussed search for an ideal male mate, a pattern critics have identified in other women writers' lives" (Scura 119). Indeed, critics, even Rawlings, spend more time conjecturing about Glasgow's potential love interests than they do in analyzing the importance of her friendships with other women. Those friendships were usually marked by mysticism, a nod to a spirituality not bound by the patriarchal religious modalities of the day, but instead awash with emotional and even romantic feelings of interconnectedness. Both the context of the letter describing Rawlings's dream and the setting within the dream acknowledge the great respect she knew Glasgow had for this kind of mysticism, a philosophy that Rawlings did not espouse as explicitly in her own writings, though there are elements of mysticism in her children's book *The Secret River*, and she frequently speaks of a cosmic consciousness when describing her novels.

After detailing the setting of the dream, Rawlings next describes Glasgow's work before she approaches her. Glasgow is seen "cutting away ice from the roadway" and "piling it in geometric pattern" (*PC* 210). The two parts to the labor described here bear the semblance of physical exertion that the act of writing represents for both women as they toil over manuscripts. To write is to "cut away" and "arrange in patterns" those semantic building blocks required by a novelist. The work, while intellectual, weighed on both women's constitutions, and required a sort of committed bodily immersion in the very act of writing. Rawlings herself admitted to undergoing hospitalization after completing *Cross Creek* due to the severely taxing nature of finishing that manuscript (Silverthorne 197). Peggy Prenshaw conjectured that the "icy blockage" of Rawlings's dream could also have "symbolized a pattern of literary criticism that she saw as dismissive not only of Glasgow's novels set in the South but of Rawlings's own Florida stories, classifying them as 'regional literature' and thus as less than 'serious' writing" (Prenshaw 222). Glasgow had a history of being strongly affected by critical writings about her work, and Rawlings was told on multiple occasions to offer Glasgow flattery and praise of her work to help her friend recover from medical conditions and her own dispiritedness.

In the dream, the younger and physically stronger Rawlings decided to lead Glasgow back into the "mansion" of the dream, serving her coffee to warm her and stimulate her mind again. Stanly Godbold points out in his biography of Glasgow that the "idea that Marjorie Rawlings could protect her from an icy world appealed to Ellen immensely," and he adds a quote from Rawlings's papers reflecting on this letter: "'It was obvious that it was I who was to attend on her. It was my feeling at the end of the dream that her original humanity and gratitude turned suddenly to self-assured arrogance'" (Godbold 283). Godbold explains that Glasgow "had an increasing tendency to cry out for sympathy and affection from literary personalities whom she hardly knew" (283). However, her lasting friendships with those personalities, especially women writers, prove that her affections were reciprocated. If she looked to other writers for approval or praise of her works, she was not alone. Rawlings also desired approbation from Max Perkins, Glasgow, and her ex-husband Charles Rawlings, to name a few.[4]

While some readers may presume a hint of eroticism in the following lines that reference enclosing Glasgow's gloved hand in Rawlings's, the line means more to those familiar with the writers' lives and experiences. It is more accurately understood as a detailed description of their stylistic differences, while alluding to Rawlings's being the successor to the literary advancements begun by Glasgow a generation earlier. Any reader familiar with the women or their novels would understand why Glasgow would wear blue silk gloves, as she lived in and wrote about the New South in Richmond, Virginia, following the Civil War. In the dream, Rawlings is surprised to find her hands larger than those of her forerunner, the renowned Glasgow, even though Glasgow was frequently noted as having exceptionally small hands and feet by interviewers (Goodman 60). Rawlings's larger hands could be seen as representative of what she knew to be her larger influence. Despite Glasgow's prolific and established career, Rawlings was first to win a Pulitzer, and has enjoyed a broader readership, historically, than Glasgow. Still, the women's hands are joined in the scene, indicating a lasting and significant connection.

Glasgow chooses her room and suggests details of its furnishings, draperies to supplement a valance, placing her again as an advisor to Rawlings. This is also the section of the dream to which Godbold points as indicative of Glasgow's "self-assured arrogance" from Rawlings's perspective (Godbold 283). In her own writing, Glasgow's attention to detail was lauded by editors and biographers alike. She was adamant about controlling every detail of her manuscripts, from the font to the binding and frontispieces. She would go over manuscripts scrupulously, and had an entire exchange of letters with Max Perkins about minor grammatical points and Oxford versus American spellings that reflect her detailed approach.[5] Rawlings shows her compassion for that attention to detail in the dream by telling Glasgow that she should stop doing "strenuous things" and let Rawlings take care of her.

In the conclusion of this intimate scene, James Branch Cabell interrupts and questions them, and is admonished in a parenthetical note by Rawlings that points out that it was just the sort of interruption they would expect from him. Cabell was a distinguished author with whom Glasgow had a somewhat conflicted relationship. As residents of Richmond and members of the same literary and social circles, Glasgow and Cabell frequently spent time together, and reviewed one another's manuscripts favorably. They became close friends. In fact, Cabell was the person, according to MacDonald, to suggest *A Certain Measure* as the title of Glasgow's collection of prefaces, encouraging her work on those prefaces and reviewing them positively in the press ("Essay in Bibliography" 201). However, he also wrote a review of that same book that Glasgow considered contentious and that resulted in a dramatic falling out between the two of them (Godbold 293). His final comment about Glasgow came after her autobiography was published posthumously. He wrote in a review that it was "her best work of fiction," one example of the snide remarks he could make, even though he appeared, overall, to respect Glasgow and her work and promote her novels (Goodman 254). The reason for his inclusion here is that Cabell was often an interloper in exchanges between the two women. He was a frequent guest at the hotel in St. Augustine belonging to Rawlings's husband, Norton Baskin, and he would provide Glasgow with details of other guests staying there; he would also often encourage Rawlings to have Glasgow come and visit (Thiébaux 28–29). Both women's communications suggest that Cabell was notorious for inserting his opinions and suggestions where they were not requested and for refusing to acknowledge Glasgow's personal life by remaining willfully ignorant of her affair with Henry Anderson, which occurred right under his nose in Richmond.[6] Cabell's appearance in the dream was most likely an example of the interruptions that Rawlings felt so keenly in her work by well-meaning acquaintances. However, Glasgow would have also interpreted it as the male know-it-all obliviously intruding upon the meaningful scene between the women. Cabell found fame in the 1920s for overly symbolic and dense fiction, like *Jurgen*, that was frequently subjected to censorship. Glasgow criticized Cabell for the ways in which he wrote women in his novels in an article titled "Some Literary Woman Myths," which included the line, "From Mr. Cabell's deceptive allegory (in which he proves with wit and learning that he knows but one kind of woman and knows that one kind of woman wrong) there emerges man, the poet and the dreamer, in perpetual flight from woman, the devourer of dreams and poets" (Raper 42). It is clear that Cabell could not understand Glasgow as a person with similar needs and passions to his own, outside of the stereotypes he ascribed to all women. Rawlings, on the other hand, comes across as manlier than Cabell. After all, she had experience hunting with crackers in the Florida scrub and engaged in drinking binges with Hemingway and Fitzgerald, among others.

Every part of this dream spoke to Glasgow. The letter was sent from Crescent Beach, Florida, to Richmond, Virginia, where it was forwarded to Glasgow at her vacation rental in Castine, Maine. And yet Glasgow was able to respond to the letter a mere five days after it was penned. Rawlings dated her letter July 19, 1941, and Glasgow dated her reply July 24th, 1941. She began her reply, "I cannot tell you how much your letter meant to me—and still means. It came last night after a trying day, and it brought a thrilling sense of friendship and sympathy" (*PC* 211). What a strange choice of words to use, to be thrilled by Rawlings's friendship and her sympathy, and how compelling that language is in describing the visceral reaction she felt at the letter.[7] Glasgow frequently bemoaned the lack of individuals who truly understood or accepted her as a writer and a person. Throughout her life, she sought out friendships with women writers, and maintained lasting friendships and correspondence with Signe Toksvig, Amélie Rives, Radclyffe Hall, and, of course, Marjorie Kinnan Rawlings.[8] Rawlings, on the other hand, corresponded most prolifically, outside of familial correspondences, with Max Perkins, her editor. She did, however, have lasting correspondence and friendships with Julia Scribner Bigham and Edith Pope, writing to Glasgow about her desire to have Glasgow visit St. Augustine in part to meet Pope, who was an admirer of Glasgow's work (Bigelow and Monti 275). The dream itself spoke strongly of how accurately Rawlings had assessed Glasgow's character, a skill in which Rawlings felt great pride. Glasgow's interpretation of the dream came in her response:

Ever since I finished "In This Our Life" I have felt as if I were drifting in an icy vacuum toward something—or nothing. I wonder whether other writers have this sense of being drained and lost and surrounded by emptiness whenever they have finished a book. . . . But the dearest part of your dream was the way you brought me in and told me I must do no more cutting of ice in the roadway. And the warmth of the red curtains and the valance! Even the way James popped in and asked what we were up to had the accent of reality. I am so glad you wrote me about it. Ever since you came to see me, so strong and warm and vital, I have felt very near to you, and you have had your own chosen place in my life, just as I had in the house of your dream. (*PC* 211)

Glasgow here extrapolates from the *ice cutting* into the nature of *iciness* in the void-like emptiness she felt after a novel had been completed and, for a while, there was nothing remaining in the creative well. Rawlings was intensely moved by Glasgow's first rule of writing from her preface to *The Sheltered Life*: "1. Always wait between books for the springs to fill up and flow over" (*CM* 210). She read the line as it was quoted in reviews of Glasgow's Virginia edition of book prefaces before she had even obtained her own copy. Referencing these lines, Rawlings wrote to Max Perkins: "I should certainly hate to think that, ego having been satisfied, I was an empty box. A more self-complimentary theory would of course be Ellen Glasgow's and that more than usual had been taken out of me in doing 'The Yearling,' and that 'the well of the subconscious' had needed this much time in which to fill again" (*MM* 414–415). This shared understanding of the need for space between creative acts was what most drew Rawlings to Glasgow initially. The act of sympathy and the permission to cease working and let Rawlings care for her came across to Glasgow as profoundly understanding of this condition. Glasgow concludes her response by acknowledging Rawlings's strength compared to her own weakened form, and then assures Rawlings that they each have carved out a home in one another's lives.

The dream stayed with Glasgow until her death, and a copy of the letter was found along with Glasgow's autobiography and a note to her literary executors asking them to include the content of the dream in its entirety in her autobiography when they chose to publish it. The attached sheet, titled "Coincidence or telepathy?," highlights how strongly Rawlings's dream recollection impacted her and was printed following the letter in her autobiography, *The Woman Within*:

> I had seen Marjorie Kinnan Rawlings only once, when she stopped on her way to Florida, and sat by my bedside for several hours. I was slowly recovering from a severe heart attack, and I had just finished my proofs, with great difficulty, while I was propped up on pillows. Marjorie and I were immediately drawn to each other, but for months I had heard nothing from her. After publishing In This Our Life, which she liked and understood, as deeply as I loved and understood The Yearling, I sank down into an icy vacuum, that living death, when I told myself that, within, I was caught in the midst of frozen fields, and could not escape. Then, last night, I had this letter from Marjorie telling me of her singular dream. I cannot explain it. One can not ever explain such things; and the extraordinary part of it is that the dream bore, in every detail, the accent of reality. I am not psychic; I am not superstitious; I seldom dream significant dreams. Yet, now and again, in my life I have known such occurrences. There was that occasion long ago, with another friend, in Dorking England . . . I may have written of this, I cannot remember now . . . I will go on tomorrow. (*WW* 294–295)

The note contains vestiges of her ailing self as she meanders into thoughts of yesteryear toward the end of her life and romanticizes the nature of the dream, but it also emphasizes the rarity of such an occurrence of complete and utter connection with another human being who understands her to her core and offers compassion from that position of understanding. From here, their friendship was solidified and future correspondences assured.

As their correspondence continued, Glasgow and Rawlings wrote in support of one another's careers, and discussed their similar interests and various relationships. Rawlings expressed her "pride and affection" for Glasgow in these letters, and the sentiments were clearly reciprocated.[9] In one of her last letters to Glasgow, Rawlings reiterated her feelings toward the older writer, reminding her of the dream that helped solidify their correspondence and, once again, inviting her to visit Florida where Rawlings and Baskin could "give [her] some warmth" and Glasgow could "let [them] warm [their] hands at [her] fire" (Bigelow and Monti 276). While many of these areas are covered elsewhere in this book, there were some topics of conversation that were seemingly innocuous and yet make up the very minutia that serves as the structural support for lasting friendships, and also became areas of particular interest to Rawlings when she began researching Glasgow's life.

Like Glasgow, Rawlings had a significant relationship to place. Where she lived was an integral facet of what she wrote. Just as Glasgow set most of her novels in Queenborough, her fictionalized version of Richmond, so did Rawlings choose Cross Creek and its surroundings as the setting for nearly all of her books. It should come as no surprise that Rawlings wrote at length in her letters to Glasgow about her various residences in Florida. While Cross Creek would always be considered home to Rawlings, she also resided with Norton Baskin in his St. Augustine hotel and at a Crescent Beach house on the shore that she purchased in order to write in seclusion after Cross Creek became too filled with distractions. Rawlings sent Glasgow a brochure of Baskin's hotel, Castle Warden, and asked her about her own plans to travel to Maine over the summer, but it seemed merely to be a way of encouraging Glasgow to come and visit, per James Branch Cabell's request.[10] At that point in Glasgow's life, she only left Richmond during the heat of the summer to escape to a rental house in Castine, Maine, ending up in a New York hospital on the way during one attempted trip because of her heart condition (PC 198). Rawlings had begun spending more time away from Cross Creek after her marriage to Norton Baskin, but she told Glasgow she had to return to the Creek every week or two, writing: "It would be so sensible to wean myself away from it altogether, but after you've read the book I think you will understand the almost unreasonably deep roots there" (Bigelow and Monti 221). After Baskin departed for India at the beginning of WWII to serve as an ambulance driver for the American Field Service, Rawlings wrote to Glasgow to let her know that she had decided to return to the Creek for the winter, hoping the isolation there would increase her productivity.[11] Following the war, Rawlings decided to turn her Crescent Beach cottage into her year-'round home to remain close to Baskin, even though she, like Glasgow, was a worshipper of trees, and found herself missing them when she was there. Her attempts to make the cottage over into her permanent residence also made it into her letters to Glasgow, as she detailed the additions she made to the house: "a studio work room with fireplace, dining room, second bathroom, and dressing room" (Bigelow and Monti 275). She also enlarged the kitchen and added quarters for a maid. These details would have been meaningful to Glasgow, who was keen on interior design and kept up a running correspondence with her brother Arthur about her own improvements to her Richmond home, many of which were funded by her elder brother. Glasgow and Rawlings frequently sent one another cards depicting scenes of Richmond or Florida, respectively, further establishing their ties to place.

The warmth that Rawlings offered Glasgow from Florida included the implied health benefits she hoped a visit would have for Glasgow. Throughout their letters with one another, the writers frequently discussed health-related issues, of which both had their fair share. Rawlings had a much stronger physical constitution, but still suffered from acute health issues like chronic diverticulitis, and died at age 57 from a ruptured aneurysm. Glasgow suffered ill health her entire life, culminating in a fatal heart condition, and while her various ailments did not keep her from taking up horseback riding or golf as an adult, they would have certainly kept her from engaging in the kinds of hunting and boating adventures that Rawlings preferred. Both writers struggled with the impact that their health had on their work and vice versa. In 1942, Rawlings mentioned in a letter to Glasgow that she had ended up in a medical center following her completion of *Cross Creek,* and concluded the same letter with her hope that Glasgow's "heart is behaving" (Bigelow and Monti 215–217). In a letter later that year, she expressed her hope that the end of winter would help Glasgow's health to improve (Bigelow and Monti 222). Winters were especially hard on Glasgow's health. Many letters included remarks by Rawlings about Glasgow's health in which she begged Glasgow not to reply to the note or gift of oranges if it was too taxing and hoped that her work was not exhausting her. As she explained in one letter to Glasgow, Rawlings felt that responding to letters could feel more arduous than "scrubbing a floor" (Bigelow and Monti 252).

As the initial dream shared by Rawlings with Glasgow suggests, both writers became close friends with James Branch Cabell. Their letters belie both their admiration for and frustration with Cabell, who dedicated books to each of them.[12] In one letter to Glasgow from Castle Warden, Rawlings told her that Cabell and his wife were "having difficulties in comparatively small quarters, as there is inevitable intrusion on his hour of work" (Bigelow and Monti 216). Cabell had apparently asked Rawlings, as a fellow writer and woman, to please speak with his wife and explain to her that he was "not being peculiar in being unable to work with two people and a dog walking in and out of the room where he is working" (Bigelow and Monti 216). The idea that Rawlings would be able to get through to Cabell's wife because they were both women illustrates many of Glasgow's critiques of Cabell's novels and their depiction of women as fairly one-dimensional. Cabell sympathized with Glasgow, however, in spite of their barbs at one another. Per his suggestion, Rawlings continuously implored Glasgow to visit her in Florida, in part because Cabell felt that the climate would be beneficial to Glasgow's health. Cabell's influence comes across in the way Rawlings posed this request, as well, by mentioning that Edith Pope would be there and letting Glasgow know how admired Glasgow was by Pope, whose novel *Colcorton* was second in the running for the Pulitzer Prize in 1945 (Bigelow and Monti 275). Cabell was convinced that Glasgow needed praise from other esteemed writers (Goodman 248). Like Glasgow, Rawlings greatly admired Cabell's writing, even when she was bemused by him. She called *The First Gentlemen of America* a "gorgeous piece of work" that will "set St. Augustine on its ear" (Bigelow and Monti 216). She also praised his nonfiction work with A. J. Hanna on the St. Johns River, telling Glasgow that she hoped the two writers would collaborate again, potentially on a history of the nation.[13] Rawlings admitted to Glasgow that she missed the Cabells after they had left.[14] It was also Cabell who alerted Rawlings to the fact that Glasgow had never received her copy of *Cross Creek*, which Rawlings, much to her distress, later found in her home unmailed (Bigelow and Monti 221). On May 30, 1940, more than a year before Rawlings was to write to Glasgow about her dream, Rawlings wrote to Glasgow praising a portrait of her that been given to Rawlings as a gift from Cabell, and a cameo of her signed by Glasgow and Cabell.[15] She candidly remarked that her time with Cabell "was almost as much aggravation as satisfaction, for there were so many things I wanted to ask him—many of them about you."[16] She explained how the portrait supplemented their discussion of Glasgow, and then wondered "who [was] the more fortunate—you, to have him to interpret you, or he, to have you to interpret."[17] In many respects, Cabell served as a physical agent in bringing Glasgow and Rawlings closer to one another.

Another experience that both authors shared was the effect that the advent of film had on their writing careers, a topic they discussed in their letters with amusement. Both Glasgow and Rawlings were of the writing generation that first saw a barrage of films being adapted from contemporary literature. Glasgow's *In This Our Life* was made into a film that she claimed never to have seen, starring Bette Davis (*PC* 217). In fact, she wrote to Anne Virginia Bennett, her personal secretary and caregiver, from a trip abroad that she hated to accept the film offer, but felt she could not refuse the extra money "in these hard times."[18] Rawlings was actually on hand for the filming of *The Yearling*, hosting Gregory Peck in her Cross Creek home. She wrote to Glasgow about the experience of watching Hollywood remake her novel into a movie, joking about their choice in actors, a 28-year-old Gregory Peck as Pa Baxter and a "20-year-old blonde glamor [sic] girl they picked for Ma Baxter," hoping that there was no plan to "have any passion between the two."[19] While the financial gains from such enterprises were great, both writers expressed skepticism at the accuracy of film representations in capturing the essence of their work.

The friendship between Glasgow and Rawlings paralleled the time frame of the Second World War, with their first correspondence occurring in 1939 and their last, along with Glasgow's death, in November of 1945. Thoughts on the war frequently entered their correspondence and demonstrated their shared melancholy over its progress. In one letter, Rawlings described being at her beach cottage "on an un-springlike day, gray with tankers sliding along as close as they dare to evade submarines" (Bigelow and Monti 221). Her interpretation of events was that they were living in "hellish times" with a "Miltonian sense of definite Good and Evil" in the conflict that had arisen (Bigelow and Monti 221). While she understood that the United States had not been "any lily," she was fairly certain that they did not "deserve" what was happening (Bigelow and Monti 222). Glasgow expressed more pacifistic leanings than Rawlings, who was never afraid to jump into the fray. In response to the First World War, "Glasgow withdrew and fretted" (Goodman 133). By the time WWII commenced, "Events in the outside world had less and less effect on her daily routine or even consciousness" (Goodman 237). However, Rawlings clearly found the extent of the conflict troubling, and the horrific nature of the Axis powers to be unconscionable. The war did affect both women's daily lives, as the gas shortage made Cross Creek feel more isolated than ever to Rawlings. By 1945, she wondered whether the heightened transportation difficulties would prevent Glasgow from traveling to Maine for the summer, and, indeed, gas rationing made the trip more challenging for her (Bigelow and Monti 251). Glasgow did, however, return to Castine that one last time before her death, with Josephine Clark (Goodman 247). Rawlings also detailed her challenges working in Cross Creek, which had become overgrown from the shortage of workers and had begun attracting the many forms of wildlife that reside in the Florida scrub (Bigelow and Monti 251–252). Additionally, she wrote to Glasgow about how the "burden of the war" seemed "inescapable," and the pressure from it made her other struggles, "mental" and "physical," weigh more heavily on her (Bigelow and Monti 251). Rawlings's anxiety over WWII closely paralleled the anxieties and depression suffered by Glasgow during WWI when she lost Henry Anderson, her fiancé, to an affair with Marie, Queen of Romania, which resulted in Glasgow's attempted suicide.[20] But Glasgow's anxiety was more focused on her personal loss during that time than on the nature of the war itself. While Rawlings seemed engaged in the war effort, Glasgow did not go so far as to volunteer for any of the relief efforts that passed through Richmond, though many of her fictional characters were known to knit socks during times of war.

Not only did Rawlings part with her husband when Norton Baskin joined the Allied Forces in World War II as an ambulance driver, but she also took part in the war effort through the donation of her many books that were packaged and shipped to servicemen and her tireless letters writing to those same troops who read her books and wrote to her about them, and even by helping to entertain officers at the hotel during their downtime. She also held a brief stint as a spotter in St. Augustine, reporting the types of aircraft she saw. Rawlings wrote to Glasgow about these experiences, claiming that the men from Camp Blanding and the Naval Air Station at Jacksonville were helping to prevent her usual "summer lethargy."[21] At the time, Baskin, who had not yet left for his own military service, was installing a cocktail lounge, and they both felt that the officers staying at the hotel would help keep it from "being rowdy."[22] Rawlings also wrote to Glasgow about the privates who would occasionally stop by the hotel for a meal and promptly depart when they saw the prices on the menu.[23] The class distinctions in military personnel that kept some men from dining at Castle Warden did not prevent Rawlings from corresponding with them overseas. Rawlings wrote to Glasgow about that correspondence, as well, admitting to feeling compelled to respond to every letter and then feeling overwhelmed when answers to her responses came back quickly with requests for additional letters (Bigelow and Monti 251).

When Rawlings decided to write Glasgow's biography, the letters she had once exchanged with Glasgow turned into letters she was now writing *about* Glasgow and the details of her life that she had uncovered. Her research led to new discoveries about Glasgow, some of which she never fully disclosed in her correspondence. Those discoveries, mentioned enigmatically in certain letters, were taken with Rawlings to the grave. In Ribblett's retelling of this experience, he points out that Rawlings told Irita Van Doren "that instead of finding the research easy and relaxing, as she had expected, she had instead been 'in a state of constant tension' and distress: 'I have felt myself a hypocrite and a sneak'" (15). Edgar MacDonald points out that her difficulty led Rawlings to decide she would, perhaps, write on Glasgow's "work alone" and not include biographical details ("Retrospective" 4). For this reason, many of the interview notes that Rawlings left behind detail mere trifles of Glasgow's life and experiences that must be run through a sieve and closely considered to obtain valuable bits of information on how she lived and who she was beneath the surface of her life.

One of Rawlings's correspondents during that time was Cliff Lyons, professor of English at the University of North Carolina at Chapel Hill. Lyons and Rawlings became friends when he was teaching English at the University of Florida in Gainesville. A fascinating note was appended by Lyons in 1988 to one of these letters, originally dated February 1953. In his note, Lyons remarked how Rawlings had stopped to see him on her way home from Richmond, where she was conducting research and interviews for the Glasgow biography. He described Rawlings as being troubled by what she had found, adding in a note included with the correspondence, "What she had learned about her [Glasgow] as a person was unexpected and deeply disturbing."[24] No other mention of that discovery was made, but several months later Rawlings wrote to Lyons again, from her vacation in New York, to tell him that she was currently on a break from the biography but had learned that two of Glasgow's closest friends were planning to visit her "and are now ready to 'tell all.'"[25] Again, that was where the correspondence ended, and no other letters between Rawlings and Lyons referred to Glasgow. Rawlings passed away in December of that same year.

Apart from any mention of Glasgow in her correspondence, Rawlings also chose to highlight certain elements of Glasgow's life in the notes she collected, including her financial situation. Rawlings herself struggled financially for many years before becoming established as an author with a generous income. Rawlings compiled an itemization of all income earned by Glasgow, including trust funds from 1931 and part of 1932, in an apparent attempt to ascertain her financial status.[26] It turned out that Glasgow's personal dividends and royalties from her major works added up to less than a third of her income, and the remainder came from the family trust fund and the trust fund enacted and managed for Glasgow by her older brother, Arthur. Other indications of Arthur's financial involvement in Glasgow's life showed up in notes regarding Glasgow's first trip to Europe, funded by Arthur. At one point in her notes, Rawlings questioned whether Glasgow was "galled" by having to accept favors from others, or whether she thought they were "her right."[27] Given Glasgow's insistence on being independent and the resentment she felt toward her father's attempts to control her mother and siblings, it is safe to assume that she did not appreciate having to rely on her politically conservative brother for her own financial well-being.

Glasgow wrote extensively of her own travels, and Rawlings attempted to trace Glasgow's experiences abroad from her autobiography and various letters and interviews to create a timeline for Rawlings's biography of her, which would have featured Glasgow's many trips. Her notes showed Glasgow with her sisters Cary and Rebe in 1898 or 1899 going to Italy, Egypt, and Norway, with a return to Italy with her sister Cary in the spring of 1937.[28] Irita Van Doren recalled Glasgow traveling mostly with Carrie Coleman Duke and remembered, as did several of Glasgow's friends, that she always requested a sitting room in her hotel for entertaining others. Van Doren explained that one of Glasgow's challenges in traveling was that she always required a traveling companion, due, in part, to her deafness.[29] Rawlings also enjoyed traveling, but her experiences were vastly different from Glasgow's. Her one trip overseas to England involved research for her second novel *Golden Apples*, and included renting her own car (without a driver, as Glasgow would have had) and "touring the countryside, staying in Quaint old country inns" (Silverthorne 91). Other trips within the United States revolved around visiting writers or family members, accepting awards, or taking a retreat to complete a novel. Such trips were much more social than Glasgow would have preferred. She was frequently admonished by her brother Arthur for visiting him in London and then refusing to attend his dinner parties.

Rawlings was also fascinated by the home that Glasgow had inhabited since her childhood. She had planned on consulting the William Byrd Branch of the Association for the Preservation of Virginia Antiquities for the history of the house. She made detailed notes on the shades of pink and white in the guest room, and recorded her own description of the wallpaper in the study as Italian and the wallpaper in Glasgow's own bedroom as English with a bird pattern. Rawlings, who was detail-oriented, wrote herself notes on everything from the bolts to the silver-plated doorknobs.[30] Anne Virginia Bennett gave her the most details, describing the Chinese Chippendale desk Glasgow used and the small Queen Anne chest in the back drawing room where she kept all her manuscripts. Bennett gave Rawlings a complete accounting of all household furnishings, down to the drapes and rugs in each room.[31] Each week, Glasgow would send Bennett to the market for fresh flowers. In her biography of Rawlings, Silverthorne noted that the former was also obsessed with flowers, "buying flowers when she was short of money for food and clothes" (3). It was one of Rawlings's "secret dreams... to have a rose named after her" (Silverthorne 1). This dream came to fruition in 2015, when the Marjorie

Kinnan Rawlings Rose was registered through a joint effort between literature professor Keith Huneycutt and rose expert Malcolm Manners of Florida Southern College. It seems Glasgow and Rawlings both enjoyed the beauty of floral arrangements. Van Doren, along with Frank Morley, sent Glasgow 70 "Better Times" roses on her 70th birthday.[32] These details helped Rawlings draw more connections with Glasgow while also creating a picture in her mind of Glasgow's home, where her attention to beauty was as strong as in her novels.

Glasgow also loved to entertain as much as Rawlings did. Rawlings once said in an interview, "I get as much satisfaction from preparing a perfect dinner for a few good friends as from turning out a perfect paragraph in my writing" (Bellman 22). Many of the stories Rawlings collected through her interviews were about Glasgow's renowned formal dinner parties. She was known for using a linen tablecloth and having Anne Virginia Bennett arrange fresh flowers and help with the menu and food presentation. She was also known for being selective about guests. The Van Vechtens once had to pressure Glasgow to include Elinor Wylie at an afternoon reception after Glasgow apparently became upset by her various marriages and affair with a married man—which seems hypocritical, given her own experiences.[33] Rawlings also learned that Glasgow had once feigned illness to keep from having to entertain Rebecca West after hearing that Anthony West, Rebecca's illegitimate son with H. G. Wells, was experiencing some personal difficulties.[34] Both Rawlings and Glasgow also enjoyed cocktails at their meals. Irita Van Doren remembered Glasgow serving "a good brand of whiskey and of sherry," but never any gin drinks.[35] Her favorite beverages to serve were "old-fashioneds" and "mint juleps" in "enormous glasses."[36] At a luncheon Rawlings attended with Henry Anderson, Maude Williams recounted how extravagant Glasgow's events were: "Where I would have 2 or 3 roses in a vase, she would have dozens. *Hot-house.*"[37] Roses grown in a hothouse were much more valuable and harder to obtain in the early twentieth century than they are today, and tended to be of much higher and more lasting quality than garden roses. Williams also remembered how Glasgow would have fires blazing in all four of her fireplaces, and lace mats on the tables for tea and dinner, so she could show off the mahogany of the table.[38] The table service consisted of fine china and silver, including extravagant silver serving bowls. Glasgow's cook, James Anderson, rivaled Rawlings's "perfect maid," Idella Parker, with his cakes, "squab-size chickens and English muffins."[39] Rawlings herself was known to have "fed her guests both exquisitely and prodigiously from her own kitchen . . . she was willing to try anything, from broiled alligator tail to the most sophisticated pastries and soufflés" (Bigelow 59). Whereas Glasgow served mint juleps, Rawlings "poured out with a free hand her prime corn whiskey made by her friends in the scrub and mellowed in a charred oak cask in the attic above her bedroom closet" (Bigelow 59). Rawlings also took a larger role in the food preparations than Glasgow, who relied exclusively on her cook for such events.

As was the custom, Rawlings and Glasgow both entertained house guests traveling to their respective towns throughout the year. Rawlings recorded interviews on what those guests experienced at Glasgow's One West Main home. Irita Van Doren described the guest room with its pair of high four-poster beds with pink curtains and bed coverings, plus a hand-woven throw on the bottom of each bed. There was an open fireplace with iron grating that burned cannel coal, which was kept nearby in a lovely tin bin. A 12-year-old "colored boy," the son of Glasgow's cook, James, would slip into the room in the morning, clean the fireplace, light a new fire, brush the hearth, and "tiptoe out again." The maid would knock on the door around 8 a.m. and put up the Venetian folding shutters and raise the shades, then close the window in the adjoining parlor and start the bath.[40] Later, she or James would bring an elegant breakfast tray covered in handmade Italian lace with Chesapeake herring roe, bacon, hot bread, coffee, rich cream, marmalade, and a small vase holding a flower, and fluff the pillows. Mornings were conducted in a leisurely fashion. When Glasgow emerged from her own room, she was typically dressed in a beautiful and frilly negligee and would visit with Van Doren before getting dressed. Her driver would take guests on day trips to Williamsburg or the James River for lunch. When she was no longer well enough to leave the house, she would ask Van Doren to stay with her and read chapters of her autobiography as she sat before an open fire covered in shawls of various colors—pink, rose, orange, red, and yellow—that had been knitted by a woman she knew in Maine.[41] During those later days, Anne Virginia Bennett would bring canapés for lunch on a silver tray with mint juleps in 18th-century goblets that were strong enough "to lay anyone out at that time of day." Bennett would join them for lunch and conversation, both of which were always in abundance. Glasgow served ham at two meals, and always had hot bread with leftover vegetables at lunch in a three-part silver vegetable dish. Rawlings, by contrast, "took her guests deer hunting or duck hunting in season, went deep-sea fishing with them on the Gulf or the Atlantic, set up river trips on the Ocklawaha and Withlacoochee, took them into the scrub on nature hikes or out on Orange Lake to catch largemouth bass" (Bigelow 59). Clearly, a trip to Cross Creek would have involved more adventure and required a heartier disposition than a stay at Glasgow's Richmond home.

Rawlings loved to cook, and wrote detailed notes of Van Doren's descriptions of food served by James at Glasgow's house: "wonderful molds of fresh strawberry ice cream or fresh peach, with fresh fruit around it"; apples that had been boiled with the stem left on and cooked in grenadine—bright pink and jellied—encircled the meat; and a dessert salad of oranges made by coring the orange, boring holes in it, and stuffing it with cherries and nuts before cooking it in a sugar syrup until tender and cutting it in quarters to be served with little cheese balls, lettuce, and endive.[42] These descriptions of Glasgow's food rivaled Rawlings's descriptions of food from *Cross Creek Cookery* and added to the bond she felt with Glasgow as she was learning more about her. Unlike Rawlings, who struggled with her weight, Glasgow ate very little but "wanted everyone else to eat a lot," and would continually urge guests to eat.

Both Rawlings and Glasgow kept unique areas in their homes set aside for working on their manuscripts. Glasgow typed at a rickety card table and kept two beautiful English oak chests and a very high secretary filled with her Buddha statue, letters, and papers.[43] At the foot of her couch she kept a great stack of newspapers and magazines. Rawlings preferred to write outdoors "on the screened veranda, from which [she] could watch the comings and goings of the birds to the feed basket in the crepe myrtle bush, and to the bird bath" (Tarr and Kinser 340). Rawlings would have no doubt found common ground with Glasgow in this mutual love of birds. Both women had a special appreciation for roses and redbirds.

In her research, Rawlings also expressed some curiosity about Glasgow's lack of religious affiliation, another commonality between the two writers. In an interview with Glasgow's cardiologist, Dr. Brown, Rawlings quoted him as saying "with a twinkle in his eye," "She wasn't a very religious person."[44] Her antipathy toward religious practices stemmed from Glasgow's own father, who was so adamant regarding the practice of religion in an overbearing and strict fashion that he did not permit any deviations from his approach. Rawlings wrote in her notes, "Every morning Ellen's father had morning prayers and read from the Bible, only the hell and damnation passages that fitted the stern Presbyterian creed. Ellen said, 'As a girl I always felt damned all day.'"[45] Rawlings also kept a letter from Emma Trigg that reveals the somewhat contradictory nature of Glasgow's religious views. Trigg described a dinner party with rector and published poet Robert Norwood, Alex and Virginia Weddell, and Glasgow, during which Norwood expressed "a joyous acceptance of Divine Love and a certainty of immortality" and Glasgow just as joyously denied those very things.[46] From Trigg's perspective, Glasgow was "aggressive" in her complaints, became "sharp," "lost her temper," and "became bitter and rude." Trigg admitted that Norwood had pushed her too far, but felt that his job as a minister required him to "save souls" and "not honorably surrender." Norwood thought that Glasgow was simultaneously the "most unhappy" and "most charming" girl that he had ever met, while Glasgow described him afterwards as "a dreadful man." Clearly, Glasgow's run-ins with religious persons did not create any sympathies for those of traditional Christian faith. Rawlings also "shared the religious uncertainty of many modern writers, having deep religious sensibilities but no formal commitment" (Bigelow 62). She attended Baptist and Congregational churches off and on throughout her childhood and college, but then stopped attending, writing to Charles Rawlings "that she found religious matters 'morbid' and full of outworn superstition" (Bigelow 62). Similar to Glasgow's mystical leanings, Rawlings espoused a Whitmanian "pantheism or the transcendentalist doctrine of the oversoul," feeling that "the best way to know this life was to live as close as possible to nature, or at least to some plot of earth where one could sense its great simple rhythms" (Bigelow 62–63).

In her notes, Rawlings highlighted Glasgow's friendship with Mary Johnston, another Virginia novelist and women's rights activist with whom Glasgow would travel and visit regularly. In some ways, their friendship paralleled that of Rawlings and Edith Pope. In a letter to Johnston that Rawlings saved, Glasgow candidly discussed her professional work ethic by expressing envy at "those systematic hardy workers who go on day after day with never a pause" because they must have found some way to "escape the fret and fever of sudden spurts and inevitable reactions" (PC 18). Describing Johnston, Glasgow wrote, "you have such courage, and suffering . . . a peaceful and strong composure" (PC 19). Glasgow also quoted a Buddhist proverb, "there are many paths down into the valley, but when we come out upon the mountain we all see the self-same sun" to express to Johnston how she understood that "the same spirit is lighting" them both and would continue to bring them together (PC 19). In a line reminiscent of her feelings toward Rawlings, Glasgow asked Johnston to "lend her a little . . . courage . . . when [her] strength gives out again" (PC 19). Her love for Johnston in these letters is made palpable by Glasgow's insistence that "the place [Johnston has] in [her] heart is a very deep and real one" (PC 23). Their correspondence also referred to their professional lives as writers. Glasgow concurred with Johnston's feelings about work "in having spent a summer staring (with newly sharpened pencils beside me) at a spotless sheet of paper" (PC 29). These shared experiences caused Glasgow to give solace to Johnston, begging her to "lose quite the 'submerged sensation'" and wishing that she could draw Johnston "not only back to work and play but back to me" (PC 30). Once again, Glasgow became overly romantic in her overtures, imploring Johnston to love her "much or little as you can, and I shall love you back in my own measure" (PC 30). Rawlings found these letters to be of particular interest, going so far as to request better copies of some correspondence, because she wanted to highlight the importance of "literary" friendships in her work on Glasgow.

Glasgow's closest companion, however, was clearly Anne Virginia Bennett, who told Rawlings she came into Glasgow's life in 1910. Rawlings made sure to win Bennett's trust and friendship, and interviewed her extensively. When Rawlings and Bennett first met, Bennett was suspicious of her motives, but she was quickly convinced of Rawlings's sincere love for her deceased friend. Bennett teared up while reading letters from Glasgow to Rawlings, and was quoted by Rawlings as saying, "Oh, she was so miserable. So little happiness. I wish I could have made her happier."⁴⁷ Bennett claimed to have convinced Glasgow to write her one collection of short stories, *The Shadowy Third*, because they needed money. Glasgow's reply to the request was, "Who do you think I am, Gene Stratton Porter? I can't turn out a story like that." In the same way that Glasgow had her dog Jeremy exhumed and buried with her, Bennett was to have their other dog, Bonnie, buried with her. Every morning, Bennett would arise at 6:30 and go downstairs to have a servant start the fires before she went to check on Glasgow, who slept in a separate, locked room from Bennett. She would have Glasgow's tray sent to her at 7 a.m., and would join her for breakfast with her own tray. Glasgow read the *Times Dispatch* each morning, and the two would plan the household meals together before they had their baths. Glasgow was in her study by 9 a.m., and was not to be disturbed before 2 p.m.⁴⁸ Bennett would take their dogs out around 10 or 11 a.m. and then work on the typing that Glasgow had for her to do. They would eat dinner at 2 p.m., and then Glasgow would rest before going out for a drive from 4–6 p.m., weather permitting. Occasionally, they would play bridge in the afternoons with Carrie Duke and Beulah Branch before eating supper at 7 p.m. Glasgow never worked after supper, but she would sometimes go on a drive afterwards. Bennett told Rawlings that Glasgow had her first car in 1925 or 1926. Bennett described her job as "to keep people away from her so she could work; to run the household; type mss [manuscripts]." In the meeting with Rawlings, Bennett lamented that Glasgow had wanted periwinkle on her grave, but it was instead covered with ivy. She broke down, telling Rawlings that the grave was "too big for her. She was so tiny." These conversations were crucial in helping Rawlings to understand Glasgow's daily routine.

Rawlings also learned about Bennett's background to understand better how her relationship with Glasgow developed. Roberta Wellford told Rawlings that Bennett had "come across as domineering at the end of Glasgow's life when she was no longer strong enough to stand up against it." Bennett's mother had been a gentlewoman who married a poor countryman, and she had walked miles to the nearest town for her education.⁴⁹ She came into the family as a nurse for Glasgow's sister Cary, and had then nursed her other sister Emily and father Francis before working for Glasgow as a secretary and, later, again a nurse. Maude Williams recalled Glasgow sitting with her back to the pantry door at dinners while Anne Virginia sat facing the pantry, so she could direct the staff, "in spite of her shyness and the fact that she did not come from the same social background."[50] Williams imagined that Bennett needed to attend these events because of Glasgow's deafness, and noted that she always looked very nice. Wellford illustrated Bennett's integrity by telling the story of how she had used an envelope full of money marked "For James for an Emergency" after Glasgow's death. She used it to help pay for James, the house servant, to have an operation he needed, and then expressed overwhelming feelings of guilt to Wellford and Carrie Duke because she felt like a "criminal" for having used the money, rather than giving it over to the estate, even though she was assured by the bank accountant that she had done nothing improper.

Recognizing the close bond between Bennett and Glasgow, Rawlings worked diligently to earn and maintain the respect and trust of Glasgow's closest companion, efforts that helped her secure countless letters and details from Glasgow's life. Bennett wrote Rawlings several letters on Glasgow's own typewriter. Rawlings sent Bennett boxes of mangoes from Florida. Bennett agreed to find homes for several kittens that Rawlings had found. After these initial overtures, Bennett opened up with her own opinions that Douglas Freeman and James Branch Cabell were both jealous of Glasgow's genius and that Arthur Glasgow should be discounted because he never understood his sister, and "could not bear to be contradicted about anything."[51] Glasgow always felt constrained when speaking with Arthur, even though she readily admitted he was very kind and generous to both her and Bennett. According to Bennett, Arthur was furious that Glasgow had left her estate to the SPCA. She encouraged Rawlings to proceed slowly with the biography, because she felt that Glasgow would have wanted her own autobiography published first. Bennett did not understand the delay in publication of the autobiography, and assumed it had to do with the choice of Frank Morley as one of Glasgow's literary executors; he had resettled in England in the time since Glasgow had named him, and did not want to work on the project. Irita Van Doren suggested the delay was due to Glasgow's request that the book not be published during the lifetimes of certain individuals named in it, almost certainly referring to Henry Anderson, Glasgow's former fiancé. James Branch Cabell and his wife, however, both agreed with Bennett that they did not believe Glasgow wanted the publication to be held until Anderson's death.

Without knowing what Glasgow had already written in her autobiography, Bennett asked Rawlings not to mention Glasgow's deafness or to make any reference to the assistance Bennett gave her, because Glasgow "hated so to be dependent." In her attempt to do right by Glasgow, Bennett tried to ensure that Glasgow would be portrayed after death as she preferred to be perceived during her lifetime. A line that Rawlings copied from Glasgow's manuscript as one she wished to remember referred to Glasgow's deafness: "This secret wolf of deafness, which is my mistaken pride, I was trying desperately to pretend away."[52] Rawlings then included an anecdote about Glasgow at 22 being asked about her deafness by a man who had attracted her interest. In these notations, Rawlings is able to illustrate with Glasgow's own words those parts of her personhood that Rawlings found most captivating.

Rawlings discovered some details about Glasgow's life and interests that she had not known before conducting research for the biography. For example, Glasgow had, from a young age, loved cemeteries and ruins, places and people abandoned over the years. She cared for the graves of former servants, and made visiting ruins part of each trip she took to Europe. She would frequently walk through Richmond's Hollywood Cemetery, the same cemetery she was walked through as a baby and her own final resting place. Rawlings had known that they both were "tree worshippers" from their correspondence, and had noticed that Glasgow always used cedar trees to represent tragedies in her novels, but had not realized that she also loved cemeteries. Rawlings, who cherished rural life, was also curious about why Glasgow never lived on a farm, given that she repeatedly expressed a desire to do so. One could surmise that Glasgow may have desired a rural lifestyle intellectually, but would not have had the physical fortitude to withstand the rougher living. Irita Van Doren supported that theory when she told Rawlings that Glasgow had "loved to drive around country in car," but that her interest in the country was "like [her] love for animals, from a distance."[53] Van Doren believed that this was in part due to Glasgow's tendency to live her life "inwardly." Another reason, according to Van Doren, for Glasgow not keeping a country place was "because of expense and because of her desire to travel." Also, Van Doren explained that Glasgow would have needed someone to run a property had she purchased one. By then, Rawlings had already learned that Glasgow's finances would not have supported another household.

During her time in Richmond, Rawlings also learned a great deal more about Glasgow's relationship with her dogs. Rawlings hypothesized in her own notes that this passion for animals could have arisen from Glasgow's "anti-humanism."[54] Glasgow had her favorite dog, Jeremy, exhumed to be buried with her, and Rawlings morbidly asked whether the bones were placed with her in the coffin or at the foot of her grave. She learned from Bennett that Jeremy's bones were, indeed, buried in the coffin with Glasgow. However, Bennett also informed Rawlings that Jeremy was *her* darling dog and that she always took care of him. Rawlings concluded that Glasgow was at once compassionate and desirous of isolation and solitude, dependent on others, but with a longing for ultimate independence. This conflictual inner self inspired many of Glasgow's best-loved characters.

Among those individuals upon whom Glasgow depended was the author James Branch Cabell. Rawlings spoke with Cabell at length when working on the biography of Glasgow, in part because she already knew him well from their time together in St. Augustine. At one point, Rawlings decided that, in spite of the fact that everyone in Richmond wanted to speak with her about Glasgow, only she and Cabell had "really loved her."[55] He recalled in his interview with Rawlings first meeting Glasgow when he was a student at the College of William and Mary in 1898 and she was doing research for *The Voice of the People*, published in 1900. They became friends in 1925 after Cabell wrote a good review of *Barren Ground*. He told Rawlings, "She liked good reviews, you know" (Godbold 147). Other writers Rawlings met had a mixture of "malice" and "admiration" for Glasgow. Glasgow earned the dislike with her own harsh criticism of the literary community, as Cabell remarked that she "was violent about Willa Cather."[56] While Glasgow liked Cabell's review of *Barren Ground*, she was upset by his backhanded compliment of *A Certain Measure* when he wrote that it was her "best-written book," especially given that *he* had done so much revising and rewriting of that manuscript, even suggesting the title. Cabell also helped Glasgow with *In This Our Life*, and was the first to point out that Glasgow's works acted as a social history of Virginia, helping her to arrange them for the Old Dominion Edition, which sold well to collectors.

Cabell also shared with Rawlings select correspondence, in part to help with the biography and in part to prove that Glasgow had, for the most part, considered him a friend. In one of these letters, Glasgow wrote to Cabell from Maine, "If only—only—only beauty were enough! But pain is sharper, and I am seldom without pain."[57] Rawlings also spoke with Cabell's wife, Margaret, but noted that Margaret's comments could not be trusted as accurate—especially when she referred to Glasgow as a "snob"—because she never really knew Glasgow. Margaret was Cabell's second wife, and did not marry him until after Glasgow's death. Arthur Glasgow explained to Rawlings that Bennett frequently denied guests access to Glasgow, including Margaret. Irita Van Doren saw the relationship between Glasgow and Cabell as one-sided. Glasgow would frequently try to talk to him about "intimate things," like "her hatred for her father." Cabell, who made an effort to avoid all emotional disturbances, later regretted that he stopped Glasgow from speaking more freely to avoid feeling burdened himself by her outpourings. He told Rawlings that Glasgow went to his house before her death to ensure certain letters she sent to him were destroyed because of the personal content in them.[58] Only a few letters remained.

The letters that Rawlings received from Cabell show a shift in Glasgow's attitude and opinions toward him that paralleled his public reviews of her work. In a letter from 1927, she wrote that she was "enchanted" by a dedication he wrote in a copy of *Something About Eve* that was, in her words, "as flattering in implication as it is graceful in gesture." Glasgow went on to write of this dedication in the comedic novel that she was more "deeply honored" because of the "diabolical innuendo of the comedy."[59] Glasgow also shared with Cabell the joy of working in isolation, writing to him from Castine, Maine, in 1939: "I work and walk and walk and work and drive. That sums up my life and my life's interest."[60] Cabell also gave Rawlings a letter from Glasgow about their collaboration on her collection of critical essays, *A Certain Measure*. Perhaps for that reason, Glasgow was skeptical about using it, writing to him that it "bother[ed] her" because it could be the name of a novel, and she was worried that the "small minority, who read critical essays" may not be drawn to it as a critical collection without a more telling title.[61] She ended up keeping the title, and the collection was a critical success that, in part, brought Rawlings and Glasgow together. Following the publication of *A Certain Measure*, Glasgow's letters to Cabell revealed how injured she felt by his review of the book and its undercutting tone. In one of the two letters regarding this conflict, Glasgow emphasized that others had also found his review to be offensive before trying to claim that its effect had lessened with the severity of the Second World War: "Even the sharpened edge of what Berta Wellford felicitously called your 'all-time low' has become harmlessly blunted" (Godbold 293). Glasgow explained her reaction to his review:

> I am willing to grant you any number of reasons, though I cannot quite understand all the long endeavor to build up a charming appearance of sympathy and comprehension, if this were simply for the need of releasing, in the end, a sudden gust of inhibited malice. Literary smartness must depend, of course, for its best effects upon caricature and misrepresentation, and, as we both have learned, from the wise or witty, caricature demands the spicy flavor of malice or flippancy. And yet, even so . . . the only literary right I deny is the right of misrepresentation. (Godbold 293)

In spite of this diatribe against Cabell, Glasgow tried to make peace with him, given the many years during which they relied on one another's personal and professional support as writers. The second letter regarding their dispute came across as a desperate attempt by Glasgow to understand why Cabell chose to write the review as he did. She asked him whether the "pleasure of releasing an inhibited gust of malice" was "worth more than it costs" (Godbold 294). Cabell tried to defend himself by claiming that Glasgow was taking the remarks too seriously, as Glasgow repeatedly responded that she did not mean to appear "over-serious." She told him in the letter that his review "would certainly be no solemn matter, if only it had not denied everything you had said or written, and I had believed, for the past thirty or forty years" (Godbold 294).

She still invited him for an old-fashioned and "a laugh together," in spite of their strained relationship, with the caveat that "ironic amusement will be the last pleasure we give up" (Godbold 294).

In her research, Rawlings was also able to share in many anecdotes that illustrated Glasgow's sharp wit, another trait the women shared. Van Doren described one incident at a New York hospital where Glasgow was convalescing. Not to be put out, Glasgow, age 70 at the time, had a private nurse, Italian pillowcases, her own manicurist, a hair stylist, and a complete wardrobe of hospital clothes. When Carl Van Vechten remarked, "Ellen, I have never seen you look so lovely," Glasgow replied, "Carl, you've never seen me in bed before" (Godbold 268–269).

Glasgow spent a lot of time in hospitals for ailments so numerous that friends wondered whether she was a hypochondriac. Rawlings investigated these suppositions by speaking directly with Dr. Alexander Brown Jr., who was brought to Glasgow by her long-time personal physician, Dr. Tompkins, after her most serious heart attack. His diagnosis was "arteriosclerosis with the heart condition."[62] Dr. Brown also told Rawlings that he concurred with statements she took from Glasgow's friends that her deafness most likely resulted from a serious bout of influenza earlier in her life, and he went further, to suggest that "the pathology of her lifelong frailty may have gone back to typhoid or scarlet fever as a child or to some undiagnosed virus."[63] When Rawlings asked Dr. Brown whether he felt her illnesses could have been, at least in part, psychosomatic, he responded, "Her illness was definitely psychopathic." He had no theories on what could have led to the psychological problems of her illness and did not know that Glasgow smoked, though Rawlings was well aware of Glasgow's smoking. He thought, rather, that "her habits were correct." Those who knew Glasgow as a child, Roberta Wellford and Lucy Scrivenor, told Rawlings that Glasgow had been "affected by the general atmosphere of her home" and recalled her "sitting on steps resting her face on little thin hands."[64] Van Doren understood Glasgow's deafness as being both inherited (a niece had the same kind of deafness) and exacerbated by a flu and intensive crying spell immediately following her mother's death when Glasgow was 20. According to Van Doren, the doctors told Glasgow that she would "clog up all the passages and make everything worse" during that period.[65] Dr. Brown described Glasgow's personality, as related to her physical constitution: "She was extremely sensitive. She had strong likes and dislikes. She was very loyal to those she accepted as friends but she was easily offended by her friends."[66] Two of those friends, Roberta Wellford and Lucy Scrivenor, also claimed that Glasgow's ailments prevented her from attending the local school as a child and kept her from taking dance lessons with the other girls in their neighborhood. When she tried to attend school at Miss Lizzie Munford's, Glasgow was "so tired and frail and had to sit down on stairs." About her deafness, Wellford and Scrivenor described Glasgow's different hearing aids, which she used throughout her life. Lucy Scrivenor told Rawlings that Glasgow addressed her deafness with dark humor, once telling her: "In a way deafness is not so bad—I can't hear men beating their wives next door." Her various ailments, both physical and psychosomatic, left Glasgow thinking about death a great a deal. Roberta Wellford told Rawlings that Glasgow believed she had been dead and come back to life, an experience that Glasgow claimed left her feeling "free" because she could say that she understood what death was.

Finally, Rawlings learned about the details surrounding Glasgow's death from Anne Virginia Bennett. Bennett told Rawlings how Glasgow had suffered a heart attack at the Jefferson Hotel Beauty Parlor while receiving a permanent ten days before her death. Bennett was with her and had already taken her hair down for a wash when the incident occurred. She sent the chauffeur home for a bottle of Scotch and gave Glasgow half a glass straight after administering a hypodermic. Glasgow said, "I think I feel a little better," and Bennett told the male operator "to hurry and finish the permanent" without waiting to have her hair washed (Godbold 298). Later, Glasgow asked Bennett, "What would you have done if I had died there?" (Godbold 298). Glasgow and Bennett had both considered Glasgow's eventual death, in part due to her long-standing health issues, but also given her earlier attempt at suicide. Bennett's reply perfectly illustrates how well she understood Glasgow's preferences: "We would have gotten you right into the car. No one would ever have known" (Godbold 298). The day before she died, she had a luncheon with her brother (and possibly Henry Anderson), hosting a meeting of the SPCA, of which she was still president, and wearing a red dress and red coat (Godbold 299). Bennett remarked to Glasgow how pretty she looked. She went to bed, as usual, with a thermos of coffee by her bed because she liked to wake at 5 a.m., have a cup of coffee, and then go back to sleep. Bennett unlocked Glasgow's door at 6:30 a.m. and found her dead with "her head half-turned on the pillow, one hand by it, half-smile on her face. So pretty in pink gown & bed jacket" (Godbold 299). Bennett notified James Branch Cabell, Dr. Tompkins, and Carrie Duke immediately. Fulfilling a promise he made to Glasgow before her death, Dr. Tompkins injected her dead body with strychnine because, as Bennett explained, Glasgow had always "had a horror of being buried alive" (Godbold 299). She then had to have a special undertaker who would agree to put the remains of her dogs, Jeremy and Billy, in the casket with her (Godbold 299). Bennett later told Arthur Glasgow, after thanking him for giving Glasgow so many comforts she could not have had otherwise, that "life was very cruel to her but Death was kind. I shall always be thankful that she died in her sleep, for the one and only thing she was afraid of, was pain."[67] Glasgow's epitaph, per a request she made to Bennett while vacationing in Maine, was from Lycidas: "Tomorrow to fresh woods and pastures new" (Goodman 250).

Despite their nearly two-decade age difference, Rawlings died from a ruptured aneurysm a mere eight years after Glasgow, without even beginning the biography she had so carefully researched. The first aneurysm ruptured while Rawlings was playing bridge with Baskin and the Youngs. Baskin immediately took her to Flagler Hospital, where she passed away the next day when another blood vessel burst (Silverthorne 348). Friends of Glasgow, like Carrie Duke, wrote letters of condolence over the loss of their friend. Glasgow's epitaph took her outdoors to "fresh woods" and "pastures new," places that had been near and dear to Rawlings's heart. Rawlings's tombstone had a different inscription: "Through her writings, she endeared herself to the people of the world" (Silverthorne 349). The difference in their grave markers could be credited to the fact that Glasgow, who saw her death on the horizon, wrote her own epitaph, whereas Rawlings was remembered in her inscription, penned by Norton Baskin, for the influence she had on people who had loved her and felt changed by her presence in their lives.

What began as a reciprocated admiration between two prominent writers of their day evolved into a relationship that enriched the lives of both Marjorie Kinnan Rawlings and Ellen Glasgow. Through Rawlings, Glasgow was able to imagine an inheritor of her craft, liberated by physical fortitude to experience the natural world in countless ways. In Glasgow, Rawlings found a sympathetic heart and a brilliant mind, a woman whose success lent credence to her assurance that a writer must wait for her "well to fill" with new springs of creativity. In their letters to one another and in Rawlings's dedicated work researching Glasgow's life, the two women formed an unbreakable bond.

2

A Certain Measure of Achievement

What honest craftsman, regardless alike of the appraisal of critics and the indulgence of readers, would squander a lifetime upon work that did not contain for him a certain measure of achievement?

A Certain Measure, by Ellen Glasgow

ELLEN GLASGOW WROTE THESE LINES in the introduction to a critical collection of her own essays on her major novels, *A Certain Measure*, published in 1938, initially as prefaces to her works. It was her own approach to writing about her craft that most appealed to Rawlings, who enjoyed these essays more than Glasgow's novels. In *A Certain Measure*, Glasgow reacts to critical responses to her works that did not fully grasp what she was trying to accomplish with her writing. By the time Marjorie Kinnan Rawlings first met Ellen Glasgow in April of 1941, both writers had firmly established their reputations in American literature, and both had received their share of praise and criticism. Rawlings earned a Pulitzer Prize in fiction for *The Yearling* in 1939, an award Glasgow earned in 1942 for *In This Our Life*. While Rawlings was at the peak of her career when they met, Glasgow was considered a revered figure in the literature of the American South, with a publishing career that spanned decades, an appointment to the American Academy of Arts and Letters, and positions on many literary award selection committees. Her first major award came after the publication of her eleventh novel, *Life and Gabriella*, when she won the Presentation Medal of the National Institute of Social Sciences for her services to literature and humanity in 1917. She was also awarded several honorary degrees, and was the guest speaker for the Modern Language Association and Southern Writers Conference.

When Glasgow first wrote to Rawlings in 1939 praising *The Yearling*, Rawlings was sincerely flattered. She knew Glasgow by reputation and admired her work. However, she correctly judged their works to be somewhat at odds. Glasgow was concerned with the human condition against the backdrop of society, whereas Rawlings focused on the human condition against nature. However, the concept described by Glasgow in her prefaces of a writer's experience, specifically the idea of the writer's subconscious springs being depleted by writing and refilled by rest, spoke deeply to Rawlings's own experiences. They each understood the challenges of the writing process and the frustrations over producing written narratives that lived up to their own expectations for the stories they told. Rawlings spent so much time investigating Glasgow's life, in part, so that she might glean more of her wisdom about the writing life. Throughout their friendship, the women encouraged one another, supplementing and correcting the critical reception their works faced.

Glasgow, it should be noted, wrote *about* Rawlings before she ever wrote *to* her in praise. In fact, her first letter referencing Rawlings was written to Irita Van Doren in 1933 in response to *South Moon Under*. The letter was not complimentary. She was asked by Van Doren, editor of the *New York Herald Tribune* and a close friend of Glasgow's, to help select titles for her *Fall Book Number*. She wrote of Rawlings's first novel, "the Southern peasants in *South Moon Under* and even the Florida swamps, all seemed to me to be made of wool" (*PC* 138–139). Her opinion of Rawlings as a writer changed after she read *The Yearling*. She wrote to Rawlings, though the two had never met, and opened the letter with a request that Rawlings visit her in Richmond to talk the next time she passed through town on her way north. Glasgow wrote, "I am watching your work with great interest. 'The Yearling' seems to me to be a perfect thing of its kind. And this can be said of few modern works of fiction" (*PC* 188). Glasgow's admiration of Rawlings was reciprocated. Rawlings responded with her own letter, stating, "I know no one whose invitation to a talk would be more welcome than yours. I have been a profound admirer for many years."[1] Indeed, copies of Glasgow's novels may still be found at Cross Creek, now part of Marjorie Kinnan Rawlings Historic State Park in Hawthorne, Florida, in Rawlings's old bedroom, resting on an end table, in memoriam to her esteem for Glasgow's work. Rawlings praised Glasgow for her prefaces in the Virginia edition of her major works, and lamented that her next trip out west would not take her near enough to Richmond for a visit. She assured Glasgow that "a little later, [she] should like if necessary to make a separate trip to talk with [her]," adding, "It makes me very happy, knowing your high critical standards, that you like 'The Yearling.' It was made out of my sweat and blood, but I hope that is not apparent even to you."[2] To be praised by Glasgow would have been seen by Rawlings to be both an honor and an opportunity. At this time, Glasgow's "name was being used to promote the works of other authors, which highlighted her own celebrity," as pointed out by Eric Leuschner, who notes that Glasgow was "associated with the top of a cultural hierarchy" by 1930 when she served as both a judge for the Harper and Brothers novel competition and a juror for the Book of the Month Club Fellowship (53–54). Rawlings was honored by having three of her books (*South Moon Under*, *The Yearling*, and *Cross Creek*) selected for the Book of the Month Club, and was well aware of Glasgow's status in the literary circles that evaluated Rawlings's manuscripts.

After James Branch Cabell sent gifts to Rawlings on behalf of Glasgow, Rawlings sent her a lengthier note on beautiful stationery decorated with a Japanese drawing of a cat reaching into a stream for a fish. Her letter focused on their admiration for one another's work and their unique approaches to writing novels that could have made a friendship between the two unlikely:

> Reciprocal admiration among writers is so rare a thing that after many years of devotion to your work, I find myself totally unprepared for your liking mine.
>
> Superficially, our aims and our material would seem so divergent that one could not conceive of common ground. Yet after reading your Prefaces and your Inscription for the delightful cameo that

comes to me with your signature and that of Mr. Cabell, it seems to me possible that our object has been more or less identical: to present human beings, as you know one type and I another, struggling against whatever is inimical within themselves or in their background. The enemy may be a complicated social fabric, or the "ironic perversity" within, or the more explicit natural forces. I happen to be more concerned with man in relation to a natural background, than with man in relation to man against a sophisticated background. And there is much of cowardice in my choice of subject matter. . . . With some trepidation, I am sending you a copy of my collected short stories. It has always seemed to me that while some deviation from a precise pattern may be allowable in the novel form, the short story, like the sonnet, requires perfection. These stories embarrass me with their distance from it. The only one that remotely satisfies me is "The Pardon," and yet my technique must have been inadequate here, for James Boyd is the only person who seems to have reacted to it as I could wish. The point I was making—the pitiful fatuousness of the man's clinging to the document that was his pardon as a formal guarantee of a new and happy life—seems not to have been sufficiently explicit. Even my sensitive friend Robert Herrick saw nothing in the story beyond a conventional sex impasse. With my most profound thanks for your interest, and with the hope that we may meet. . . . [3]

Rawlings found their mutual understanding in their shared instincts for characterizing the individual, specifically that individual in conflict with self, society, or environment. Their differences in craft, according to Rawlings, were that her novels focused on nature while Glasgow's works focused on society's influences. Most notably, Rawlings was moved to send (with trepidation) a collection of short stories to Glasgow, along with her personal notes about various stories in the collection as an apology for parts she felt were lacking. Rawlings began her career with successful short fiction she published in *Scribner's Magazine*, and wanted Glasgow to read and appreciate what she was trying to accomplish in those early works. Their friendship was built upon the foundation of their writing lives.

Rawlings admired Glasgow as a writer, but she also sought to be admired by Glasgow and other writers of her respectable status in the literary community. In a letter to Max Perkins, after receiving Glasgow's praise but before meeting her, Rawlings referred to a note and pamphlet Cabell had sent her that described Glasgow, "signed by her 'With tremendous admiration'" (Bigelow and Monti 186). Rawlings reported feeling "overcome," and then asked Perkins, rather earnestly, whether he thought that Rawlings could have been the author Glasgow meant when she told Cabell that she only admired two women writers, one of them Jane Austen (Bigelow and Monti 186). Rawlings visited Glasgow two years later, on her way through Richmond, demonstrating that the letter and its content had had an impact on her. The meeting had a lasting effect on both women, as they found kindred spirits in one another.

As their friendship developed, their lives as writers continued to be the focal point of their letters. When Rawlings first wrote to Glasgow after their initial meeting, she closed her letter with a description of her writing process and the frustrations accompanying it:

> I am at my cottage on the ocean, and have been working very hard on my book, so hard that I put myself in the hospital for a week. It wouldn't seem necessary to tie oneself into knots to get out a few ideas, but while I *feel* at the drop of a hat, thinking is terribly hard work for me! The first draft of the book is nearly done. Much of it is very bad indeed, and after Max Perkins has seen it and given me, I hope, some of his marvelous suggestions, I shall go at it again. (Matthews 210)

Rawlings viewed Glasgow as one of the few women who could understand completely the anxiety that she felt when working on a novel. Glasgow felt a similar kinship with Rawlings, and replied to this letter that she felt as if she were "drifting in an icy vacuum toward something—or nothing" since finishing *In This Our Life*, her last novel (*PC* 211). She then elaborated on her own condition when finishing a book to see whether Rawlings could commiserate with her: "I wonder whether other writers have this sense of being drained and lost and surrounded by emptiness whenever they have finished a book" (*PC* 211). After this attempt at validating her own experiences, Glasgow encouraged Rawlings on her new book project, *Cross Creek*. She assured Rawlings that the final product would be good, and gave her a beautiful account of how writing a book felt: "But there is a kind of slow agony, after the first rush of impulse, in bringing a book into the world. I shall send my helpful wishes to you every day, with the hope that you may feel them" (*PC* 211). Glasgow knew that Rawlings shared this agony, and hoped to emphasize their commonality.

These remarks were especially haunting to Rawlings, who had written just a few years earlier to Max Perkins about a nearly identical quotation from one of Glasgow's prefaces. In her letter to Perkins, Rawlings wrote:

> It was a life-saver to my conscience to come across a statement quoted from one of [Glasgow's] prefaces, in which she said that the writer must wait between books for the well of the sub-conscious to fill. I haven't been able to understand why I couldn't get to work, when on the surface at least I thought I wanted to . . . the Glasgow theory is profoundly true . . . I do not believe a writer can go ahead with a new piece of work until he is entirely free of the old. (Tarr 366–367)

For Glasgow later to reiterate these sentiments in a personalized note further illustrates the intimate connection they shared as writers. Throughout their correspondence on Rawlings's difficulty in beginning her next writing project after finishing *The Yearling*, Rawlings and Perkins referred regularly to the "Glasgow theory" of why Rawlings was struggling (*MM* 366). The letter from Rawlings inspired Max Perkins to secure proofs of Glasgow's prefaces and send them to Rawlings from his own press records, asking only that she "return them some day" (*MM* 369). Perkins, who helped edit and publish the prefaces, had written earlier that he was not particularly fond of Glasgow's works, but he found her work on writing to be "enlightening" (*MM* 368). He later requested that the prefaces be returned, but soon replaced them with a copy of Glasgow's *A Certain Measure*, containing all the prefaces along with some new material. That same year, Perkins told Glasgow how much value Rawlings placed on her works, including the fact that Rawlings had named her prefaces "as one of the three things [she] had most enjoyed reading during the year" (*MM* 383). Playing, perhaps, as much of a matchmaker between the two writers as Cabell, who is sometimes given credit for Glasgow and Rawlings having met, Perkins wrote of the exchange to Rawlings and included Glasgow's reply:

> And she says: "I am very much pleased by what you say of Marjorie Rawlings and her liking for my prefaces. Few books have ever moved me more deeply than 'The Yearling.' The tragedy of the end seemed to me almost too intense to be borne. It is a perfect thing of its kind, with the accent of inevitability that tempts me to use the word 'genius.' And genius as a term in literary criticism does not often appeal to me." I thought this from her might please you. (*MM* 383)

Perkins's work with Glasgow, at the time when the two women began writing to one another, was still brand new. Glasgow changed publishing companies and editors from Harcourt to Scribner's just before releasing the prefaces. Rawlings, however, had a strong professional and personal friendship with Perkins that spanned her career as a novelist. The fact that the two writers were able to share their admiration for one another's work through correspondence with one of the great American editors of their day is another remarkable aspect of their friendship. A few months later, Rawlings was able to write to Perkins to let him know that Glasgow had invited her to visit and that she "should gladly go far out of [her] way to meet" Glasgow (*MM* 397).

In addition to their similar experiences with the writing process, Glasgow and Rawlings both felt that their writing lives took a toll on their physical health. After completing *Cross Creek*, Rawlings ended up "collaps[ing] gratefully at Medical Center" in New York (Bigelow and Monti 215). She wrote of the experience to Glasgow and included an aside on receiving the book's page proofs. Even in this letter of relief over her completed manuscript and her description of her recent marriage, Rawlings made sure to ask Glasgow about her own work, and returned the same encouragement that she had received from Glasgow. Glasgow was considering writing a follow-up novel to *In This Our Life*, which she decided against publishing. The short sequel, *Beyond Defeat*, was published in 1966 by Glasgow's literary executors. Rawlings declared the idea "fascinating," just before she told Glasgow that a recent "list of the ten most evil women in literature included Stanley" from *In This Our Life* (Bigelow and Monti 216). Both writers obsessed over their craft and always had the beginning of another project in mind, even though they found themselves unable to work on a new project prior to waiting for that well of the unconscious to refill.

After she finished *Cross Creek*, Rawlings was upset that Glasgow did not congratulate her or offer any thoughts on the new book that they had so frequently discussed in letters. She then found the package she had intended to send Glasgow with her early copy of the manuscript in her rooms at Castle Warden, unmailed. Rawlings was "horrified," after having feared Glasgow "had been too ill or busy to read it—or, horrible thought, that [she] hadn't liked it and wouldn't say so!" (Bigelow and Monti 221). She hoped the book would help Glasgow and others to understand better the "almost unreasonably deep roots" she had planted at Cross Creek (Bigelow and Monti 221). After apologizing to Glasgow for the oversight, Rawlings admitted to feeling "itchy at not working," but had found "comfort" with a "remark in [Glasgow's prefaces, published as *A Certain Measure*] about needing to let the well of the subconscious fill up again between books" (Bigelow and Monti 221). This oft-repeated phrase, the same one she used in the letter to Max Perkins mentioned earlier, continued to have a strong effect on Rawlings. Those moments of depletion before inspiration returned were keenly felt by both women.

When Glasgow finally received and read her copy of *Cross Creek*, a very different sort of book from *The Yearling*, she was quick to offer Rawlings not empty praise, but a heartfelt commentary on the content of the essays included in that autobiographical work. Describing the book as full of "magic," Glasgow highlighted Rawlings's writing style in her review:

> The writing seems less a vehicle of expression than a luminous web, which captures and holds some vital essence of a particular place and moment in time: heat, light, color, scents and sounds. Even the primitive enjoyment of killing, from which my inadequately covered nerves are inclined to flinch, I recognize as an essential part of

the truth. Too well I know the cruelty that runs through the beauty of all things Southern—perhaps, though I am less sure of this, through the beauty of all things human. (*PC* 214)

Glasgow called the book "flawless," and pointed out the very qualities Rawlings was most anxious to bring out in her work by telling Rawlings that she had "uprooted a landscape, with its tendrils still living" and "made it over into a book that would bleed if you tore it apart" (*PC* 214). As a lover of trees, Glasgow most enjoyed "For This is an Enchanted Land" and "The Magnolia Tree" (*PC* 215). However, she was appalled by the treatment of Leroy, the yellow catch dog, who she felt was sorely abused in the book, however well-written the story about him was (*PC* 215). Glasgow lifted Rawlings up with encouragement both as a writer skilled in technique and as a kindred spirit with the same passion for landscape and the natural world that Glasgow shared. In a literary climate that was moving toward a grittier and more grotesque realism, Rawlings and Glasgow both maintained a love for the beauty of their environments and described even the harshest settings of the natural world with a reverence that revealed their own romantic leanings.

Rawlings continued to share her writing challenges with Glasgow as she struggled to begin *The Sojourner*, while worrying over her husband, Norton Baskin, who had left for India as a volunteer ambulance driver during WWII. She wrote to Glasgow, "I have been totally unable to work, great relief though it would be. I made two forced beginnings, so bad that I was appalled at my delusion that I could write! But I shall go back to it again, and probably find no loss in the waiting" (Bigelow and Monti 251). In a follow-up letter, she described being "in a dreadful state of mind, from being unable to do anything with a novel that has been long on [her] mind, and on which [she has] made eight or nine beginnings" (Bigelow and Monti 275). Rawlings was so dissatisfied with her work on *The Sojourner* that she "tore it all into irretrievable shreds" after finishing "a quarter" of the book's length (Bigelow and Monti 275). Rawlings knew intuitively that Glasgow would understand why she felt so much "better" after destroying part of the manuscript, even though "the new beginning [was] no better" (Bigelow and Monti 275). Glasgow, whose high standards for writing led her to complete a multi-draft process (three drafts was her standard) for all of her novels, commiserated with Rawlings's struggle. In her letter to Glasgow, Rawlings grappled with her problem at length: "The characters, the setting, the general theme, are clear as crystal to me—and it emerges as pure tripe" (Bigelow and Monti 275). The distance between Rawlings's understanding of her story and the written words expressing that story was a problem Glasgow found in her own writing.

Between 1944 and 1945, Glasgow had her own trouble with writing as her health deteriorated. Rawlings learned of her troubles through their mutual friend James Branch Cabell. Repeatedly begging Glasgow not to exert effort in replying to her correspondence, Rawlings nevertheless wanted to convey her deep concern over Glasgow's health, in particular because of the way it prevented her from being able to write, her one true passion in life. Rawlings wrote:

> How I suffer with you, for it puts one into an acute state of melancholy and frustration. Being obliged to write is a strange curse. With the impressive true literature to your credit that you have already, it would seem that you could rest on your laurels, but I know that you must be chafing at the bit. I understood that you have been working on something of an autobiography. You MUST finish it!!!!! Your prefaces are of course a most valuable piece of autobiography, but you MUST do more, giving more of a personal nature. Not that you should "tell all," but posterity must have more of what you have thought and done and how your mind and emotions have functioned. (Bigelow 275)

Rawlings emphasized the life of a writer in this letter that begged Glasgow to return to her writing as soon as she was able. In fact, Rawlings implored Glasgow, "But your work is so much more important than mine, that I pray you will find strength from somewhere to go at it again" (Bigelow and Monti 275). She also apologized in a self-deprecating way "for including myself in your, and [James Branch Cabell's], genre" (Bigelow and Monti 275). Rawlings preferred Glasgow's nonfiction, and worried that she would not complete her final autobiography. She invited Glasgow to visit her in St. Augustine for both the milder climate and the camaraderie of other writers who "would give [her] as much companionship as [she] wanted—or have the grace to leave [her] alone when [she] didn't want to be bothered" (Bigelow and Monti 275). Glasgow was known for being fond of flattery, especially from other writers.

In her final letter to Rawlings, written a few days before her death in 1945, Glasgow offered a kind of charge and benediction, as if she knew that it was the last time she would be able to communicate with Rawlings. She advised Rawlings to continue work on *The Sojourner*, a novel that Rawlings was still struggling to complete after many renewed attempts, and after the death of Max Perkins, her beloved editor. Glasgow's final thoughts to Rawlings were, "Do not give up. You have great gifts" (*PC* 253). For Glasgow, there was no predecessor of equal acclaim to reassure her of her talent. She had only the sale of her books and some rather uneven critical support from the likes of Cabell. What she felt herself offering Rawlings was the support that she so desperately wanted for herself, support given in earnest by an admirer of her work who was an accomplished writer in her own right, someone who had suffered the same trials in her attempts to succeed as a writer.

Rawlings and Glasgow offered one another public support as well. When Rawlings was asked to help select a winner of the Gold Medal of the Institute for Fiction in 1943, she chose Ellen Glasgow over Hemingway, Dreiser, Cather, and Lewis (Bigelow 244). In a presentation to the Annual Luncheon of the National Council of Teachers of English in New York in 1939, a work that was later published in both *College English* and *English Journal*, Rawlings asserted, "Ellen Glasgow stands alone in our generation as the only unmistakable regional literature of the South" (Tarr and Kinser 277). She went on to declare how surprising it was that Glasgow had not earned a Pulitzer Prize, comparing her with Thomas Hardy and wondering why Hardy was never dismissed as a "regional" writer. When Glasgow finally did win the Pulitzer, Rawlings refused to congratulate her for it, offering instead to write a letter of congratulations to the selection committee for finally getting it right.[4]

Rawlings's biography of Ellen Glasgow was the first project she took up after finishing *The Sojourner*. In a letter to Norman Berg after beginning that project, she indicated her horror that her Aunt Wilmer was "astonished" that Rawlings was working so hard after finally having completed *The Sojourner*, referring to Glasgow as "some obscure person" (Bigelow and Monti 390). Rawlings exclaimed to Berg, "My God, if 'Richmond' heard of this!" (Bigelow and Monti 390). In a letter to Maxwell Geismar, an American critic who had written an extensive analysis of Glasgow's literature that Rawlings found compelling, Rawlings poignantly declared her affection and great esteem for Glasgow by writing, "I loved her as a woman, and admired her books, with some of your own reservations, and others of my own" (Bigelow and Monti 402). By publicly supporting Glasgow, Rawlings refocused critical attention on her works in Glasgow's final years and after.

Glasgow also praised Rawlings publicly and reserved a section in the epilogue of her autobiography, *The Woman Within*, to highlight their friendship. In that section, she wrote, "After publishing *In This Our Life*, which [Rawlings] liked and understood, as deeply as I loved and understood *The Yearling*, I sank down into an icy vacuum, that living death, when I told myself that, within, I was caught in the midst of frozen fields, and could not escape" (*WW* 294). She then included the full text of the letter she received from Rawlings that solidified their friendship and wondered at how perfectly it answered her every need at the moment of its arrival, as if the two women shared a psychic connection.

After Glasgow's death, Rawlings had to decide how she would represent Glasgow's literary impact in the biography that she was writing. She began collecting critical reviews of Glasgow's work that detailed the influence her novels had on American literature. These materials were meant to become part of the biography Rawlings never completed. The items from this collection, when compared with similar materials in Rawlings's archive that deal with her own writing, reveal some of what Rawlings had intended to write and why she chose particular attributes of Glasgow's writing as her focus.

Many of these articles described Glasgow straddling the line between realism and sentimentalism. Rawlings did not lean toward sentimentalism until her final novel, *The Sojourner*. Following that novel, she began her study of Glasgow, whose work, at least according to its critical reception, evolved from the realism of *The Descendant*, with its socialist protagonist, into more conscious sentimentalism with General Archbald in *The Sheltered Life*, and his realization that tradition has both its costs and its merits. One reviewer remarked on Rawlings's *The Sojourner* that it was "often sentimental, often beautiful, sometimes profound."[5] Other reviewers claimed that women, especially, would love the novel for its sentimental qualities, describing it as "a pastoral novel with a dark thread."[6] Their eras added to both writers a measure of reticence at any revolt against traditions, and an acknowledgment of a broader worldview that admired certain traditional traits as valorous.

Rawlings followed up on criticism Glasgow received when compared with emerging writers, like William Faulkner, in order better to understand how Glasgow fit into the writing of the new South. The trend toward these grittier modern authors meant that Glasgow received criticism for being romantic rather than realistic. In an interview with Glasgow's cousin, Frances Williams, Rawlings learned that Glasgow "called certain of the 'modern' writers the 'Sewer-Realists,' in a resigned mood, when you felt the world-weariness on her. She said, 'You don't have to kick the chamber-pot under the bed to know you are in a bedroom, do you?'"[7] Her simultaneous rejection of sentimentalism and naturalism is evident, according to Francesca Sawaya, in her "economic and political critique of them" (Scura 133). Sawaya finds Glasgow equates sentimentalism with slavery, and naturalism with capitalism (Scura 133). Sawaya argues that naturalism, according to Glasgow's *A Certain Measure*, "is associated with masculinity and male authorship," while "sentimentalism is associated with femininity and female interests" (Scura 134). Glasgow refused to adopt either style. While Rawlings confided to Norton Baskin how distasteful she found Douglas Freeman, a critic and acquaintance of Glasgow's, she included in her critical materials a somewhat indulgent article he wrote on Glasgow's *Vein of Iron*, titled "Idealist." In this musing, Freeman argued that Glasgow would "go through the muck if she has to," but that she would not "deliberately choose a path of filth for sensationalism" (11). This refers to one of Glasgow's most commonly misread stylistic choices. Coming from a background in which education and intelligence in writing were crucial elements for a woman attempting to succeed in a male-dominated literary canon, Glasgow found decorum to be a dying trait among an emerging literary culture that thrived on the "muckiest" material simply for its shock value. In an interview for the *New York Times Book Review*, she described the "nullity" and "emptiness" of much contemporary writing. She found too much of the literature contemporary to her own works to be "raw" and admitted to preferring the journals of Dorothy Wordsworth, which had just been released, to the new, sensationalist Southern writers.[8] In one interview, Glasgow quoted an Arabian saying that "Allah delights in the truth, but not in the whole truth," and said that "the truth must be slowly processed through a vital and discerning mind into literature and not just blurted out."[9]

As she studied these reviews, Rawlings was most likely reminded of similar reviews she had read of her own novels. In one of the earliest reviews of *South Moon Under*, Rawlings was distinguished from other Southern novelists, namely Faulkner and Caldwell, for not "bringing into such great prominence the biological functions of her characters," choosing instead to "submerge the sensational aspects of the lives of her characters to the main theme of how they live and why they live as they do."[10] At the same time, Rawlings was not considered a sentimentalist. Reviews of *The Yearling* emphasized "the genuineness of the feeling . . . that never for a moment slips into sentimentality."[11] Another reviewer praised the language in *The Yearling* as "so real and so unsentimental."[12]

Rawlings found other articles that declared Glasgow to be the precursor to the Southern literary revolt. Sara Haardt was surprised, in "Ellen Glasgow and the South" (1929), that the author's anti-sentimentalism, which had been a key feature of Glasgow's work for fifteen years prior to the current tradition, had not been heralded as part of its foundation. In a disappointing turn, Haardt went on to praise Glasgow for not needing to "raise her voice" in such matters as women's suffrage, and then described Glasgow's home decor and extraordinarily feminine physical features, including her small feet (13). The article, written in part as an interview with Glasgow, gave voice to Glasgow's predictions at the time, ones that have in large part come true, regarding how the "patriotic materialism" of the modern South could cause it to lose more of its individuality "by conforming to the accepted American pattern of standardization and mass production" (29). Haardt made the astute comment that Glasgow was, paradoxically, trying to "resurrect the true romantic tradition and defend it" against modern industrial forces after she "achieved a revolt from the debased romantic tradition of the Victorian era" (30).

Rawlings took a decidedly different approach in her writing by making an exodus from literary circles and creating compelling narratives about those people who lived outside the boundaries of social niceties and lingering Victorian dramas. Her move to rural Florida and decision to work her own orange grove before writing of the real-life struggles that existed in the area came with their own challenges, like how she should represent the Florida Crackers. Reviews of *South Moon Under*, her first novel, teetered between complimentary local reviews that noted her "accuracy," claiming she had "not misused" the local population in her portrayal of it, and misguided attempts at praise from national, mostly Northern-based presses that described how well she "delineate[d] the odd characters who reside in the southern part of the United States," referring to them as "elemental folk."[13] Other reviews described the characters as "primitive, earth bound souls" who "would rather starve there than enjoy whatever plenty anywhere else might provide."[14] One review went so far as to describe the Florida Crackers as "the outcasts or the survivors, those illiterate and uncivilized persons who live in a locale made up of rattlesnakes and alligators and stunted trees," people of "crude" standards.[15] Another reviewer claimed that these kinds of portrayals should be considered for "ethnography" studies and not literature, because they were merely a camera-lens view of the inhabitants of the region, with no beauty and too much crudity.[16] Most reviewers, however, praised Rawlings's expert use of dialect and the literary quality she lent to her realistic characterizations of the Crackers. They also focused on her depiction of a land "untouched by industrial civilization," and the people who had chosen to live removed from that civilization, bordering on a noble-savage idealization that Rawlings never intended.

In addition to reviews, Rawlings collected images and notes on Glasgow's writing that were used to help her narrate the settings in her novels more accurately. In this area, Rawlings was a much more effective illustrator of landscape than Glasgow, because she worked from personal experience, rather than books and photographs. As one Philadelphia reviewer wrote of Rawlings's first novel, "It would be difficult to say whether *South Moon Under* is the story of Lantry Jacklin or his mother, Piety, or of the Florida scrub itself."[17] Both Glasgow and Rawlings were well-versed in the natural features and foliage in their novels, but Glasgow worked from photographs of environmental features. Rawlings's firsthand descriptions of Florida in *South Moon Under* and *Golden Apples* were selling points for those early works, as Northern readers clamored to learn more about vast wilderness of Florida. Reviewers commenting on *Golden Apples* described the "wild sprawling acres" of "lush, jungle-like hammocks," along with the "dignity and value and human qualities of the poor Florida Cracker."[18] The only negative comments she received for these works focused on character development or commonly used sentence structures that may have indicated writing that was overly self-conscious, and even those critiques made sure to give Rawlings credit for the scenic descriptions and the concept behind "golden apples."[19] In praise of *The Yearling*, a local Florida newspaper claimed that Rawlings had "found beauty in our backwoods, and has preserved it for future generations to enjoy."[20] One reviewer of *The Yearling* praised her writing, but wondered why so many recent Book of the Month Club selections had been "bucolic," hypothesizing that 1938 may have been a time during which the depiction of rural struggles was particularly desirable to a people emerging from the Great Depression.[21] As well, few reviewers of *Cross Creek* were able to complete their critique of that autobiographical work without mentioning the snake encounters that were a common occurrence for Rawlings in Florida. The characters in *Cross Creek* were said to share the "common ground of their love for the soil and their daily needs and interests."[22] *The Sojourner*, Rawlings's final novel and the only one not set in Florida, related the farming lifestyle to the rhythm of the narrative, as the changes of the seasons and the farmers' reliance on that pacing bled into the narrative, giving it a slow, lyrical feel.[23]

Several articles collected by Rawlings suggested that she would be writing about Glasgow's use of irony in her biography, a tack that led to many misinterpretations of Glasgow's literature, especially by the feminist recovery efforts of the 1970s. Rawlings copied out a single quotation from *Lucifer at Large* (1937) by C. John McCole that claimed Glasgow should have been considered for the Nobel Prize for her "richly textured and superbly ironic style" (McCole 294). Glasgow opened her critical prefaces, *A Certain Measure*, with the italicized quotation, "*What the South needs is blood and irony . . .*" (*CM* 2). Rawlings also found an article on Glasgow by Majl Ewing titled, "The Civilized Uses of Irony:

Ellen Glasgow," in which he argued that Glasgow's earlier work was "a revolt against sentimentality" that stayed true to realism, while still holding onto the idealism of the confederate cause (Ewing 81). Ewing praised Glasgow's comedies and more mature, later work for "the deft paralleling and counterbalancing of characters and situations" by which Glasgow "sheds ironic illumination on her immediate story," specifically those comedies of Queenborough, which offer a more sophisticated critique of Southern romanticism (Ewing 86). As Ewing explained, Glasgow "explores the lives of her old and young happiness hunters in a disintegrating society which acknowledges with its lips a code that it does not practice in its life" (85). Such work, which Ewing calls "Meredithian" after George Meredith, whom Ellen Glasgow admired, demonstrates that Glasgow "knows men and women" but does not "expect too much of them," though she does "hope for good" (85–86). According to Ewing, Glasgow was able to see the "folly of luxuriating in feeling" and developed a detachment that allowed her to see the difference between word and deed, ideal and reality, employing a "civilized use of irony" (90). The juxtaposition of Glasgow's ironic wit with novels that resemble dramatic works and contain an elevated prose form caused Glasgow's ironic insertions to be overlooked or ignored by her readers, but not by all of her fellow writers or critics. The emphasis placed on these articles by Rawlings indicates that she intended to explain Glasgow's irony and correct for the misreading of her works.

Rawlings's work with the Florida Cracker community took on great anthropological value as well as literary import. Anna Lillios has compared her work extensively with that of Zora Neale Hurston, herself an anthropologist turned writer, in *Crossing the Creek: The Literary Friendship of Zora Neale Hurston and Marjorie Kinnan Rawlings*. Rawlings found a different anthropological approach to literature in Glasgow's work than she did in Hurston's. Unlike Rawlings and Hurston, both of whom immersed themselves fully in the lives of their communities, Glasgow studied the people and places she characterized by reading histories and visiting her settings as an outsider. She was meticulous about changing the names of people and places to protect any actual persons from feeling misrepresented, and to give a sense of universality to her writing. When working on *Vein of Iron*, Glasgow described reading "innumerable records of the frontier and frontier warfare," searching through "several volumes in order to verify the state of the weather or the month of the year" before deciding to "dismiss it in a parenthetical clause" (CM 168). She questioned everyone, "old and young," and "devoured every record [she] could find of the earliest settlers in the Valley of Virginia," only to discover that all of her research together resulted in "exactly two pages of print" (CM 169–170). Glasgow's characters had to be fully realized in her mind before her stories could take shape, and were, in many respects, an intellectual exercise born out of her attempts to grapple with the world around her. Rawlings must have found many of Glasgow's exercises tedious and unnecessary. Many of the best-known characters in her own works, including Jody from *The Yearling*, were based directly on real individuals with whom Rawlings interacted daily.

Glasgow was, additionally, seen as a social historian, with many of her novels paralleling the social and political upheavals of the South following the Civil War and transitioning through Reconstruction to the beginning of WWI. James Branch Cabell wrote of Glasgow's social histories in "The Last Cry of Romance" (1925) that what is most compelling about *Barren Ground*—her best novel, in his opinion—is the way in which all those "things which ought, by every rule of tradition, to have mattered most poignantly have in reality meant nothing" (29). His one critique of her work was the way in which she consistently ends her characters' "trials and defeats and losses" by focusing on their "unshaken faith in an immediately impending future wherein everything will come out rather more than all right," a faith that Cabell found to belie "the ironist dismissing her sport" (30–31). In a bibliography of works by and about Glasgow that Rawlings intended to use in her biography, William H. Egly described Glasgow as a prominent "interpreter of the transition period in the Southern states after the Civil War" and argued that her vivid, realistic manner adeptly portrayed the change from the old South to the new.[24] Van Wyck Brooks, in another article Rawlings planned on using, described Glasgow's novels as indicative of the "confliction regimes of the South, rising industrialism and the twilight of agrarian culture."[25] He went on to point out that Glasgow only sided with the "new life" when it was "generous or positive in its change for the individual suffering people at the bottom."[26] In the summary of an address sent by Edward Mims to

Arthur Glasgow and then forwarded to Rawlings, titled "Ellen Glasgow, social historian of Virginia" (1947), Mims recounted the historical period of Glasgow's novels from 1850 to 1939, and explained how she intended to compile a social history of Virginia that would detail its manners and morals. Mims saw Glasgow's novels following *The Battle-Ground* as exemplary of the rising middle class in its struggle against the old aristocracy for positions in politics and business. He claimed that she saw the vast possibilities in a democracy, in spite of its crudity and vast wreckage, because of the ways in which it permitted this class mobility.[27]

Though Glasgow's works may be read as those of a social historian, Rawlings was more interested in the ways in which those same novels transcended place and time. Rawlings also aspired to this universal experience in her writing. Reviews of *The Yearling* pointed out that, "far more than a picture of life in inland Florida, Jody's story touches the universal."[28] Another review qualified it as a "universal" and yet "sectional novel" in which the characters become "of all time, anywhere in the world, yet retain the flavor of their own country," detailing the novel's "versatility" in spite of the static location.[29] Glasgow wrote in her preface to *Barren Ground*, part of the collection of prefaces that Rawlings most admired among her works, that "I had learned that there are many facets of human nature and the aspect we call the regional is only the universal surveyed from a shifted angle of vision" (*CM* 153). Both writers were noted by their reviewers as capably conveying universality in their narrowly located landscapes of Virginia and Florida, respectively.

As she was collecting materials, Rawlings looked for comparisons that had been made between Glasgow and other authors to illustrate better the quality of Glasgow's writing. Rawlings had already compared Glasgow, as mentioned earlier, to Thomas Hardy in her own presentations. In one article by Van Wyck Brooks, Rawlings found Glasgow compared to Thomas Jefferson in her knowledge of the intermixing of races in the Tidewater region of Virginia, and to Thomas Nelson Page in her celebration of the South, which seemed to occur even in her revolt against the "evasive idealism" that had developed in Southern literature.[30] Edward Mims, a prominent literary critic at Vanderbilt, named Glasgow and Willa Cather the "two leading American writers of prose fiction."[31] Radclyffe Hall, after having read Glasgow's *Vein of Iron*, wrote her a letter in which she likened Glasgow to herself, writing, "This book makes one realize the misery and courage brought about by the terrible years of depression. Ellen, I see that like me you hate the times in which we live."[32] Glasgow's nephew, Carrington Tutwiler, completed a study of Glasgow's library that he presented after her death at Glasgow House. He found that she was influenced early on by Darwin, Maupassant, and Flaubert, and later turned to Proust and the German idealists, writing on less intensively researched themes.[33] Glasgow herself admitted to reading Maupassant and Henry James (some critics comparing her to the latter for their similar "prefaces" on writing) for style and realism, but she swore that her writing was never meant to seem imitative of any of those works she read for edification.[34] Rather, she worked to find her own style and created her own sense of perfection in narrative. Later, Rawlings's own novel *The Sojourner* was also compared to works by Thomas Hardy, indicating further potential influence of Glasgow on Rawlings. A better comparison, however, is made between *The Sojourner* and the works of John Steinbeck, with the main difference being that Steinbeck more accurately developed his unfavored characters into violent ones.[35] Characters in *The Sojourner* were also compared with historical and literary figures that may have influenced their conception. Ase Linden is compared with Abraham Lincoln and Job. Biblically, his struggles are also compared to those of Cain and Abel, or to Eden with its serpent. *The Yearling* was compared time and again to both *The Adventures of Huckleberry Finn* and the *Adventures of Tom Sawyer* in expressing a timeless narrative in the guise of a "boy's book." Rawlings's *Cross Creek* was described as a "kind of Walden" to which Rawlings escaped after being a "sob-sister" for newspapers in a number of cities.[36] The comparison to Thoreau's *Walden* is further described in a *New York Times* article (1942) by Robert Van Gelder: "the anonymity of life in a large city, that seclusion that is at once a blessing and a perhaps not altogether healthy insulation of the spirit, is nonexistent."[37] All of these comparisons reveal the standard to which Glasgow and Rawlings were held in their careers.

Finally, Rawlings collected several articles that reviewed Glasgow's portrayal of gender norms, specifically in her satirical comedies. In "A Virginia Lady Dissects a Virginia Gentleman" (1926), Carl Van Vechten characterized Glasgow as having a "malicious feminine wit" in *The*

Romantic Comedians (40). In his summary of the novel, the disillusioned gentleman believes he can hold the affections of a young woman, while elsewhere a woman may "lose her virtue ... several times in Paris without forfeiting caste" when she returns to Virginia (41). In that novel, gendered expectations are shown to be superficial and contradictory, with most characters simply playing a game based on the rules they have been taught, even when their behaviors devolve into impropriety by social standards. At the end of "The Fighting Edge of Romance" (1925), Stuart Sherman described Glasgow's distinct feminist vision as one that claims "the average woman's life is founded on a lie, a vital illusion, namely, that the sexual attraction which draws her to her man in the mating season is enough, is her supreme and sufficient affair with life" (9). In "An Appreciation of Ellen Glasgow" (1946), Van Wyck Brooks found that Glasgow was able to portray "new and old style women" equally well, but that she found the "bad but bold" women to be far better than the "good and soft or weak."[38] Edward Mims claimed that Glasgow was unique in writing not for the political rights of women but for their "personhood," their right to exist outside of their relationship to men and families and to be financially and emotionally independent from the men in their lives.[39]

One can only imagine how Rawlings interpreted Glasgow's representation of women. After all, Rawlings frequently chose to privilege male characters in her literary works, which included some rather horrid depictions of women, like Ma Baxter, in *The Yearling*. Rawlings, however, upset a different set of societal norms by deciding to portray the economically disadvantaged, including race relations between impoverished groups. Reviews of her autobiographical work, *Cross Creek*, revered its "pioneer spirit" in the portrayal of characters "white and black," arguing that it would "sway others" to want to "retreat from the cluttered existence of the urban haves to the more unimpaired life of the Cross Creek have nots."[40] Proving that Rawlings had, in some respects, worked on overturning common prejudices against the poor, one reviewer wrote of *Cross Creek*, "the shiftless and the ornery wear the same brand of overalls as the pure in spirit. You can't be too certain."[41] Glasgow also wrote about the poor, but only from the perspective of an outsider. She never lived among people outside her economic class; instead, Glasgow viewed herself as a benefactor to the less-privileged members of her community, a concept that was seen by writers like Brooks (1946) as evident in the way that her poorer characters and black characters were frequently helped up through society by the ruling gentry.[42] In an interview late in Glasgow's life, she explained how she had recently discovered her first story, saved in a desk, titled "A lonely daisy in a field of roses."[43] She went on to say that she felt this had been the theme of all her writing—the unprivileged rising in society, the outcast, etc.[44] Through the articles and interviews she reviewed, Rawlings emphasized the pivotal role Glasgow played in disrupting static definitions of gender and misperceptions of the economically disadvantaged.

While Rawlings was compelled to include Glasgow's work with gender, which was vital to her narratives, she repeatedly returned to Glasgow's craft of writing in her research, and focused on the ways in which those methods overlapped with her own. Rawlings found a clipping from the *New York Times Book Review*, in which Glasgow claimed that people's only connection with reality is "to seize the flying thought before it escapes us" (Raper 170). The quotation was taken from her address to the Modern Language Association in 1936, and came after her realization that she had "never seen an idea so antiquated that it was not at one time modern" and that "no idea is so modern that it will not one day be antiquated" (Raper 170). By 1936, Glasgow had been in the literary world long enough to recognize that the posturing around new styles and methods of narration was not only contrived, but also derivative.

This same obsession with the craft of writing led Rawlings to work doggedly on draft after draft of her own novels until finally finishing them and then feeling completely dissatisfied with what she had produced. Glasgow's similar drafting process reassured Rawlings by showing her she was not alone. After finishing *South Moon Under*, Rawlings wrote to Max Perkins that she would "swap it for a hunting license" (*MM* 76). She was then embarrassed by its positive reviews and the publicity being given it by Scribner's "because I am acutely conscious of how far short the book falls of the artistry I am struggling to achieve. It's like being caught half-dressed" (*MM* 91). In a lengthy autobiographical sketch for the *Los Angeles Times* (1953), Rawlings admitted that "none of [her] novels has satisfied [her]" (Tarr and Kinser 351). She found through Glasgow's writing and their discussions that her feelings were not uncommon. In a 1913 interview with the New York *Evening Post*, Glasgow described how "slowly" she needed to progress, writing a novel every two to three years, and then shared her dream to "write each novel and keep it ten years" before publishing it (Raper 118). Rawlings found that Glasgow was similarly compelled to draw out the process of creation and revision as long as possible.

Rawlings found that Glasgow had also struggled with the rise of commercial publications and the pressure to write for hire as a way of financing more artistic ventures. Early in her writing career, Glasgow was told by a publisher that she "must write historical romances if [she] wish[ed] to be popular," to which Glasgow responded that "popularity, though agreeable no doubt, was not, as [she] vainly tried to convince him, the ultimate standard" (*CM* 29–30). As Glasgow explained in her preface to *The Deliverance* (1904), it had never occurred to her that she "should ever become a popular writer," because she had purposefully "taken the wrong turn and was still moving steadily in the wrong direction," having understood early on that "to be honest and yet popular is almost as difficult in literature as it is in life" (*CM* 30). Rawlings agreed with Glasgow. In an article on regionalist literature, she told the story of a businessman who speculated to her that "the big market right now would be for war stories" and asked her whether they were not the "easiest trash in the world to write" (Tarr and Kinser 275). Rawlings replied tersely, "I wouldn't know. I never wrote trash on purpose" (Tarr and Kinser 275). She then explained, "Regional writing done because the author thinks it will be salable is a betrayal of the people of that region" (Tarr and Kinser 275).

Rawlings explained the difference between her craft and that of a writer who writes to "make a living" or "commercial writing" in an article for *The Book of Knowledge Annual* (1948). The kind of writer she strove to be

> writes out of the inner depths of his heart . . . because life seems tremendously exciting, because it seems beautiful or sad, because he understands people better than the average person, because he burns to express in words the things that he sees and feels. He writes when he is cold and hungry, although he could keep warm and well fed in some other kind of work. He writes even when

everyone tells him that his work is of no account, when magazines and publishers refuse his stories. (Tarr and Kinser 325)

This sentiment that writing is something one is compelled to do, regardless of success or lack thereof, is echoed in the earlier writings of Glasgow, who admitted that she "began being a novelist, as naturally as I began talking or walking, so early that I cannot remember when the impulse first seized me" (Raper 153). The fact that both women wrote in secret long before they were published and continued to write unceasingly in a variety of forms, from Rawlings's early work in journalism to both her and Glasgow's less-successful attempts at poetry, denotes their *identities* as writers.[45]

Rawlings discovered that this shared identity had given Glasgow the same desire for isolation that she herself felt. Like Rawlings, Glasgow's writing process was easily disrupted by the most minor distractions. Glasgow insisted that she "remain, or try to remain, in a state of immersion" while working on a book (Raper 159). Rawlings removed herself entirely to Cross Creek, and, later, to her Crescent Beach home, to write more or less in seclusion. By the time she received the O. Henry Prize money for "Gal Young Un," Rawlings, living alone at Cross Creek, was down to "a box of crackers and a can of tomato soup" (Tarr and Kinser 345).

For Rawlings, the decision to remove herself fully to Cross Creek led to her breakthrough as a writer, and also to her decision that she would "never again try to write stories with one eye on possible sale and publication" (Tarr and Kinser 345). She instead began to write of "this land and these people as I saw them, stirred by my new love," in an "unpopular style" that would nevertheless be true to those stories she wanted to tell (Tarr and Kinser 345). In the midst of the Florida Crackers on Cross Creek, Rawlings was able to mature as a writer and produce her best prose.

Her research on Glasgow revealed to Rawlings a different approach to the same need for seclusion in order to write well. Glasgow needed to "get at some distance and obtain a perspective, especially for realistic writing" because, as she explained, "realism isn't a photographic reproduction of life. It is rather the truth of life portrayed—and in the novel, with an interpretation, for one must put oneself into the writing" (Raper 119). Glasgow's novels were largely character-driven, but her characters were more loosely based on real individuals. She developed character templates into psychological portrayals of universal struggles between the individual and his or her social environment.

While Rawlings was able to view the social consciousness in Glasgow's work, her research also uncovered Glasgow's desire to present it in a way that was largely apolitical. Glasgow wanted her novels to target the problems "an individual life may present" to a character (Raper 120). She did not want to be seen as writing "propaganda" (Raper 120). Glasgow saw her characters as going through the same universal struggles faced by humans through the millennia, and wanted to capture those experiences without judging the environments that produced those problems. One of her repeated critiques of American fiction was the "evasive idealism" that they promoted, in spite of the harsh realities of life outside the novel (Raper 123). Glasgow complained in a 1916 interview with Joyce Kilmer for *New York Times Magazine* that people in America seemed to want "a sugary philosophy, utterly without any basis in logic or human experience. They want the cheapest sort of false optimism, and they want it to be uttered by a picturesque, whimsical character, in humorous dialect" (Raper 123–124). Rawlings determined that Glasgow shared her wish to capture the untold stories of struggles faced by common individuals in turmoil with their environment.

Glasgow's ability to articulate her own writing process and experiences accurately comes across as having inspired Rawlings more than any of Glasgow's literary accomplishments. The most salient inspiration came in Glasgow's own personal rules of writing. In "One Way to Write Novels" (1934), Glasgow breaks her writing method down into three rules:

1. Always wait between books for the springs to fill up and flow over.
2. Always preserve within a wild sanctuary, an inaccessible valley of reveries.

3. Always, and as far as it is possible, endeavor to touch life on every side; but keep the central vision of the mind, the inmost light, untouched and untouchable. (Raper 162)

These rules describe the innermost writing life as set apart from other facets of one's experiences and inviolable, and the writing process, with its ebbs and flows, as coming from some natural inner reserves that can be depleted as easily as they fill up.

3

Blood of My Blood

For we are strangers before thee, and sojourners, as were all our fathers: our days on the earth are as a shadow, and there is none abiding. I Chronicles 29:15

Epigraph from *The Sojourner*, by Marjorie Kinnan Rawlings

THE IMAGE OF Rawlings taking Glasgow's hand in hers after leading her in from the cold in her dream served as a foreground for the Glasgow she would come to understand even better as she spent time with Glasgow's closest friends and family members to learn more about Glasgow after her death. Rawlings's early glimpse into what was later published as Glasgow's autobiography, *The Woman Within*, revealed to Rawlings a baby being carried about on a pillow and a child with nervous headaches that kept her from attending Miss Lizzie Munford's school. Richmond had a different sort of elite from the political figures that were part of Rawlings's childhood in Washington, D.C. Glasgow's childhood summers in the country at Jerdone Castle were also no match for the time Rawlings spent living in tents on her father's farm, separated from the dairy herd, including a bull, by "three strands of barbed wire and a stile" (Silverthorne 14). Time and again, however, Glasgow's friends recounted her sense of justice and devotion to the poor, the elderly, her African American nurse, and all manner of animals. When Rawlings read from *The Woman Within*, she discovered a young Glasgow who, despite her frailty, fought aggressively on behalf of her mother's dog, Toy, and her mother's beloved mare, Winnie, when they were being abused by Glasgow's father—one put to death and the other turned into a workhorse for the Tredegar Ironworks (*WW* 86). While she was physically no match for her father, Glasgow found she could protest his actions by refusing to go to church or by using headaches to get out of chores. Rawlings was fascinated by Glasgow's childhood relationship with her father, which was so drastically different from her own experiences. Rawlings had been nicknamed "Peaches" by her father, and was his shadow on the farm and in life. Arthur Kinnan Sr. once wrote about Rawlings to his wife Ida, "She is the joy of my life. I never knew I had so much love in my heart" (Silverthorne 13). Her mother also seemed to spoil Rawlings as the firstborn child, allowing her to neglect chores when she was writing. After Arthur Kinnan passed away, Ida made sure that Rawlings received the education her father wanted for her, while toiling to keep her dressed well for social occasions. Rawlings may have rejected Glasgow's works initially because they were the kind of writing her mother would have wanted her to produce. As Rawlings got to know Glasgow better through her research, however, she learned how Glasgow's writing was intended as a revolt against the very themes and styles that pervaded her writing.

From the beginning of her career, Glasgow strove to write what she considered to be substantial literature, along the lines of the French realists Balzac and Flaubert, and feared having her work dismissed as local drivel. At the same time, she wanted to gain financial and physical independence from her family. This second goal was only partially realized in her life. Rawlings could relate to these challenges, having learned to make a living through journalism before succeeding with her fiction. She had gone so far as to gamble her financial security on Cross Creek when she purchased the grove and relocated to give her writing a fresh start.

When Rawlings began work on her biography of Glasgow, she studied the history of Glasgow's family, using documents provided by Glasgow's brother, Arthur. These included extensive genealogical records of the Glasgow family, tracing Glasgow back on her mother's side to Virginia's founding families, the Randolphs and the Yates. Family portraits saved by her great-aunt from General Hunter's invasion during the Civil War remained with Ellen Glasgow in her One West Main home until her death.

Surrounded by artifacts of a more affluent time before the family had emerged from the war as working-class—not poverty-stricken, but with a much smaller fortune than they had once possessed—her father adopted a strict policy of financial austerity, and her mother took on more domestic work than she could handle with her ailing health. Former slaves and their families were kept on as servants and given pay, regardless of their aptitudes. Anne Gholson Glasgow, Glasgow's mother, picked up the loose ends and managed what was left undone. Glasgow grew into a woman with distinct tastes for antiques and the finery of Victorian décor, while simultaneously championing racial and economic parity.

Rawlings had an interest in family legacies from her study of her own genealogy. She knew that members of both sides of her family had been captured by Native Americans and that one, Mary Kinnan, who was captured in 1791 by a band of Shawnee in West Virginia, had written a suspenseful narrative of the event. Her earliest known ancestors in the United States were men of the cloth, including Dominie Bogardus of the Dutch Reformed Church and, later, the Reverend Asahel Simeon Kinnan, a Methodist minister. Rawlings felt most connected to her maternal grandparents, Abram and Francis Traphagen, farmers in Michigan.

As Rawlings read about the death of Glasgow's mother and learned of its effect on her from family and friends, she was reminded of the painful loss of her father at a similar age. The legacy of her father played a role throughout Rawlings's life. He was the one who wanted her and her brother to attend the University of Wisconsin in Madison after he became friends with Senator La Follette from Wisconsin (Silverthorne 27). Rather than establishing herself financially with a lucrative career or marriage, Rawlings chose to be a journalist because she had a passion for writing that paralleled her father's passion for farming. She took work wherever she could get it, claiming at one point that her "Songs of the Housewife," published in Rochester's *Times-Union*, was evidence of how "she avoided one kind of prostitution by practicing another" (Silverthorne 54). Rawlings plunged into a writing career with the same relish with which her father had once plunged into farming, publishing anything and everything that would result in a paycheck. Her goal was to make a living doing what she loved.

Rawlings also saw in Glasgow's anger with her father a reflection of Rawlings's feelings about her own mother. In her scathing fictionalized memoir *Blood of My Blood*, Rawlings described her mother unambiguously:

> The physical ugliness of my mother was the bitter drop that tainted the fluid of her life. In her ugliness, she was guilty of the same spiritual inadequacy that so often characterizes beauty: she did not comprehend that the mind and soul, being intangible and therefore more closely related to the eternal, are worthier of service than the eye. She accepted her appearance as a calamity and early decided that the desirable things of this world are those likely to fall to the lot of the beautiful woman: wealth, position, fine raiment and the homage of men. (xxi)

The entire memoir focused on the story of Rawlings's mother, Ida May Traphagen Kinnan, unapologetically, and was not meant to be a truthful exercise. Though she initially submitted the manuscript to a writing contest, Rawlings wished to forget it ever existed, requesting that it never be published, a request that was contentiously overlooked after her death when the manuscript was discovered in a collection of materials belonging to Julia Scribner Bigham, Rawlings's friend and protégé. In the same way that Glasgow was resentfully dependent on her father financially, so did Rawlings depend on her mother to support her, especially during her college years. Ida Kinnan, like Francis Glasgow, made sacrifices for her daughter, many of which are detailed in the later sections of *Blood of My Blood* when Rawlings describes how she "took in greedily everything her mother tendered: dropped her nightgown and soiled underwear on the floor of her room for her mother to bend her back over" (128). At one point, she tried to explain her conflicted relationship with her mother to her husband, Norton Baskin, by describing a nightmare in which she was seeking a place to call home and ended up begging her mother for help. She analyzed the dream as indicating that "some sort of betrayal on the part of my mother made me feel without ground to stand on, while at the same time leaning on her" (*PM* 112). Most of her writings about her mother demonstrate exactly this kind of push-pull relationship.

Her mother's devotion to Rawlings came at a price. Rawlings complained in letters to her future husband, Charles Rawlings, about her mother's snide comments during their apartment-hunting in New York City after Rawlings had finished college. Ida Traphagen Kinnan felt that her daughter owed her. The price was to conform to social norms, be the kind of daughter her mother could brag about to her friends and possibly use as a stepping-stone in her own attempts at upward mobility. When it came to her daughter dating, she never approved of Charles Rawlings or of any of the women her son, Arthur Kinnan Jr., dated. None of her children's potential mates lived up to Ida's own standards, or the standards she expected of her children.

Rawlings found it difficult to escape her mother's influence early in her career. She began writing professionally for organizations like the YWCA, the *Louisville Courier-Journal*, and the Rochester society magazine *Five O'Clock*. Most of these pieces were society pieces, at times satirical, but largely geared toward women of a certain social class. This writing echoed her mother's admonitions to Rawlings when she was a young girl not to "write such queer things" because, after all, "people want to read happy things" (*BB* 79). Ida Kinnan feared that her daughter would not "make any kind of name" for herself if she was "peculiar" (*BB* 79). Yet Rawlings wanted the very things her mother disliked: to live off the land, trade good manners for brash acts that were honest and bold, and, most importantly, to indulge herself, rather than living to please others.

When Rawlings read about Ellen Glasgow's relationship with her mother, she found a reversal in roles, with Glasgow wanting to protect her mother against a harsh world. She fashioned one of her most pathetic characters, the title character of *Virginia*, after her mother. Virginia is a young woman who believes in the precepts of Southern culture and morality. Her father, Gabriel, the rector of the local Episcopal church and a man of honor, loses his life defending a black man from a lynch mob. Her mother is a saint who works her fingers to the bone, so her daughter will never have to lift a finger. Buying into the self-sacrificial lifestyle of her mother and her faith in the nobility of men, she places all her hopes in a relationship with a young socialist playwright, losing any remnant of her own identity by transforming into his helpmate. Marriage becomes their downfall, as it does in many of Glasgow's novels. To support his new wife and their future children, Oliver must compromise his ideals and take a professional position that leaves him little to no time for his writing. Virginia trades her loyalty to her husband for an obsession with her children, refusing any assistance in the home. Her son inherits her feelings of maternal obligation and abandons his aspirations to care for his mother when Oliver leaves her for another woman. Glasgow's mother never had the luxury of an empty nest because she was constantly bearing children—eleven in all, two of whom died in infancy and a third before he was grown, as well as one who was stillborn. With the sheer volume of children, Anne Gholson Glasgow was heavily reliant on inherited black nurses, or "mammies." Glasgow maintained close, somewhat filial relationships with her former "mammy," her mother's former "mammy," and their families throughout her life, helping them financially and caring for their family plot at the cemetery for "colored people" in Richmond.

Rawlings read about the trials faced by Glasgow's mother in *The Woman Within* before Irita Van Doren had it published. Anne Gholson Glasgow, who married at 21, had her first two children before the Civil War. Her second two were born during the conflict, and she had trouble feeding them, partly because food so often ended up in the hands of the scavenging remnants of passing armies who would invade her home and raid her larder. The remainder of her children came immediately following the war, when the South was still experiencing the devastating effects of the Reconstruction Acts. In spite of all these trials and her mother's struggle with anxiety, Glasgow remembered her as a positive figure in her childhood. Glasgow wrote of her own birth in her autobiography: her father recorded "the unhappy event as occurring on April 21st." Her mother always celebrated Glasgow's birthday on the 22nd. As Glasgow had come into the world at four in the morning, "I suppose Father had considered it was still night, while Mother, a more sanguine spirit, who welcomed ten children with joy, had dreamed of the more confident morning" (*WW* 5). She used this example to explain why she sympathized with her mother and mistrusted her father. Glasgow wrote:

> My mother was the center of my childhood's world, the sun in my universe. She made everything luminous—the sky, the street, the trees, the house, the nursery. Her spirit was the loveliest I have ever

known, and her life was the saddest. I have two images of her, one a creature of light and the other a figure of tragedy. One minute I remember her smiling, happy, joyous, making gaiety where there was no gaiety. The next minute I see her ill, worn, despairing, yet still with her rare flashes of brilliance. (*WW* 13)

Glasgow's desire to bring joy back to her mother's life propelled Glasgow onward, even though at times it seemed nearly impossible.

Rawlings received many different reports of the life-changing experiences at Jerdone Castle that Glasgow described in her autobiography. Glasgow's later biographer, Susan Goodman, speculated that around this time, Glasgow's father, Francis, was found having an affair with a colored servant, a reason for Anne Gholson Glasgow's not wanting to keep a maid. Speculations about the affair appear in various letters and interviews collected by Rawlings, as well. Arthur Glasgow speculated to Rawlings about his mother's unhappiness at Jerdone Castle: "Except my poor mother, who had the burden of housekeeping, I think we all more or less enjoyed Jerdone Castle."[1] Whatever the reason, Anne Glasgow suffered a mental and emotional collapse, witnessed by her children that summer. Francis Glasgow remained in the city, visiting the family over the weekends that summer. In *The Woman Within*, Glasgow wrote that when she was ten, her mother became a chronic invalid, due to a "severe shock, in a critical period [originally written as 'climacteric']" (*WW* 311n1). Glasgow and her younger sister Rebe slept in their mother's room when their father was away and in an adjoining room with the door open when he was there, leaving them completely exposed to her breakdowns. She refused to take medicine to help her sleep and paced the floor during the night. Glasgow lamented that her mother could have been treated medically, but her physicians downplayed her illness and suggested that she think happy thoughts or try a change of scenery. While her father appeared to be devoted to his wife and children when they were sick, he did not understand or respond sympathetically to mental illness in his wife or, later, in his son, Frank, who took his own life as a young man.

Rawlings did not expect to find in Glasgow the protective spirit she showed toward her mother. The Glasgow that Rawlings knew experienced her own nervous conditions and anxiety. Her sympathy for her mother's condition, however, extended to Glasgow's brother, Frank, during his own mental decline and following his suicide. Glasgow wanted her mother and Frank to prefer her, given her willingness to speak up for them. Her mother instead grew closer to Glasgow's younger sister, Rebe, when the two of them traveled alone to Mississippi to visit Anne Glasgow's brother (*WW* 73). Whether or not she actually played such a role in her mother's life, Glasgow perceived herself to be an advocate and caretaker for her, as she did after her mother's death for her sister Rebe. Rawlings came to see Glasgow as less frail and more iron-willed when compared with her mother. She also learned that Glasgow had, like herself, transformed out of her family's expectations for her into the writer that she became.

Rawlings learned that Glasgow had complicated feelings for her father, whose work ethic and charitable giving she admired, even while she condemned the strict line he took with sensitive family members like her mother and brother. The love-hate relationship mirrored Rawlings's own feelings for her mother. In one portion of her autobiography, Glasgow felt compelled to clarify that her father had never physically abused anyone in her family, but then chose to excise that portion from the final manuscript as unnecessary (*WW* 311n2). Francis Glasgow once paid Ellen Glasgow to stop asking him questions after work. He later offered to pay her not to read Lecky's *European Morals* and *Rationalism in Europe*, a work anticipating the New Deal principle, which illustrates both his respect for his daughter's intellectual prowess and his desire to direct her thinking to be more in line with his own (*WW* 25). Glasgow presented an image of her father that may be best described as a series of contradictions that she was trying to reconcile.

In a way not uncommon for this time period, Glasgow's father misunderstood the nature of mental illness in the family and lacked empathy for the emotionally vulnerable, behavior at odds with his devotion to family members suffering from physical ailments. Her father's alleged affair with a house servant caused Glasgow's mother not to want a maid, even when she needed the help (Goodman 19). This affair coincided with Anne's most severe nervous attack. While she was never able to prove it, Glasgow "believed [her father] a contemptible philanderer" and spread rumors to this effect "by confiding his sexual proclivities to close friends"

(Goodman 21). Irita Van Doren told a mutual friend "that Glasgow had a black half-sister" (Goodman 21). Her sister Rebe's son, Carrington Tutwiler, corroborated this view, remembering that neither his mother nor Glasgow ever "forgave their father for keeping a black mistress during their mother's illness" (Goodman 20). Glasgow wrote characters based on her father's infidelity in her novels, like George Birdsong from *The Sheltered Life* and Cyrus Treadwell from *Virginia*, whose affairs with "mulatto" women in the community were depicted as betrayals of both their wives and the women they manipulated. In spite of his philandering, Francis Glasgow posed outwardly as a very righteous Presbyterian, known in his community for helping the younger employees at Tredegar Ironworks and serving as an advocate for prison reform (*WW* 16). He was so strict with the children that Glasgow frequently feigned terrible headaches to keep from doing what he wanted her to do (Goodman 22). Francis Glasgow was also inordinately compassionate to family members during times of physical suffering, frequently staying by a bedside throughout a long illness without rest for himself, as if his suffering might help ease another's (*WW* 86).

Francis Glasgow was able to compartmentalize and order suffering based on his own ethical hierarchy, which he believed to be based upon a Protestant worldview. Mental illness paralleled personal weakness to Glasgow's father, while physical suffering, like the suffering of Job, could not be helped and could be endured with comfort and understanding. This same hierarchy applied, much to Ellen Glasgow's chagrin, to animals, which he felt were meant to serve mankind and which were incapable of personal salvation. Abusing or even destroying animals was, in his estimation, mankind's right, and not the great sin that Ellen Glasgow attributed to such acts. Rawlings, who enjoyed the occasional hunt but kept beloved pets like her pointer dog, Moe, sympathized with Glasgow's childhood experiences as she learned these details about her friend. Glasgow characterized her father in her autobiography:

> My father had little compassion for the inarticulate, and as his Calvinistic faith taught him, the soulless; and because of this and for many other reasons, including this iron vein of Presbyterianism, he was one of the last men on earth that [my mother] should have

married. . . . His virtues were more than Calvinistic; they were Roman. With complete integrity, and an abiding sense of responsibility, he gave his wife and children everything but the one thing they needed most, and that was love. Yet he was entirely unselfish, and in his long life he never committed a pleasure. For pleasures were not only unnecessary to the scheme of salvation, they were also extravagant, and he held fast to property, not for his own sake, but for the sake of his family. He spent nothing on himself. (*WW* 14)

One could speculate that Francis Glasgow applied this same hierarchy to servants, especially former slaves in the family's employment. While too little is known to corroborate fully the details of Francis Glasgow's affair, Ellen Glasgow explored examples of similar relationships in her fiction, the most damning in the novel *Virginia*, whose title character Glasgow admitted was a caricature of her mother. In that novel, Cyrus Treadwill, the uncle of Virginia's love interest and a perfect example of the Calvinistic industrialist, sires a child by a black servant and then refuses to support or even acknowledge him. Cyrus's resemblance to Francis Glasgow goes further. His only redeeming qualities are those of frugality and loyalty, and his loyalty is given only to those who fit certain criteria, namely Gabriel, who served with him in the war, and Oliver, the son of his deceased brother. Everyone else he considers beneath him, including women, servants, and African Americans. Rawlings would have seen the same contradictions in Francis Glasgow. In fact, one of the letters she discovered in her research on Glasgow came from a former employee, and described how Francis gave the man, a stranger to him, employment and helped train him in the lumber business, even getting him "a decent suit of clothes" when he did not have one to wear to church (Goodman 114).[2]

Rawlings had not expected to learn the depths of Francis Glasgow's cruelties. Her own father, Arthur Kinnan Sr., inspired her. She remembered him as the father who had once rescued her from the rough seas off the coast of Maine when their dinghy overturned near the wharf: "although Arthur cut his hands badly on barnacles trying to hold the dinghy close to the steps, it overturned . . . in heavy oilskins and rubber boots . . . he said quietly, 'Put your arms around my neck.' She did so, clinging to him without fear until they were rescued and rowed to shore"

(Silverthorne 17). Memories like this one of her father recur in Rawlings's novels through characters like Pa Baxter in *The Yearling* and Lantry Sr., Piety Jacklin's father, in *South Moon Under*. Rawlings saw that she and Glasgow had each dealt with their fathers in their writing—just in different ways.

Glasgow's father also lacked the physical aptitude of Rawlings's father. In Rawlings's notes, she wrote how Glasgow's mother told her children that their father tried to join the active Confederate army and even drilled his workers, but he was sent back to his job at the Tredegar Ironworks and told that that was more important for the cause.[3] Francis's uncle sent him to take charge of the blast furnaces to supply the ironworks with pig iron. According to Arthur Glasgow, their father never mentioned the war; Arthur was born one month after Lee surrendered. Francis Glasgow retired at eighty after a lifetime of being the manager at Tredegar, and then died at eighty-six.[4] The few commendable remarks Rawlings could find that Glasgow made about her father related to his treatment of employees at "the Works" and his early activism with prison reform. Glasgow wrote of her father: "But we were made of different clay, and I inherited nothing from him, except the color of my eyes and a share in a trust fund, which he had accumulated with infinite self-sacrifice. Everything in me, mental or physical, I owe to my mother; and it is possible that from that union of opposites, I derived a perpetual conflict of types" (*WW* 16).

Marjorie Kinnan Rawlings could relate to the lifelong influence Francis Glasgow had on his daughter, but her experiences had come from the severe trauma of her father's early death. In a letter to Norton Baskin, Rawlings admitted to having "nightmares of homelessness . . . all probably Freudian in that I have never had a true home since my father's death, yet I have understood and outgrown my childish attachment to him" (*PM* 130–131). Her father was principal examiner in the U.S. Patent Office, but according to Rawlings, "he lived the true life of his mind and heart on his Maryland farm" (Tarr and Kinser 343). Rawlings claimed that she "learned her love of nature" from her father. Her mother's family was from southern Michigan, and she also spent her summers on their farm. Living close to the land as she was growing up "planted deep in

[her] a love of the soil, the crops, the seasons and a sense of kinship with men and women everywhere who live close to the soil" (Tarr and Kinser 343). Rawlings realized, however, when researching her grandparents' life for *The Sojourner* that their lives were not exactly as she had imagined them, just as she recognized later in life that she had idealized her father. Her maternal grandfather, for instance, was better educated and more articulate, with a passion for violin that his religious mother discouraged (*MM* 550). She even found a receipt for a book on astronomy that she imagined her grandfather to have read in detail. It became a reference text for her work on *The Sojourner*. Her maternal grandmother and her sister both wrote poetry, mostly religious, "but very vivid" (*MM* 550). These discoveries shaped the way in which Rawlings constructed characters in *The Sojourner* to have qualities of tortured artists thinking "along cosmic lines" (*MM* 550).

From time spent in primitive camping on the land to listening to her father's lectures on the value of crop rotation, Marjorie Kinnan Rawlings developed a passion for the natural world, where she was allowed to run wild, wear overalls, and bathe in the creek with her younger brother (*BB* 76). In a letter to William Kelley about her father's property, Rawlings explained how her father "was one of the first to co-operate with the U.S. Department of Agriculture on experiments with the inoculation of seed, rotation of crops, and the planting of alfalfa to be turned under a certain number of years to enrich the depleted land" (Bigelow and Monti 395). (Coincidentally, the rotation of crops with alfalfa is a major theme in Glasgow's *Barren Ground*. She uses it to demonstrate the education and success of Dorinda Oakley after her tragic romantic failure and subsequent experiences in New York.) Rawlings was proud of her father's farm, begun with no capital and developed during evenings and weekends around his full-time job in D.C. He traveled ten miles to and from the farm by train. The farm was a dairy farm with a registered Holstein bull, and became self-maintaining the same year her father died (Bigelow and Monti 395–397). Rawlings remembered it as an idyllic place where they would stay in tent colonies (which her mother hated) during the summer. Her father would use a special bird-like whistle intended just for her as he approached (Bigelow and Monti 395–397). What Rawlings does not describe in her letters is the distance that the two experienced in her teenaged years, at least according to her fictionalized autobiography *Blood of My Blood*, as she took on a more active social life. In her works, Rawlings lives out her father's dream by conveying the beauties and harsh realities of living off an inhospitable land.

Rawlings also enjoyed the compassion of a father who lauded childhood and play in a way that Francis Glasgow would never have considered. In one childhood incident, Rawlings remembered climbing out of her bedroom window to "[dance] madly in her nightgown around and around the chestnut tree . . . the full moonlight plain on the flesh of her gay and spindly legs" (*BB* 58). When her mother upbraided Arthur for encouraging Marjorie, he responded, "She's doing the only sensible thing on a moonlit night like this" (*BB* 58). His declaration to her that night became the title of her fiction-memoir: "You'll never know how much your father loves you. You're mine—blood of my blood, bone of my bone, flesh of my flesh" (*BB* 59).

Glasgow never had the kind of advocate that Rawlings had in her father. Arthur Kinnan would stand up for Rawlings whenever he felt that her mother's plans for her were harmful. Glasgow's mother might have played this role had she been stronger, but her weakened state led to Glasgow advocating on *her* behalf more often than not. When Marjorie Kinnan Rawlings was offered a place in an exclusive girls' school as an attempt on the school's part to inspire the wealthier, "indifferent protégées," Arthur Kinnan protested that she would be socially ostracized and potentially viewed as a charity case (*BB* 90). In Rawlings's mind, her father's protestations came from his consideration for her happiness, while her mother, though convinced by these arguments, was more concerned with her daughter's entrance to society, going so far as to move the family to apartments in the northwest section of the city where the public schools drew from the "better classes" (*BB* 91). Arthur Kinnan gave his wife the authority to make such changes as long they continued to fit within the family budget, in part to placate her for going along with his Rock Creek farm venture.

As she read about Glasgow's traumatic loss of her mother when Glasgow was a young adult, Rawlings recalled her own loss of her father in her adolescence. Her father's death of "acute uremia"—what today might be associated with kidney failure—was hard. She judged herself harshly when relating the story in *Blood of My Blood* by focusing on her distracted attentions to a young man who had come to take her on a date. In this narrative, she maintained her composure, prepared a meal for her brother, and helped deal with the physicians and her suitor when it became apparent that the situation was critical. Rawlings comes across as her own harshest critic in the scene, writing herself as a self-involved teenager, annoyed with her parents, even as her father lay dying.

Her parents were a primary influence in Rawlings's writing and career. Her mother's role comes across in her early journalism, and her father emerges as a key figure in her Florida fiction. Rawlings was able to find the same strong influences in Ellen Glasgow's writing career. In Glasgow's case, her experiences with her parents led her to become a staunch supporter of social justice and individuality.

Glasgow and Rawlings contended with siblings during their careers, as well. During her work on the biography of Glasgow, Rawlings received innumerable pieces of correspondence and material from Glasgow's brother Arthur, the same name given to Rawlings's brother and father. She also had to navigate the possessiveness that both Arthur and Glasgow's sister Rebe felt over Glasgow. Rawlings only had one brother, but that relationship had taught her, as well, the challenges that being a successful writer could impose on a sibling relationship.

One sibling of Glasgow's whom Rawlings did not meet was her sister Cary, who was also one of Glasgow's closest friends. Cary and her husband, Walter McCormack, educated Glasgow in those subjects her father disavowed, introducing her to the works of Charles Darwin and John Stuart Mill (Thiébaux 14). Cary helped Glasgow publish her first novel by using connections with a friend who was a professor at the University of Virginia in the economics department. She even gave Glasgow fifty dollars to have her first manuscript reviewed by a literary agent in New York (Goodman 41). Rebe and Cary were the first two people with whom Glasgow shared her first published novel, *The Descendant* (Goodman 47). A close family friend, Roberta Wellford, told Rawlings that Cary was brilliant, and saved Ellen Glasgow in more than one way.[5]

According to Wellford, Cary helped Glasgow cope with her deafness after an operation that increased the severity of it. Glasgow had become a recluse who worked all night and slept all day. Cary encouraged her by telling her that the deafness could help her work, and helped her to enter the world again. After her terrible descent into isolation, Ellen Glasgow and Cary were able, with the financial assistance of Arthur Glasgow, to take a long trip that brought Ellen out of seclusion (Goodman 57). By then, she had a hearing device that she kept in a discreet silver mug (Thiébaux 26). The two sisters traveled together regularly, relying at first on the generosity of their older brother Arthur before gaining some financial freedom from Glasgow's earliest earnings. Tragically, Cary became ill and died when they were both still young women, following the early death of her husband. Glasgow did everything she could to ease Cary's discomfort during the final stages of her illness, purchasing her dressing gowns and renting a summer home for her convalescence (Goodman 120). The last words Cary read were the inscription to Glasgow's *The Miller of Old Church* (1911), which Glasgow dedicated "To my sister Cary Glasgow McCormack in loving acknowledgment of help and sympathy through many years" (*WW* 120). Her death devastated Glasgow. She ended up renting an apartment in New York to get away from Virginia for a time. Cary was instrumental in launching Glasgow's career, and her death had a lasting impact on Glasgow's writing.

Rawlings was much more familiar with Glasgow's younger sister, Rebe, who grew to think highly of Rawlings after meeting her. Glasgow was overly maternal toward Rebe, whose marriage upset her. Rebe was Glasgow's only younger sibling, and Glasgow remembered crying when she first saw her mother holding Rebe as a baby for fear that her affections had shifted to the new child (*WW* 17). The two girls were very close, and traveled together frequently as adults. After Rebe married, they began having conflicts. Carrie Duke, one of Glasgow's close friends and a neighbor of the Glasgow family, told Rawlings that Rebe's husband Carrington came across as unpleasant and even "cross."[6] According to Arthur, Glasgow and Rebe had another falling out after Glasgow criticized Rebe's son, also named Carrington, and his fiancée prior to their marriage. Arthur advised Rawlings not to include any of those details in her biography because they were family matters that should not be aired.[7]

Glasgow and Rebe made up with each other in two back-to-back letters, written by Glasgow and reviewed by Rawlings in her work on the biography, that illustrate their closeness:

> Your letter has made me cry, for I know I oughtn't to have written what I did to you—but conversations like that with Cary somehow seem to make me lose all my balance. If I have ever loved anybody I have loved you, and I thought I had always been as good to you as I was able to be during all these years. I suppose it's silly to get upset by what Cary says, but she made me feel that I never wanted to see any member of my family again. Of course you are the only one that has ever come in any vital way near to me, and it was because I cared more for you than for myself that I was always eager for you to marry, because I realized that my work took up so much of my time and you had nothing in your life that corresponded to it. I shall always love you in this way, but I have a terrible temperament to deal with, and I have always felt satisfied simply to know that you were well and happy however far off you were. For years you were the only thing that kept me alive and yet I know that because of my own absorbing wretchedness, I never was as great a pleasure to you as I might have been. However, that's over, and you are, I think the dearest and sweetest human being on earth. Be as happy as you can, but if you ever need me, I will come through fire and water to help you. . . . It is terrible that you should feel so badly. . . . You know I love you, my darling little sister. (PC 38–39)

The next letter, sent the very next day, continued to try to explain Glasgow's actions and to solicit sympathy from her younger sister:

> I am distressed that I have hurt you, and yet I don't suppose under the circumstances that I could have helped it. In New York I did feel a change (I thought you seemed to enjoy everybody else more than me,[8] but I reconciled myself to it, though not so pleasantly as I might have done, I suppose. Then I had that talk with Cary, and I felt suddenly that I'd never been any use to anybody and this made me want to get away from there for good. Life is very difficult here; it wouldn't be perhaps for another person, but I'm too nervous to

fit into it. I cried over your letter yesterday and my eyes have filled with tears whenever I've thought of it—but if I could feel that you are perfectly well and cheerful I shouldn't mind so much if I had to give you up. What worries me is the thought that you are sick. I love you better than I've ever loved anybody in my life, I know. (*PC* 39–40)

Glasgow needed the affirmation of Rebe, as much as she needed affirmation about her writing from friends and critics. Rawlings understood this about Glasgow early in their friendship and was always careful to include words of praise and admiration in her letters to Glasgow.

In her notes on Rebe Glasgow Tutwiler, Rawlings remarked how similar Rebe and Glasgow looked, yet Rebe claimed the two did not resemble each other when younger. Rawlings also described Rebe harshly after meeting her: "ostensibly sweet, but filled with hate, hypocrisy and malice" and with "a strident, nerve-wracking voice."[9] Glasgow's letters indicate that she and Rebe shared a love for ruins and that she had seen Rebe look into the eyes of the sphinx in Egypt when the two were traveling like one older than her years. However, most of her letters are to Rebe were filled with maternal nagging about Rebe's health and habits, frequently chastising her about what she should do and why, or even what she should wear. Rebe admitted to Rawlings that she had destroyed much of Glasgow's correspondence, presumably to censor information she deemed too personal or inflammatory. Her destruction of letters did not begin to compare with what Glasgow's eldest sister, Emily, did after moving in with their father to care for him when Glasgow was in New York following Cary's death. Sometime between 1911 and 1916, while Glasgow was in New York, Emily found all of her manuscripts and letters in the top of a closet and burned them, so she could clean the closet shelf on which they had been placed (*WW* 278). Emily never liked Glasgow, and was one of the two sisters who had intercepted the letter Glasgow wrote to her mother to tell her that Glasgow's father had killed her pet dog while her mother and Rebe were visiting a brother in Mississippi.

Rawlings interacted most with Glasgow's brother, Arthur, who had supported Ellen Glasgow's career and was immensely proud to have an accomplished writer as a sister. Rawlings had first written to Arthur in

1953 to explain that Glasgow's literary executors had asked her to write the biography, even though at one point Arthur had thought such a book unnecessary. Rawlings told Arthur in this letter that her emphasis "will almost certainly lie on the body of her work which I believe will become increasingly important as time passes, so that she will take her place along with Jane Austen and Maria Edgeworth as a social historian."[10] These sentiments would clearly have appealed to Arthur, who seemed to feed off his sister's literary fame in his own personal connections. Rawlings also ensured Arthur that she "dearly loved Ellen Glasgow the woman and admired her profoundly as a writer" and that she planned on using any personal material about her life "with great discretion."[11] As a final nod to Arthur, Rawlings wrote that she understood how much he "did for [Glasgow] . . . how greatly [he] helped her."[12]

Glasgow published most prolifically during the 1920s and 1930s when the book trade was economically depressed. She came to depend upon financial assistance from Arthur, but she also shared with him professional ambitions that he respected. Glasgow once wrote to Arthur, "I can never understand the way you and I appear to have exhausted all the ambition in the family."[13] Arthur Glasgow took an engineering degree from Stevens in 1885 and worked as the chief engineer for New York Gas and Light, later establishing his own gas and light company, Humphreys and Glasgow, in London, where he lived for many years and was the sole establisher of gas lines for the Eastern Hemisphere. Arthur funded Ellen Glasgow's many European tours, which included visits to his illustrious London home, visits that Ellen Glasgow often resented because of the intense social schedule her brother and his wife kept. Near the end of Glasgow's life, Arthur retired to Norfolk, Virginia, later purchasing a house in Palm Beach, Florida. It was here that Rawlings was able to meet with him while researching her biography of Glasgow.

Arthur enjoyed showing off his sister, the best woman writer in the state of Virginia. In one letter, he wrote, "Everyone I meet puts me on a far higher plane in their regard when they learn that you are my sister."[14] Arthur encouraged Glasgow and her friend Carrie to stay with him in London, where they would be free to come and go, except that he expected them to attend any parties he hosted while there. He regularly expressed his sincere admiration for Glasgow, pointing out in one letter:

Blood of My Blood · 87

"Life takes a lot of courage, but I know you will not fail in that respect."[15] After reading *Barren Ground*, Arthur wrote poignantly to Glasgow, "It is without question a great work of art, and the greatest of your productions. I have never seen the curtain raised so completely on all the actions and reactions of a human body, a human mind and a human soul, nor have I ever read a book so absolutely devoid of 'thrills' which is so thrilling. I am immensely proud of you."[16] Not to be outdone, Arthur wanted to ensure that his own intellectual merits were equally understood, frequently pointing out to Rawlings his own honorary doctorates of science from Washington and Lee and Wabash, after recognizing his sister's five honorary degrees, not including the ones she turned down due to health reasons. He made sure to send Glasgow his own letters to newspapers and political pamphlets, despite the fact that they did not agree on political issues. When Glasgow died, Arthur vigilantly promoted obituaries and memorials written in her honor, which he collected, and wrote letters of thanks or corrections to publications mentioning Glasgow's career.

As Rawlings familiarized herself with Glasgow's financial background, she learned that Glasgow's lifelong home, One West Main, had been purchased by Arthur Glasgow after their father died. He allowed Glasgow to remain there and even financed home improvements over the years, but the deed stayed in his name. Their father, Francis, left the contents of the house to Glasgow with the stipulation that she take care of him in his last years, but Arthur was the only family member with the financial resources to purchase the house outright. Glasgow did stay with her father at the end of his life, but Anne Virginia Bennett, who remained with Ellen Glasgow as her trusted secretary, provided most of his end-of-life care. Bennett eventually became a leader of the Richmond SPCA with Glasgow. In one letter to Rebe, Arthur wrote that Glasgow, despite being his "greatest beneficiary," met his pleas that she "adopt a similar attitude," to his, presumably toward other family members, with resentment.[17] Arthur wanted to donate the house to a historical society after Glasgow's death, but was challenged by Glasgow's own will, which stated that Bennett could live in the house as long as she was able to maintain it. At that point, Glasgow wanted the house to go to the Richmond Society for the

Prevention of Cruelty to Animals (SPCA). This left Arthur, the owner of the house, with a great dilemma.

Rawlings learned more than she wanted to know about Arthur's political views when he voluntarily sent her stacks of pamphlets and political tracts he had written. These post-WWII pamphlets espoused his strongly worded views on a number of current issues, including the consequences of unrestricted suffrage.[18] He opposed trade unions, argued for an extended workweek, and believed in paying women lower salaries to discourage them from keeping their jobs once the war ended. Arthur also differed from his sister in his proposition that the "problem of the Negro" in the South would best be handled by leaving the South alone to figure out its own problems.[19] Glasgow frequently addressed the harsh reality of such policies in her novels, which included stories of men being lynched, as seen in *Virginia*, and various experiences of former slaves in their respective communities, as seen in *In This Our Life*, based largely on the integrity (or lack thereof) found in the white power structures of those communities.

Arthur Glasgow's greatest outpouring of political unrest appeared in his writing on suffrage. He argued for intensive voting restrictions to ensure the democratic process occurred fairly. He wanted to suspend or revoke suffrage for people living on public relief, those who refused to pay a poll tax to cover the cost of elections, criminals and reckless drivers, citizens who opposed the Constitution, and the vague category of those "otherwise proving unfit even to govern themselves," as demonstrated, for example, by government-blaming and supporting revolutionary change.[20] He also opposed lowering the voting age from twenty-one to eighteen, asserting that eighteen-year-olds were still dependent on parents or legal guardians, and people under the age of twenty-one committed the most post-war violent crime. Other measures in his pamphlets called for stricter term limits.

In her interviews with Rebe, Rawlings quickly saw that both Rebe and Arthur competed for Glasgow's loyalty and affection. Rebe offhandedly remarked to Rawlings, "I hope you will want to use the poem she wrote to me in your Biography, to show Arthur that Ellen loved me."[21] She then proceeded to tell stories from their childhood of how close she and

Glasgow had been, with Glasgow nicknaming Rebe "Shadow" for always trailing her. Rebe then told Rawlings exactly what she thought about Arthur: "Arthur is my brother, but I hate him. Oh, you saw the best side of him. You just don't know him. He's perfectly hateful. He insulted Ellen, to me. He said she was rude. Why he's the rudest person himself."[22] Rawlings took careful notes on her interviews, and viewed Rebe with suspicion and skepticism. Rebe was not likable, but Rawlings won her over in order to learn more about Glasgow from a different perspective.

Rawlings could also tell that Arthur was not as knowledgeable about Glasgow's personal affairs as he pretended. In a letter to Edwin Mims following Glasgow's death, Arthur wrote that he knew nothing about his sister's autobiography, published several years later as *The Woman Within*. Rawlings was given immediate access to Glasgow's autobiography by her literary executors, and knew how long she had been writing it. Arthur also claimed that Glasgow only had a few letters and that he did not think she wrote many, a clear misconception. The volume of letters that she did not destroy attests to the fact that she was an ardent letter writer. The arm's length at which Glasgow kept her brother may be measured by his ignorance about to whom Dr. Mims should inquire regarding the autobiography, Anne Virginia Bennett or Carrie Duke. Arthur assumed that one of Glasgow's closest companions might know about such a manuscript, but he had no idea that she had appointed literary executors to handle an autobiography she wanted published posthumously. He was, however, aware that Glasgow preferred any personal effects remain unpublished until the people who could be hurt by them had passed away, wishes that were indeed expressed by Glasgow before her death. Arthur was similarly unaware of the extent of Glasgow's deafness for many years (Goodman 59). Her sisters knew about the deafness and frequently discussed it with her and helped her in social situations, but Arthur remained in the dark about it, according to interviews with Rawlings, and interpreted the social anxieties surrounding her deafness as the thought that "she repelled him."[23] He later learned enough about her disability to ask her for a recommendation of a hearing device for a close friend. Letters from Glasgow to Arthur later in her life did refer to her deafness. She even used the condition as an excuse for not visiting him in England by herself, and wrote to him about the device she used for hearing, the Mears Ear Phone.[24]

In a rare moment of brutal honesty with Rawlings during an interview, Arthur confessed that his sister "simply had no use for any of her family."[25] He admitted, "She had no use for me. Except for what I did for her."[26] In Glasgow's defense, she wrote Arthur many letters of thanks and praise, one of which even hoped for some record of Arthur's life to be published and claimed that he had always been a wonderful brother to her. In one example of her praise for Arthur, Glasgow stated, "Nobody in the world was ever more generous, but I always feel that you do so much more for others than anyone is able to do for you."[27] Arthur had made most of his sister's financial and business arrangements, in addition to supporting her with various financial trusts and gifts.

Rawlings had more difficulty discussing Glasgow's relationship with her other brother, Frank. She knew that Glasgow experienced a dark period in her life when Frank killed himself in his early twenties while working with their father at the Tredegar Ironworks in Richmond (Goodman 113). Frank, two years her senior and her most beloved brother, had always been a sensitive young man, much to his father's chagrin. Francis Glasgow, in an attempt to toughen up his son, sent Frank to the Virginia Military Institute. Frank's desire to please his father left him withdrawn and anxiety-ridden for his brief life, the majority of which he spent trying to impress his father through his obedient tutelage in the family business. Frank's suicide and the information she gathered on Glasgow and her sisters led Rawlings to conclude that the whole family was morbid. In her notes, Rawlings asked herself whether this morbidity was the fault of the mother or father or both.

Rawlings experienced a much less dramatic childhood, with only one brother—who was not planned by her parents, at least according to her somewhat fictionalized memoir, *Blood of My Blood*. She must have been amused to read about and interact so much with Glasgow's brother of the same name, Arthur. Arthur Kinnan Jr. could not have been more different from Arthur Glasgow. If anything, Rawlings treated Arthur like Glasgow treated Rebe, telling him what to do and occasionally joining forces with him against their mother. Rawlings's brother was a womanizer, and consistently needed financial support from his successful sister. In one letter to Max Perkins, Rawlings asked for an immediate cashier's check, so she could send Arthur a $4,500 loan to help him with business expenses (*MM* 387). Nevertheless, Rawlings loved her brother, naming him heir and executor of her will prior to her marriage to Norton Baskin (*MM* 354). She and Arthur shared a love of adventure and nature, even though he was also an instigator who knew how to set off her short temper. When the family relocated to Madison, Wisconsin, so that Rawlings could begin her university education, Arthur, the younger brother, had to move as well, and also attended the University of Wisconsin per his father's wishes. He did not suffer from the move, as Rawlings once remarked that the Delta Gammas were after him—"the good-looking Devil" (Bigelow and Monti 31). His problems with women worsened in his adult life. He had three failed marriages, and many more failed relationships.

Arthur and Rawlings shared a fierce temper that caused them many intense arguments with each other and their loved ones. In one scene from *Crossing the Creek*, Anna Lillios described how Arthur once visited Rawlings at her Cross Creek home only to find, along with Rawlings, who was returning from a trip to North Carolina, that the house was in a horrible state and not suitable for entertaining. Arthur convinced Rawlings to confront the servants in their home: "I've seen what you have to put up with. We're going over to the tenant house and run that black ape off" (Lillios 144). They burst into the servants' bedroom to find one of the servants, Kate, fully clothed, lying between two naked men, Kate's husband and a "sweetheart." Both men ended up running away, never to be seen again, and Rawlings felt "sad" that she had lost the chance to rehabilitate them into good servants. Later, she found that Kate had stolen money from her brother's wallet, further dampening his visit, a visit in which she hoped that they would spend the day hunting and then come "home at night to an orderly house and a waiting and edible dinner" (Lillios 144). Rawlings and her brother fed off one another's vitriol, making it worse.

Arthur Kinnan Jr. also influenced Rawlings positively in some areas. They loved hunting together. Rawlings visited her brother in Seattle and Alaska on hunting expeditions, and brought him to Florida to hunt with her. Rawlings considered writing a novel, tentatively titled *Tidal Highway*, about her experiences traveling from Seattle to Alaska with her brother (Bigelow and Monti 103–104). Rawlings must have wondered about Glasgow's views of these hunting expeditions, given her work on animal rights. However, Rawlings was motivated by a passion for the outdoors that Glasgow shared. After Rawlings forewent hunting in her later years, "when her love of animals overcame her enjoyment of the sport of hunting," she still preferred to accompany the hunters as an observer "for the pleasure of the company and the enjoyment she got from being outdoors" (Silverthorne 66).

Arthur gambled on his professional life as Rawlings did, but without as much success. He moved to Alaska, where he operated a boat for fishing and tourism. During WWII, he shifted to independent contract work for the government and barely broke even financially. Like Cross Creek, the harsh Alaskan environment led to frequent breakdowns of equipment while Arthur was transporting defense workers to nearby bases. Rawlings believed that those bases were constructed in Alaska to give the U.S. a location from which they could launch an attack on Japan. She seemed, however, to buy too easily into her brother's assurances that profit was always just around the corner in his various ventures, and was torn between a desire to have him closer to her and the knowledge that he annoyed her to no end. She wrote to Baskin, "In a way, I want Art to come very much, and in a way I don't" (*PM 203*). Rawlings compared Arthur's work strategies with their father's after Arthur described the challenges he was having with an engine replacement for his boat that led to the discovery of dry rot and cost him two thousand dollars to repair. He was constantly struggling just to stay on top of things. Rawlings wrote to Baskin, "It seems to me that he is repeating Father's performance right over again, killing himself with overwork and nervous strain, to do the type of thing and live the type of life he wants to. I believe in living as one wants to, but not in killing oneself at it" (*PM 256*). His work vacillated among private passenger work, government contracts, and fishing charters, but the work was scarce enough that at one point he contemplated joining the navy. Rawlings cared deeply for her brother, in spite of the many financial and physical risks he took. At one point, she encouraged Art to come and support her during her legal trial when Zelma Cason sued her for invasion of privacy over her portrayal in *Cross Creek*.[28] She explained to Baskin that she really wanted Art there because she thought he was depressed and it would cheer him to visit her, but encouraged him not to come when she realized it would further complicate his situation as he worked doggedly to ready his boat for the upcoming season. Her concern, repeated in so many of her letters about Art, was that "There is so much more in his letter, and he isn't off the beam at all, as I feared, but only harassed to death for several good and valid reasons . . ." (*PM* 461). Her worry over Arthur, compounded by her concern for Baskin during WWII and strain over the lawsuit with Cason, led to a lengthy delay in her completion of *The Sojourner*.

Arthur's multiple marriages and children from different wives also exasperated Rawlings, who was childless and had approached her second marriage cautiously after the failure of her first one. She disliked her nieces and was convinced that they feigned an interest in her for her money. She told Baskin about a letter from Arthur's daughter Marjorie Lou before her marriage, remarking:

> Something about it disgusted me and made my blood run cold. She gushed so about wanting me to know, and she was so thrilled, etc., and of course all she is doing is making sure of as sizable a check as possible. I couldn't possibly mean a damn thing to her—we spent one day together when she was about nine years old. I'm just the rich relative who by God ought to come across. It makes you understand why old aunts and uncles ignore nieces and nephews and leave millions to homes for cats and dogs! (*PM* 151)

This letter is especially amusing, given that Ellen Glasgow did just what Rawlings described here by leaving the bulk of her estate to the Richmond SPCA. In spite of her harsh words, Rawlings did send a generous check to Marjorie Lou for $300, a gift that purportedly led Marjorie Lou and her mother into crying fits. It also inspired Barbara, Marjorie Lou's sister, to ask Rawlings what she would like for Christmas, a note Rawlings translated into, "You came across for Marjorie Lou, now don't forget Mother and I are around, too" (*PM* 180). She lamented Arthur's marriage to his first and second wives, the second of whom she felt was "BORN to be a kept woman" (*PM* 180).

Most of her letters to Norton Baskin about Arthur refer to his third marriage, a union that seemed destined for failure from the beginning. Rawlings's frustration over her brother's rash decision to get married again is palpable in these letters: "A letter from Arthur, I do love him so, and miss him, and he is about the most *impossible* human being I have ever known. He is *considering* marrying—but not the Seattle Miriam. I begged him not to marry anyone at this stage of his work" (*PM* 549). Rawlings was disappointed in and concerned for her brother after he justified this marriage to a woman named Grace by saying, "[she] has enough fine attributes and few enough faults so that I feel I'm not to be able in the future to do better" (*PM* 552). He admitted that he was not exactly in love, "but very fond of her" and wrote that "her worst fault is her poverty," by which Rawlings wondered "if he means she has a large and impoverished family he would have to help" (*PM* 552). Rawlings bemoaned this union to Baskin and accurately predicted the outcome of the marriage when she wrote: "Did you ever hear of a drearier prospect for a marriage? He will get fed up with her in no time, and have to split his property in half once again. I shall say nothing further, however, to him. But he can just sweat this out alone" (*PM* 552). Rawlings was correct about the end of the marriage, but did not foresee the worst part of the split: a fight over a newborn nephew who ended up becoming, in her mind, at least, the son she never had.

Arthur's third failed marriage was a devastating blow to Rawlings, and contributed to her struggle with *The Sojourner*. It began for Rawlings with a letter from Arthur's wife that arrived before Arthur even confessed to Rawlings that he had gone through with the marriage, against her advice. Grace's letter informed Rawlings that she had a seven-year-old son and was expecting "another offspring with Arthur" (*PM* 586). She claimed to have read Rawlings's letters to Arthur, making Rawlings a bit worried about what she had written. She later learned Arthur did not know his new wife had written to her. Grace included a picture of them. Rawlings generously hoped that Arthur's "loveability [*sic*]" would make up for his "Kinnan neuroticism" (*PM* 586). She let Grace know that she expected to hear back from Arthur and not "through his wife" in future (*PM* 586). The letter marked the beginning of the end of that marriage, and could be interpreted as an attempt by Grace to make good with Arthur's wealthy sister. She was clearly interested in using Arthur for financial security, and was not interested in the child over whom she tried to retain custody. Relatives raised her seven-year-old. Rawlings summarized Arthur's relationships as springing from his desire to have whatever he wanted without waiting for it, which is "Not too bad about a little boy's circus, but another matter when it comes to a grown man's wives—and their babies" (*PM* 594). Grace and Arthur's relationship was a rebound from the woman he had written of in letters directly preceding these, the aforementioned Miriam from Seattle. Grace was a Canadian whom Arthur had sponsored to remain in Alaska with him. Arthur believed Grace's letter to Rawlings was vengeful, despite the tone seeming pleasant enough to Rawlings, who worried he was showing signs of being "demented" with all these hasty decisions (*PM* 594). Between Arthur's letter and her worries over the lawsuit with Zelma Cason, Rawlings's writing suffered. While she continued to produce shorter works, there was a long dry spell between *Cross Creek* and *The Sojourner* that included her trial, Arthur's troubles (especially over his infant son), and Baskin's deployment during WWII.

Rawlings was particularly annoyed by Arthur's criticism of Grace's sexual history, especially given her own sexual liaisons that included two marriages and an alleged affair with a married man, Otto Lange. She sarcastically described what Arthur would want in a wife to Baskin: "she should be raised in a Catholic orphanage to be frugal and appreciate everything he does for her. She should have her virginity tested by the whole College of Physicians and Surgeons. Then when he instructs her in the delights of love, he must explain to her that he is the only man in the world with such a gadget. When she begins to enjoy it, she should refuse firmly to allow him to ever touch her again, so he will respect her" (*PM* 596). Rawlings struggled to explain her brother openly and honestly to her husband, worrying that she was "betraying" him in some way by discussing his flaws (*PM* 596). After all, she once told Max Perkins that her brother was the only close relative who thought her to be the "one perfect woman in the world" (*MM* 111). Rawlings's relationship with Arthur was much more genuine than Glasgow's relationship with her own brother Arthur, on whom she was financially dependent. Their mutual independence and struggles with work and relationships helped justify Rawlings's brutal honesty with her brother.

Arthur's final failed marriage upset Rawlings the most because it produced the son she had always wanted. As Rodger Tarr pointed out in his introduction to *The Private Marjorie*, "Her need for a son, hauntingly addressed in 'A Mother in Mannville' (1936), and later rekindled in her thoughts of adopting her brother's child, is a recurring subject. Her lamentation at one point about the 'false alarm' when she once thought she had 'killed the rabbits' (7 April 1944) was not lost on Norton" (4). Killing the rabbits was a way of denoting a positive pregnancy test and was based on an early 1930s test that involved injecting a woman's urine into a female rabbit. The injected rabbits were killed and their ovaries removed for examination. Rawlings grappled with her own anxieties about her brother's son more than she had regarding any of his daughters. She told Baskin that she would have felt the same way about any boy as she did about her nephew, Jeff, but that had the baby been a girl, "he could drown her for all of me" (*PM* 611). Rawlings traced her own distaste for women touching her to "the physical revulsion [she] felt for [her] mother" (*PM* 416). She criticized Arthur's parenting of Jeff, worrying that her brother's overindulgence of his son "was likely to make Jeff not only totally unadapted to normal living, but even homosexual" (*PM* 12). After writing such crass and offensive lines to her brother, Rawlings must have been bewildered by the language Glasgow used with her brother. They filled their letters with flattery and formal descriptions of events, mostly writing about medical treatments.

Arthur's son, Jeff, became his final means of retaliating against Grace once they separated. Rawlings was terrified that Arthur's rash acts would result in him losing Jeff permanently in a custody battle. He threatened to kidnap Jeff and "get him placed somewhere," "possibly with [Rawlings]" (*PM* 607). This suggestion infuriated Rawlings, who was torn between considering the possibility and feeling unduly pressured into it. Baskin had suggested that she should have a child because it "would be a stabilizing influence on her, but she [thought] that the long rope he [gave] her with freedom to do as she please[d] and not feel trapped at the cottage [had] been good for her" (*PM* 607). A child could have also been another obstacle to her creative output. After going through the pros and cons, Rawlings decided that the only way she could take Jeff would be through "adoption, to make him permanently theirs," so that she and Baskin would not have to worry about Arthur and Grace fighting over him and potentially taking him back (*PM* 607–608). She recommended that Arthur find a family near him to board the child during his work absences, so he could stay close to his son. Rawlings, even at this early stage, was devoted to Jeff, worrying that Arthur would lose affection for the boy as he "had periods of coolness with the girls and then spurts of longing and suffering over them" because of the distance from them (*PM* 607–608). She did not trust Arthur to find a new woman to be a mother for Jeff because she "wouldn't trust him to find a foster mother for a rabbit" (*PM* 608). Baskin proved to be the one with the calmest demeanor during this crisis, demonstrating his level-headedness and desire to see Rawlings happy. He encouraged her to advise Arthur not to kidnap the child, but to go through the legal process to gain custody, and to stay in the marriage, if possible, until Jeff was school aged, at which point he could consider divorce and custody appeals. Baskin threatened to write Arthur himself to let him know how much emotional distress the situation was causing Rawlings. She convinced him not to write the letter, admitting that hysteria ran in her family (*PM* 609). Baskin even convinced her to write to Arthur about the situation without having taken a drink (*PM* 610). Most of her letters to her brother, and husband for that matter, were composed while she was intoxicated. These more objective letters received the harshest response from Arthur, who systematically denied ever having considered giving Jeff to her, pointed out her shortcomings as a wife, and told her to be better to Baskin. His defensiveness at the change in tone in Rawlings's letter was because of the way it exposed his own instability by not berating him in kind. They quickly returned to civil exchanges with one another, bearing out the emotional rollercoaster that the two siblings experienced with one another throughout their lives. Rawlings's writing went through similar ebbs and flows as she tried to get it right and was easily influenced by her interactions with family and friends and the moods produced by those relationships.

Eventually, Grace initiated divorce proceedings, doing so while Arthur was on a hunting trip so she could tie up his assets. She filed for "separate maintenance," so Arthur would need to support her and Jeff financially in their own lodgings (*PM* 624). He tried for reconciliation until he could position himself better with his own attorney and move them from Juneau to Seattle, where the courts were not as biased toward mothers. These ploys eventually failed, and Arthur took off with Jeff. Baskin welcomed the two into his home while Rawlings was in New York working on a book. When Baskin described to her the ways in which Arthur struggled with Jeff's temper tantrums, Rawlings remarked that they must be hereditary, describing to Baskin in detail the kicking and screaming tantrums Arthur had as a child (*PM* 643–644). Baskin was quite taken with Jeff from the start, and expressed his love for the child in a way that suggests he would have liked to have adopted the boy.

When Rawlings finally met Jeff in New York, she thought he was adorable, but she was concerned about Arthur's obsession with the boy and how spoiled he was. He refused to have Jeff outside while the two talked and insisted on taking away the Pablum cereal she made for him, giving him instead "a buttered blueberry muffin," "strawberry jam," and "some of his coffee with cream and sugar in it" (*PM* 646). Rawlings imagined Jeff growing into a resourceful, outdoorsy boy, and did not think these indulgences would get him there.

Her experiences with Arthur colored Rawlings's writing of *The Sojourner*. She left Arthur to find lodgings for himself in Syracuse while she went on to Rochester for a time, only to return feeling like "Ase Linden going into Benjamin's slum room to find her lost brother" (*PM* 653–655). By that point, she had offered her brother any financial and emotional support she could render, in spite of her wariness that he would want help with some business schemes when she meant to help him only with basic living necessities. The rooming house she discovered in Syracuse was impoverished and crowded, with the landlord sleeping in the living room area of the house behind a piano and magazine pictures stuck to the walls. Arthur and Jeff had been "amicably" evicted (*PM* 653). Rawlings gave up her hope for the boy, telling Baskin to hold off on sending a crib. The last in this series of letters shows Arthur preparing for his trip back west with Jeff to try his hand at the legal proceedings, and Rawlings writing various checks to cover Arthur's third bankruptcy. His daughter Barbara had also run away with a married man, leaving a young child and baby behind.

It was following these traumatic times with her brother and the completion of *The Sojourner* that Rawlings began her study of Glasgow. She met Glasgow's brother and sister, read her letters, and learned from her autobiography and close friends about her childhood. In so doing, she found that Glasgow, like herself, had developed her identity as a writer to assert herself against the expectations of others. Conversations with Arthur Glasgow reminded Rawlings of her own Arthur and the frustrations that siblings contribute to the writing life. She found a commonality, once again, with the woman whose life she wanted to write because she felt the world needed to understand her.

Figure 1. Ellen Glasgow's house, One West Main, Richmond, Virginia, circa 1933 (photograph courtesy of the Richmond Society for the Prevention of Cruelty to Animals, Albert and Shirley Small Special Collections Library, University of Virginia).

Figure 2. Ellen Glasgow, n.d. (photograph courtesy of the Richmond Society for the Prevention of Cruelty to Animals, Albert and Shirley Small Special Collections Library, University of Virginia).

Figure 3. Col. Henry W. Anderson, 1917 (photograph courtesy of the Virginia Historical Society).

Figure 4. Cross Creek, 1939 (photograph courtesy of the University of Florida, Smathers Library Special and Area Studies Collections, Literary Manuscript Collection).

Above: Figure 5. Marjorie Kinnan Rawlings seated at her typewriter at home in Cross Creek, 1940s (photograph courtesy of the University of Florida, Smathers Library Special and Area Studies Collections, Literary Manuscript Collection).

Right: Figure 6. Norton Baskin, n.d. (photograph courtesy of the University of Florida, Smathers Library Special and Area Studies Collections, Literary Manuscript Collection).

4

Women Who Will—Do

A memory stirred him. He had come here a year ago, on a bland and tender day. He had splashed in the creek water and lain, as now, among the ferns and grasses. Something had been fine and lovely. He had built himself a flutter-mill. He rose and moved with a quickening of his pulse to the location. It seemed to him that if he found it, he would discover with it all the other things that had vanished. The flutter-mill was gone. The flood had washed it away, and all its merry turning.

The Yearling, by Marjorie Kinnan Rawlings

DURING THEIR BRIEF YEARS OF CORRESPONDENCE, Rawlings and Glasgow frequently touched upon political matters that were of interest to each of them. They were not shy about using their literary celebrity to promote causes close to their hearts.

The two women shared an opposition to the prohibition of alcoholic beverages, enacted by the Eighteenth Amendment and repealed by the Twenty-first Amendment in 1933. Glasgow was an animal rights activist who helped to found and promote the Richmond SPCA. Rawlings focused on ecological concerns, namely the preservation of the Florida landscape and its wildlife. Both women shared concerns over WWII. In their letters, they supported one another's causes.

When Rawlings met Glasgow, she was expecting the socialite from Richmond known for her regional novels to be well-dressed and accustomed to the comforts of life in the city. Instead, she came to know an iron-willed woman who played that role, but had hidden depths that would take time to uncover. In an interview that Rawlings intended to use in her biography of Glasgow, Glasgow described her three lifelong desires: "I always have wanted to go around the world quite alone, but I never have been able to do that because of partial deafness. I have always wanted to live on a farm.... And, third, I always wanted to write. I have written."[1] Glasgow only achieved one of her lifelong dreams, but she found in Rawlings a woman who had achieved them all, independently. Rawlings preferred the isolated rural life of which Glasgow dreamed. She explained to Glasgow: "The conflict, for me, lies not in any adjustment to [Norton Baskin], but in the pull of the isolated rural life against the more or less sophisticated and urban life that we must share" (Bigelow and Monti 216). For Rawlings, furniture shopping in New York was no more or less enjoyable than making scrapple from a freshly butchered hog. She needed both experiences. Glasgow admired her friend's ability to traverse those borders effortlessly, and envied Rawlings's strength.

Their friendship paralleled, nearly exactly, the Second World War, the letters they then exchanged providing a treasure trove of their personal views about the war. As writers, they poignantly expressed their complicated feelings over the conflict. Rawlings shared her anxiety over Norton Baskin's service with Glasgow, who had experienced similar anxiety and a broken engagement to Henry Anderson during the First World War. Rawlings learned the details of that failed romance much later. Rawlings was extraordinarily sympathetic toward the American troops because of her husband's service. Her books were released in Armed Services editions, and she saved and responded to frequent correspondence with soldiers who had read them. She also entertained troops at Baskin's hotel. In one letter, she explained to Glasgow how the officers would typically stay at Castle Warden, where Baskin was installing a cocktail lounge. However, they would occasionally have privates pass through the lounge or restaurant without knowing of its prestige. Two of those privates left as soon as they saw the menu, exclaiming, "We were looking for fried 'possum, and they didn't have it."[2] After Baskin left for India with the

American Field Service, Rawlings was more subdued in her discussions of military operations. In one of these later exchanges with Glasgow, she wondered "whether the inertia comes of being more disturbed about my husband than I will admit."[3] She detailed Baskin's military training in "motor-mechanics, against the day, I am sure, when Mountbatten makes his push to re-take the Burma Road."[4] She was too worried about Baskin's safety to complete any of her own work.

Rawlings discovered Glasgow's remarks on war to be largely abstract and centered on the destructive forces that accompanied conflicts. She understood the sometime necessity of war in preventing larger wrongs, but disapproved of most military conflicts. One of her nuanced protestations to war had to do with the destruction of natural beauty. A *Richmond-Times Dispatch* article that Rawlings included in her files quoted Glasgow as saying that "generals may not mind the men they kill, but they should at least consider the beauty they destroy."[5] In a 1942 interview from the *New York Times Book Review*, also in Rawlings's collection, Glasgow claimed, in response to the war, that there was only one sin, "cruelty;" everything else could be called an "error in manners," if anything.[6] That cruelty, she claimed, was against humans and animals alike. Glasgow feared that war caused people to regress from advancements made in reducing cruelty and caring for the poor and defenseless, including animals, and felt that she could not have lived in the Renaissance, in spite of its glorious artwork, because of its cruelty.[7] When the Second World War began, Glasgow felt overwhelmed by it, and admitted to Rebe that she was trying to forget it, "since there is nothing to be done about it" (*PC* 192). She had no sympathy with either side, viewing Hitler as a "psychological tornado" who should have been left alone "to spend himself in Eastern Europe" (*PC* 192). By entering the war, the other nations were, in Glasgow's opinion, going "out of their way to be destroyed," along with democracy (*PC* 192). In a letter to Van Wyck Brooks, Glasgow wrote, "the world seemed to go deranged with war madness" (Rouse 255). In her correspondence, her understanding of the conflict appears limited, and she comes across as an isolationist; Glasgow argued in a letter to Rebe that "England would be mad to get entangled with any other Continental quarrel, or to defend any border, except her own" (*PC* 181).

Glasgow thought that allying Britain with Russia and France would lead to the end of the English government and of English democracy (*PC* 181). She contended that Communists and Fascists were the ones trying to bring on the war and have England enter it (*PC* 181). Of course, these were all sentiments expressed early in the war that were shared by many Americans who did not want to face another global conflict. In another letter to Rebe near the end of the war, Glasgow wrote that she was saddened over the loss of so many young lives that she was sure would be forgotten "when victory comes, as it must and will" (*PC* 249). Rawlings must have found these remarks difficult to read when she found them, especially given her personal investment in the conflict.

Rawlings had initially steered clear of the topic of military conflicts. She attended the University of Wisconsin during the First World War and did not engage deeply in discussions about it. She wrote one article for the *Kappa Alpha Theta Magazine* on how fortunate the university was to attract so many prominent speakers during the war, and praised the profits being given by student organizations to war funds, but the piece did not go into any of the politics surrounding the war effort in depth (Tarr and Kinser 140). Other students at the university wrote strongly worded opinion pieces that resulted in Rawlings's name being attached to a letter from the editors of the *Wisconsin Literary Magazine* to the President of the Board of Regents apologizing for recent publications and agreeing to send material to the University censor in the future (Tarr and Kinser 143). She took a stronger stance during WWII. Rawlings, as noted previously, responded at length to letters from soldiers. She wrote a touching introduction to a series of letters from Caleb Milne, a stretcher bearer with whom she corresponded, after his death in a German mortar shelling while "giving aid to a wounded French Legionnaire." Rawlings wrote, "One feels humble and a little frightened that such a man has died for us, untimely" (Tarr and Kinser 309). She supported the troops serving with Norton Baskin in India by writing anonymous parodies of Emily Post that were published in their company's newspaper. These parodies were full of booze and risqué humor, certain to entertain their mostly male audience (Tarr and Kinser 298–302). In one sample, she responded to a letter asking for the correct response when a man accidentally walks in on a woman using the toilet; his initial response of "excuse me" had resulted in screams (Tarr and Kinser 301). Rawlings responded as Emily Post by giving a perfunctory speech, including the line, "Your functional purposes are your own affair. But I cannot help admiring you perched there with your paradisical dress histed [sic] up to reveal so many charms" (Tarr and Kinser 302). She had an intimate connection to the men serving in the war and wanted to do whatever she could to ease their burden.

Rawlings moved back to Cross Creek for the winter after Baskin left, "because it feels like home and is unusually isolated with the gas situation being what it is."[8] Back at the Creek with her pointer dog, Moe—the one she got after her beloved pointer Pat was struck by a car—and a new Siamese kitten, Rawlings hoped to calm her mind and work on *The Sojourner*. Instead, she spent most of her time responding to overseas correspondence from servicemen, feeling obliged to "answer them all," even when, to her dismay, letters sent as far away as the Aleutians and South Pacific were answered within ten days with remarks like, "Hope to hear from you soon" (Bigelow and Monti 251). Rawlings shared the general effects of the war on her mental and emotional state with Glasgow, as it weighed on her with "a great pressure" that seemed to exacerbate "whatever else one is battling, mental or physical" (Bigelow and Monti 251). The war also took a toll on her orange grove, with shortages in fuel and in the help she needed to plow and maintain the property. Cross Creek returned to a jungle-like state, full of wildlife that encroached upon her home. Rawlings turned these same problems into questions about Glasgow's experiences, wondering whether fuel shortages would keep Glasgow from traveling to Maine, where she spent most summers.

Rawlings, who had been a college student during WWI and fairly detached from the war effort, found herself overwhelmingly engaged in WWII. Glasgow, on the other hand, was older and not in good health by the time WWII began. Rawlings had a bird's-eye view of the war from her Crescent Beach cottage. Passes were required to drive on the roads leading to her cottage, where "convoys went by, bombers droned overhead, and big ocean tankers could be seen sliding along close to the shore to evade submarines" (Silverthorne 206). Both Baskin and Rawlings volunteered as "fire wardens and aircraft spotters, and twice submarines were spotted from the post where they did duty" (Silverthorne 206). Rawlings raised funds and purchased bonds while privately lamenting her novel, *The Sojourner*, which she could not even begin amid the chaos of the war.

Rawlings knew from her visit with Glasgow that the author had a special interest in protecting and promoting the lives of domestic and wild animals. She respected Glasgow's passion for animals, but took a slightly different view as a woman who had learned to live on the land. In her nonfiction book *Cross Creek*, Rawlings described the harsh realities of life in the Florida wilderness on her orange grove. One section in particular upset Glasgow because it described Rawlings throwing rocks to chase away a dog that she had previously befriended. It was the only part of the book that Glasgow disliked. Rawlings defended the story by claiming she had "exaggerated to make a good story, even at my own expense."[9] In her revised version of the story, Rawlings admitted that the dog "was only a casual acquaintance and walked with me just twice."[10] Glasgow's reaction to the story was doubly funny to Rawlings because Baskin had reacted in the same way, "sulking" for "two days" before demanding to know how Rawlings "could treat that dog that way[.]"[11] When Rawlings pointed out that she had merely thrown "a handful of light gravel in his direction," Baskin countered, "Well, it *feels* as though you threw rocks in his face."[12] Rawlings relayed this story in its entirety to Glasgow to justify her inclusion of the story and to let Glasgow know she was not the only person to object to it.

One of the side effects of the war effort was the lack of available labour needed to tame the wilderness around Cross Creek. Rawlings wrote to Glasgow that she felt "obliged to kill the possums, for they eat not only all the eggs, either fresh or under setting ducks and hens, but the biddies" (Bigelow and Monti 252). The possums were cooked and eaten, along with turtles, by "old Martha" Mickens who lived and worked for Rawlings at the Creek along with her family. Rawlings told Glasgow that she would not bother most of the snakes because they were harmless, but she would "dispose of the chicken snakes, who also eat eggs and biddies" (Bigelow and Monti 252). As much as Glasgow loved animals, she had never had to respond to the challenges of a predatory food chain, replete with reptiles that would take an egg out from under a roosting hen. She took a harsh view of hunting, particularly for sport, as was common among the gentlemen of Virginia, but she was by no means a vegetarian.

Rawlings shared her love for Florida and desire to preserve its natural landscape with Glasgow in her letters. She wrote to Glasgow about a publication on the St. Johns River, composed by their mutual friend and writer, James Branch Cabell, and co-authored by A. J. Hanna, that paid homage to its rare beauty and diverse wildlife. Glasgow, in turn, sent Rawlings a copy of an article she had read, titled "Notes on the Breeding of the Ground Dove in Florida," by Donald J. Nicholson, in 1937. She inscribed the article with the note, "Thought this might interest you. Isn't it amazing? Wish I had been able to observe too. Still missing you. Much love.—E."[13] The article described the mating habits, nest-building, and shared parenting of ground doves, and would have appealed to Glasgow, who kept her own garden as a kind of bird sanctuary, and to Rawlings, who favored red birds in her own writing.

Nature was also a crucial element in the works of both authors. Rawlings found herself more concerned with "man in relation to a natural background," while Glasgow was more interested in "man against a sophisticated background."[14] However, Rawlings wondered whether her choice was not indicative of her own "cowardice," without explaining how it could be seen as cowardly.[15] These differences figured into the women's activism as well. Rawlings preferred a grassroots style of activism by working with people in her community to help them set their own standards for living as their needs demanded in a harsh rural climate, while Glasgow endowed the SPCA with financial gifts and then created a formal organization to operate at her behest for the good of the animals.

Glasgow chose to write and speak on behalf of her causes, and did not back down from a fight when she felt one was warranted. In an essay on Glasgow by Douglas Southall Freeman, a prominent historian and biographer of the day, he referred to her as an "idealist" for her defense of social justice issues. While Freeman highlighted her important work with the SPCA, he also alluded to the fact that she would find the ablest attorney among her friends to defend any "wrongly accused Negro" and that she would fight the hardest for the poorest sufferer (11). Rawlings read this and other articles, including one in the *New York Herald Tribune Books*, in which authors described Glasgow as an opponent of "inhumanity" wherever she found it, for man or dog.[16] These progressive views on class and race did not extend to the sexual liberties that were emphasized in the writing of her day. Glasgow despised the representation of perversion and obscenity in much of the latest fiction (Freeman 11–12). Rawlings agreed. She lived a life free of sexual repression, but chose to write about sex "chiefly as a biological, creative process relating to animal life and not as sensuous experience relating to human life" (Bigelow 60). Rawlings respected Glasgow's ability to speak out constructively for those causes she supported without jumping on the bandwagon too quickly for causes she felt needed more careful consideration.

Rawlings found that most information about Glasgow's activism related to her work as a founder and president of the Richmond SPCA. Her love of animals came across in nearly all of her literary works. Catherine Rainwater examined the use of the "predator-prey code" in *Barren Ground* and *Vein of Iron* and the ways in which Glasgow's narrators in those novels "attempt to drive 'wildness' to the margins of the narrative universe" (Scura 215). She cited many examples to illustrate the "the rise of female, articulate power over inarticulate males" and the establishment of a "female-dominated domestic world" through references to animal voices (Scura 217). This symbolic domestication would have been a reason for Rawlings to dislike Glasgow's literature, as she did initially. Her own place was with the wildness on the margins.

Glasgow had a great sympathy for birds, which Rawlings shared, and kept a garden with feeders meant to attract birds. In a letter to Rebe that Rawlings saved, Glasgow wrote about her concern that the birds would not get enough food in the snow and recounted an article she had read about the flight of birds to the South that was "of unusual quality" (*PC* 234). Glasgow lamented that some of the birds she was caring for in her garden during the winter were being killed by boys, "terrible about destroying birds with air rifles" (*PC* 174). In one news clipping that Rawlings retained, the Richmond SPCA, under Glasgow's advisement, pleaded with local residents to help birds during an upcoming cold spell by putting out pans of unfrozen water and fat or suet. The article reminded pet owners to maintain good bedding and keep their pets exercised during the freeze.[17] While Rawlings would not have gone out of her way to protect birds from natural events, like freezes, she enjoyed the diversity of avian life around Cross Creek, and empathized with Glasgow's attempts to protect birds in Richmond.

Anne Virginia Bennett shared with Rawlings many of the documents associated with Glasgow's work for the SPCA, including a poem titled "A Plea" in which Glasgow complained of the way in which God was revealed by man, and claimed that she had never taken Communion and found only anger and shame among those who "speak for God."[18] The poem concluded with Glasgow asking to be judged by God on her standing up for and having pity upon the "hunted and injured" animals of her day, rather than for her doubt.[19] In another poem by Glasgow, "A Creed," each stanza ended with "Lord, I believe" and included her beliefs that the greater should help the lesser, and that Buddha and Christ alike, and weed, flower, worm and man, "result from one supernal cause" (Freeman 15). Rawlings shared Glasgow's cosmic understanding that superseded any particular religious affiliation and emphasized instead the connection of humans to their natural world.

Rawlings found that Glasgow had traced this cosmic understanding back through the ages. In one letter to the SPCA, Glasgow quoted a younger writer: "Man's inhumanity to man is the milk of human kindness compared to man's inhumanity to animals."[20] She then cited historical figures who urged better treatment of animals: "From Plutarch, protecting worn out beasts of burden, from Leonardo da Vinci, buying caged song-birds to release them into the blue sky, down to the little American boy who gave his life yesterday for his dog, there is a strong, unbroken bond of fellowship."[21] Glasgow included a poem by Ralph Hodgson, "Bells of Heaven," that depicted the bells of heaven ringing when parson and people knelt to pray for suffering animals, "the tamed tiger, the dancing bear, blind pit ponies, and hunted hares."[22] Rawlings may have started her life with a similarly idealized version of man and nature, but her views were transformed by the act of making a living off the land. As Bigelow points out in *Frontier Eden*, Rawlings "often spoke about the grievous contrast between the *idea* in Rochester of running an orange grove and the *fact* of running the grove, where insects, drought, windstorm, and freeze all compromised the pleasant pastoral vision she had before she came" (Bigelow 57). It is difficult to philosophize about the plight of suffering animals when one is living as a suffering animal.

One of the views most divergent from her own that Rawlings discovered among Glasgow's letters was the hard line she took against hunting.

In one letter she found from Glasgow to her sister Rebe, the former declared that she was "sick to think of the hordes of savages roaming the woods and killing all the little wild things that I love" (PC 171). She hoped that Rebe, who lived in a more rural area near Lexington, would make her place a refuge for these animals and feed them. Glasgow tried to make a refuge at her own home, but ended up with mostly pigeons. Rawlings also loved wild animals, enough to adopt a baby raccoon named Racket during her writing of *The Yearling*, which features him as a pet of Fodder-wing (Silverthorne 119).

Rawlings shared Glasgow's affinity for dogs. In one letter she saved that was written by Glasgow to Rebe at Christmas, Glasgow wrote about finding a fox terrier puppy wandering in the neighborhood. She took him to the shelter, where they already had eighteen other dogs and received three more from the pound on Christmas Eve (PC 79). Christmas was always a busy time for the shelter because people would visit it looking for pets to be given as gifts: "One, a beautiful hound we got a home for at once and a small female poodle went in half an hour" (PC 79). Rawlings, who also loved dogs, was so distraught over the death of her pointer, Pat, that her friend, fellow writer Edith Pope, told Baskin, "I'm so glad it didn't happen before you were married.... You can more or less take Pat's place," to which he replied, "I just hope nothing happens to Dora" (Silverthorne 211). Dora was Rawlings's Jersey cow, whose milk or cream is required in so many of the recipes in *Cross Creek Cookery* that one friend suggested "she give away a Jersey cow with every book" (Silverthorne 211). The anecdote was deemed acceptable for the cookbook when it was released, and served as a perfect example of the sense of humor shared by Glasgow and Rawlings, both of whom were known to possess a sharp wit.

When she was working on her biography of Glasgow, Rawlings got to know Margaret Dashiell, a local Richmond artist and friend to Glasgow, very well. Dashiell told her the story of a time when Glasgow was very ill but still had several young SPCA members visit her in her home at her sick bed.[23] She wanted to encourage their participation. According to Dashiell, Anne Virginia Bennett told the women to "go up softly," where they encountered Glasgow lying on old-fashioned fluted pillowcases in a room filled with white camellias.[24] She was so fragile that she could not speak, but she was still determined to inject young blood into the organization, which had some "cranky" older members.[25] Running the organization became a strain on Glasgow, even though Bennett handled most of the day-to-day operations. In another letter Rawlings obtained from Glasgow to Rebe, Glasgow commented on her struggle to find help with "the Shelter" after one of the managers "began to drink" and the replacement was not suitable for the position, all during a time when "money was tight."[26] She called upon Rebe to help her place a dog she liked, telling her that Bennett would have it spayed if Rebe could find it a really good home.[27] Glasgow felt that the process of spaying a female was necessary but "dreadful," and that mixed breeds were the most attractive dogs.[28]

When reviewing Glasgow's estate plans, Rawlings discovered that her support for the Richmond SPCA extended beyond Glasgow's own life, much to the frustration of her fiscally minded brother. Glasgow chose to leave the bulk of her estate and all rights to her literary works and other documents to the organization in which she had invested so much of her time and resources (Goodman 246). She left most of her financial resources in a trust fund for Bennett's use during her lifetime, with the intent that they would revert back to the Richmond SPCA "in memory of Glasgow's dog Jeremy" after Bennett's death (Goodman 246). The Richmond SPCA continues to function as a strong advocate for animal adoptions, and rescues animals from municipal centers where they risk being euthanized. The Society houses animals in its main headquarters, where they are cared for until they can be adopted. Ellen Glasgow would be proud to revisit the organization she started and see the impact it is still having on the lives of abandoned animals.

Rawlings included many notes in her files that described Glasgow's exaggerated affection for her pets. She left notes reminding her survivors of her desire to have her deceased dog, Jeremy, exhumed and his body reburied alongside her in her casket. A 1952 article from the *Richmond Times-Dispatch* referred to one of her dogs, Bonnie, as the "Thousand Dollar Dog." Her cook, James, had told the local children of Richmond not to mess with Bonnie because Glasgow would not sell her, even for $1,000.[29] The children were so impressed that some of them got together and charged a cent per child to "see the thousand dollar dog."[30]

Bonnie slept on Glasgow's chaise lounge and was included in her will, with an allowance of twenty-five dollars per month should Bennett pass away before Bonnie. The story in the paper, which was also found among Rawlings's notes, noted how Bonnie's keepers before and after Glasgow's death would spell out "bath" and "doctor" around the dog because she would flee upon hearing either of those words.[31] Irita Van Doren told Rawlings that Bennett bathed the dogs regularly in her own bathroom.[32] Van Doren remembered Jeremy, a Sealyham terrier, white with some black spots, and Billy, all white. According to Van Doren, "Some of the things Ellen Glasgow said about dogs nauseated you."[33] After Glasgow's death, Bonnie did not like visiting Hollywood Cemetery, where her mistress was buried. Bennett told Rawlings that she believed it was because Bonnie remembered Glasgow and was unsettled by the gravesite.[34] Margaret Dashiell told Rawlings that Glasgow had offered her garden where her own dogs had been buried as a place for Dashiell to bury her dog "little Billee."[35] During her first trip abroad after the death of Jeremy, Glasgow wrote frequently to Bennett of the grief she was experiencing. In one letter that Bennett shared with Rawlings, Glasgow admitted that Bennett was closer to Jeremy, as his principal caretaker, and wondered how Bennett was able to "get any peace" (PC 116). Glasgow concluded these thoughts with, "But life has to be lived as long as you can't die & I must at last, I suppose, get my mind on something else" (PC 116). Glasgow's obsession with her pets was occasionally referred to as a "fetish" by friends and interviewers in these collected papers, and would have seemed excessive even to Rawlings, who frequently traveled with her pets.

Trips with her pets meant that Rawlings spent more time with her dog, Moe, and her cat, Uki, than she did with Baskin, who stayed behind when she traveled to manage the two restaurants and bar they owned at Marineland after he sold Castle Warden (Silverthorne 245). Glasgow would have liked to travel with her pets, but was not adept at caring for them or even managing them by herself. When she was still a young woman vacationing with her father at White Sulphur Springs in West Virginia, Glasgow left her dog Joy at home in Richmond because she was worried she wouldn't be able to manage him alone on the ride back. She missed him, even though he was terribly behaved. At one point, Glasgow tried to get a new dog, but had to give it up because Joy nearly killed him (*PC* 34). After she gave the new dog away, he ran away from his new owners and showed up outside her home. Glasgow took him in again and let him sleep under her bed, in spite of the fact that Joy "falls on him tooth and nail whenever he sees him" (*PC* 35). Later, her decision to bring her dogs Jeremy and Billie along with her on vacation was largely determined by Bennett's presence.

Rawlings's research also revealed that Glasgow had been an avid equestrian when she was younger and stronger, falling out with her father over his donation of her mother's horse Winnie to the Tredegar Ironworks to be turned into a workhorse (*WW* 86.) Rawlings came across in her writing as a rugged frontierswoman, but in fact "was only a mediocre swimmer and horsewoman, and had scarcely hunted so much as a rabbit" before moving to Cross Creek (Bigelow 58). Cross Creek did not have much in the way of horseback riding during Rawlings's time there. Glasgow, however, grew up surrounded by horses in Richmond and its surrounding countryside, and frequently witnessed domesticated horses being mistreated. After a local man was beaten by one Joe Johnston for whipping a horse when Glasgow was still a young woman, she concurred with her friend Anne, who remarked, "I always said there was good in Joe" (*PC* 36). In a letter Rawlings found from 1907, Glasgow wrote to Rebe about her stay at White Sulphur, where she was summering with their father, to describe "a dreadful man" who ran the stables and gave her a horse that was so old it could not "go above a walk unless he kicks him."[36] He also charged too much.

Rawlings clearly planned to focus a large portion of her biography on Glasgow's love for animals throughout her life. She kept a receipt of Glasgow's for the purchase of a plot in Bide-a-Wee cemetery in Nassau, New York, for pets, at a cost of twenty-five dollars.[37] Margaret Dashiell told Rawlings about the time when Glasgow came across a boy with a broken-down town horse that he was too poor to feed.[38] Glasgow fed the horse and outfitted the boy at Miller & Rhoads. As Dashiell told Rawlings, people knew to go to Glasgow about animals because she insisted, "I'm never too tired for that."[39] One of the physicians who treated Glasgow, Dr. William Porter, explained to Rawlings that Glasgow "*personified* animals."[40] He remembered her telling him, quite intensely, that she was "going to stop all animal experimentation."[41] Porter thought that Glasgow's love for animals could have been an "aberrant emotional outlet," related to her lack of sexual fulfillment in life.[42] Irita Van Doren also referred to Glasgow's love for animals as a "fetish," telling Rawlings that Bennett took care of Glasgow's pets and would "once in a while" bring them for Glasgow "to make a fuss over—then she was through with them."[43] One of Glasgow's relatives, Frances Williams, told Rawlings that she thought Glasgow's love of dogs "was a compensation for her deafness" because she could "talk to a dog, and need no answer."[44] She also thought that Glasgow found dogs to be more loyal than people, recalling her saying, "They never turn on you as humans do."[45] A more empathetic friend of Glasgow's, Roberta Wellford, told Rawlings about Glasgow's defense of animals as a child. She remembered Glasgow hurling herself out of a carriage to protect a dog being mistreated by a man.[46] Wellford remembered Glasgow holding the man's coat with one of her "tiny hands," while she beat him with the other.[47] During a trip to Spain with Rebe, Wellford recalled Glasgow vehemently explaining to a driver why they would not be going to a bullfight.[48] In one report Rawlings collected from the Richmond SPCA, Glasgow had written about the atrocities committed against animals in Virginia, as compared to laws protecting animals in New England, especially Massachusetts.[49] She included a letter that had been written by an unnamed citizen asking for better laws relating to the treatment of animals in Virginia, in which the letter writer claimed to have never seen such horrendous treatment of animals, even abroad in the Orient.[50] Even as her health was failing at the end of her life, Glasgow took the time to write to her sister Rebe about a person in Lexington who was trying to start a humane society and needed additional funds.[51] She asked Rebe to call on people she knew in the area to try to help fund it.

Rawlings was given a collection of letters sent to Bennett from Glasgow when she was traveling in Europe, many of which commented on the state of animals there. Glasgow frequently visited animal memorials and humane societies while abroad, and gave money whenever an organization impressed her. She wrote to Bennett from Scotland about visiting the grave on which the "blessed Bobby had slept every night for 14 years from puppyhood until death" (*PC* 122) As the story went,

"Canting piety would not allow him to be buried in the grave," but the old sexton buried him secretly under a rose bush in a flower bed (*PC* 122). Glasgow decided that she distrusted the Scottish religion (*PC* 122). She was pleased to report to Bennett that the war memorial in Edinburgh included every creature that had shared in the war "from man to carrier pigeon . . . even . . . mice that helped the men in the tunnels and little birds in cages," with the face of a dog in the "bronze frieze" (*PC* 122). Her only criticism was the way in which the war was romanticized, in spite of the "cruelty and brutality which are the seeds of war in reality" (*PC* 122). While on this particular trip in 1930, Glasgow encountered a Sealyham like Jeremy, for whom she was still grieving, and offered to buy him, only to be told by the wife of the man who agreed to sell him that she would sell the dog "over [her] dead body" (*PC* 123). Glasgow had lost Jeremy just before this trip, and spent the voyage across the Atlantic weeping inconsolably for him (*PC* 118). She told Bennett that she looked forward to joining Jeremy in Hollywood Cemetery (*PC* 119). During an earlier trip abroad, Glasgow had come across the Animal Rescue League in the poorest part of London while trying to find the Shelter of our Dumb Friends League (*PC* 99). It was located in a little house "founded by one woman, & now run by three women" that did more work than any other similar organization; unfortunately, that work was largely euthanasia (*PC* 99). Glasgow wrote to Bennett that the organization had put 51,000 animals to death during the last year because they were unable to keep them or find them homes (*PC* 99). While the visit made her feel sick, she was glad that she had seen it, and still felt that the animals in London were "the best taken care of" that she had ever seen, mostly because there were not as many work animals as in the United States (*PC* 99). Glasgow fretted over the driver provided to her by her brother Arthur on the trip because he drove too fast, and she was afraid he might run over a dog (*PC* 98). As they returned from Canterbury, she saw a dog killed by a Buick in front of them (*PC* 98). She insisted they stop, but the people had already sent for the "humane killer" because the dog was too far gone (*PC* 98). Glasgow marveled that everywhere a village existed in England there seemed to be some branch of the Humane Society (*PC* 98). It was the only place she had ever travelled where her heart was not "constantly wrung by dreadful sights," and she wished she could take some of the animals home with her (*PC* 98). She preferred Sealyhams, her dog Jeremy's breed, because they were "fashionable" there (*PC* 98). Jeremy, the dog that Glasgow had buried with her, was distinctive. His half-brother "Barking Hill Bootlegger" had won the "best dog of any breed at Westminster Kennel Show."[52] Rawlings preferred a good hunting dog and must have been amused by Glasgow's careful detailing of Jeremy's lineage.

Rawlings learned that Glasgow's fondness for her could have originated in Rawlings's own writing on animals and been cemented when Glasgow learned she also kept a dog. Glasgow frequently judged writers and dignitaries by their relationships with their pets, most notably in her extensive review of Virginia Woolf's *Flush*, which she admitted to "over praising" (*PC* 141). *Flush* was a biography of Elizabeth Barrett Browning's cocker spaniel, told from the dog's perspective. Glasgow also appreciated Thomas Hardy, whom she visited at his home while traveling in England, writing to Anne Virginia Bennett in one of the letters given to Rawlings that he was "attractive," "modern," and possessed of a heightened "sensibility," in part because he was "sympathetic about animals, as in his books, especially *Jude*" (*PC* 106). Glasgow became fond of Hardy's terrier during their visits and mourned his passing in her letters to Bennett. She thought May Sinclair, whom she met, was "nice, but pathetic," with some form of paralysis, but made sure to include a note to Bennett about Sinclair's love for her black cat (*PC* 100). When she visited Charles Dickens's home, Glasgow was pleased to find "planted in flowers and ivy the graves of his bird and two cats. The boards at the graves read (all marked by him) 'This is the grave of Dick, the best of birds,' and on another of a cat, 'Thou, O Lord, will save both man and beast'" (*PC* 97). She was sincerely impressed by the Duchess of Hamilton, whom she met at her brother Arthur's house over lunch. The duchess had given her life over to work for animals "and against vivisection in particular," and attended the lunch to discuss plans for an international humane congress with Margaret Glasgow, Arthur's wife (*PC* 83). Glasgow felt drawn to the duchess, in spite of the fact that her views were much more ardent than Glasgow's own: "She, however, is a vegetarian, does not wear fur, and appears to be as consistent as Mary Johnston, which is the most one can say" (*PC* 83). In all these instances, Rawlings must have wondered how much the theme of *The Yearling*, rather than its writing style, appealed to Glasgow.

Some of the activism Rawlings discovered was self-serving on Glasgow's part. Glasgow vigilantly supported individual liberties, and deplored the prohibition laws, which never kept her from serving her favorite beverages: mint juleps, old fashioneds, and sherry. In an article by Burton Rascoe on Glasgow that Rawlings saved, he wrote that she was a staunch opponent of prohibition who was simultaneously concerned with her "dwindling shelves of fine wines and liquors" and with the "cheap 'corn' being consumed" in lieu of mint juleps made with high-grade bourbon.[53] On her trips abroad, Glasgow complained that the ship would not serve ale on the first day because the law required them to be "three miles out before it could be served" (*PC* 120). On one trip, Glasgow celebrated having a "glass of wine with every meal," telling Rebe, "Nothing has ever given me the feeling of uplifted spirits like escaping from prohibition!" (*PC* 84). Rawlings was also a staunch opponent of prohibition. She defended moonshining in her novels and letters. Moonshining in Florida was a way for people to recover financially from failed crops or other causes of impoverishment (Silverthorne 71). Rawlings understood it to be one of the most "dangerous way[s] to eke out a living," more so than "illegal trapping or seining," because the courts were so intolerant of it, despite displaying some flexibility when it came to other activities that were "wrong according to the law but right according to [Cracker] code" (Silverthorne 70). Rawlings and Glasgow both enjoyed drinking and serving alcohol to guests, even when it meant illegal procurement.

Rawlings also learned in her research that Glasgow wanted to preserve the historic Richmond of her youth as adamantly as Rawlings wanted to preserve the natural landscape surrounding Cross Creek. Glasgow "deplore[d] real estaters" and "real estate subdivisions," which had a direct impact on the shifting culture and community of downtown Richmond.[54] Glasgow's house was described as "one of the few ancient houses in the section which [had] not been demolished to make way for the industrial expansion of the new South."[55] This statement echoes Glasgow's writing about the ruins of Europe, which she preferred to the architectural restorations that so frequently replaced them. Rawlings had letters from Glasgow to Rebe that described how much she disliked the "disfiguring preservation" going on everywhere in England because she preferred to visit the untouched ruins (*PC* 108). Glasgow felt that the "ruins and enchanted forests" encouraged her belief in "fairies and dryads" and were a revelation of the "spirits of trees" (*PC* 97). Her complex views regarding urbanization caused Glasgow to speak out against human welfare demands, saying, according to Frances Williams, a relative whom Rawlings interviewed, "I am for the down-fall of the up-lift."[56] In a letter to Rebe about the construction of a garbage disposal plant in the middle of the valley near Lexington, an area known for its beauty, Glasgow claimed that such desecration would never happen in Connecticut (*PC* 249). John Selby with the *Richmond Times-Dispatch* defended Glasgow's decision to leave New York and return to Richmond by explaining how Glasgow was both socially and politically active in Richmond, gathering together the Richmond elite to protest depression-era budget cuts to the Humane Society and running a bird sanctuary on her back porch in winter.[57] Rawlings recognized in Glasgow an affinity for place that rivaled her own.

Most of Rawlings's support for the ecology of Florida comes across in her representation of landscape and rural dwellers in her writing. However, Leslie Kemp Poole points out in *Saving Florida: Women's Fight for the Environment in the Twentieth Century* several instances in which Rawlings specifically pointed to ecological problems that needed to be resolved in her writing. Poole noted in Rawlings's works mentions of the decline of several species, "including the limpkin, a wading bird, and the Florida panther, which is now critically endangered" (84). As Poole points out, Rawlings wrote that she saw no reason to destroy black bears, yet she also offered "three recipes for bear meat to her cookbook's readers" (84–85). Rawlings also argued against clear-cutting measures that were destroying the longleaf pine forests in an article titled "Trees for Tomorrow" for *Colliers* and the U.S. Forest Service (Tarr and Kinser 289). The article began with a character sketch of a young boy in Mississippi, and then reached across the southern states to comment on the timber industry before pointing out that "the American forests are not infinite" (Tarr and Kinser 289). During World War II, the clear-cutting of forests in the southern United States intensified to the point at which it was creating ghost towns, as areas supported by sawmills became unlivable once the trees were completely eradicated. Rawlings found these practices atrocious, especially since most of the owners "of the 190,000 acres of commercial timber" did not live on the land but were "absentee owners" who called the timber "investment" (Tarr and Kinser 290). She argued that such practices were handled more responsibly by small owners and farmers than "big owners" who "have handled timber through greed, and thoughtlessness," even though a small owner might be thoughtless in his "need," as, for instance, if he had a sick child, which is more justifiable (Tarr and Kinser 291). Rawlings pointed out that trees were different from gold or coal because they could, and should, be grown and farmed. Her proposed solution to the problem of clear-cutting of native forests was the establishment of tree farms, like ones in the Osceola National Forest of Florida and the W. T. Smith forests in Alabama (Tarr and Kinser 292). She profiled two small farmers, each of whom was embracing scientific methods of tree farming to create a sustainable crop (Tarr and Kinser 293–295). Rawlings's outspoken dedication to trees was another reason why Glasgow, a professed "tree worshiper," was so attracted to her. Poole points out the importance of Rawlings's home and land now serving as a Florida state park, where her house is preserved, along with her orange grove, so that future generations can savor the beauty of the natural Florida habitat (Poole 85).

Her affinity for place also comes across in the support that Rawlings lent to ecological approaches that promoted the natural landscape of Florida. She wrote a lengthy review complimenting a work by James Branch Cabell and A. J. Hanna, "A River that Flows through Florida History," on the St. Johns River. In her own sketch of Florida, "Florida: A Land of Contrasts" for the *Transatlantic*, Rawlings described the history and people of the state along with the pros and cons of the tourism industry. As the wife of a hotelier in St. Augustine, her views on tourism were complex: "Those of us who prefer Florida's lush wildness to profitable commercialization regret the increasing so-called 'development.' But it would be selfish to deny a share in the bland sunshine, in the enjoyment of the palm trees, the exotic birds, the fishing and the hunting, to 'transients,' and it is only to be hoped that while more and more travellers

[sic] come inevitably to the State, the natural beauties, the native flora and fauna, will be preserved" (Tarr and Kinser 305). Rawlings fervently supported efforts to protect endangered species in Florida: "Social consciousness toward preservation of the irreplaceable is increasing, and the once almost extinct egret with its beautiful white plumage, the prehistoric alligator, are now protected by law and may be seen in their natural habitat" (Tarr and Kinser 305). She worried that the attractive climate would attract too much industry and too many people, resulting in the destruction of the very habitats that drew people to the Sunshine State (Tarr and Kinser 308). When asked by Florida congressman Joe Hendricks "to describe the beauties of Florida," Rawlings explained that she had attempted to do just that with her six full-length books, but then gave a few cursory highlights of the natural landscape before writing her political thoughts on the matter in "Florida: An Affectionate Tribute":

> If human wantonness and human greed have here and there destroyed Arcadia, with the careless cutting and burning of forests, the useless and destructive draining of lands that were refuges for all the wild things; with the erection of billboards and transient camps, if avid purveyors of Florida's great cash crop, the tourist, have a little spoiled the beauty and overcharged the seeker of loveliness, lay the blame fairly where it belongs, as all such things as greed and war and man's general inhumanity to man, must be laid, on the frailty of human nature, and not on Florida, great and gracious tropical queen. She waits, as she has done through the centuries, to be all things to all men. (Tarr and Kinser 311)

This commentary, published in the 1945 *Congressional Record*, indicates that Rawlings took a keen interest in the political movements aimed at preserving the landscape and resources of Florida during a time in which those landscapes were being threatened. Her activism led Rawlings to support Marjory Stoneman Douglas openly in a review of her book, *The Everglades: River of Grass*, which preceded Harry S. Truman's dedication of the Everglades National Park by one week (Tarr and Kinser 324).

In spite of her comments on human welfare in Richmond, which may have been exaggerated by Williams, Glasgow came across to Rawlings as sympathetic to the plight of the poor. During one of her trips to England,

Glasgow visited an almshouse, claiming in a letter to Rebe from Rawlings's collection that she always visited such places. There she met an old woman with a rose garden and a daughter who had been crippled by tuberculosis (PC 108). The woman and her daughter lived in the same room, and seven other older women stayed in other rooms of the house, each with its own small garden. They grew their own roses from slips. The woman told Glasgow that she was planning to grow a new salmon-colored rose and name it for her, evidence that Rawlings may not have been alone in having a rose named for her. The chapel notice indicated the house's endowment as being only "12 shillings six a quarter" (PC 108). Glasgow was so moved by the women's plight that she gave her "a quarters [sic] allowance and Carrie gave her something too" (PC 108). At another almshouse near Dorchester, Glasgow gave a gift to the prior and was taken aback when he insisted on giving her something in return, "a little old glass bowl from his bureau" (PC 105). She wrote to Rebe that she needed to send him some Virginia tobacco when she got home, and went after lunch to purchase tobacco for the men and candy for the women who lived in the almshouse (PC 105). In the letter, she told Rebe that one old woman lived in the almshouse with six old men, "and the old woman complained of the old men to us exactly as if she had been married to all of them!" (PC 105). These actions must have appeared to Rawlings, who lived among the Florida Crackers as one of them, to be those of an outsider or tourist among the poor, but they still indicated an empathetic response to poverty.

In her research, Rawlings was able to detect in Glasgow similar views of religion to her own. Glasgow strongly opposed religious movements that she found to be detrimental to personal liberties, primarily Fundamentalism.[58] Like Rawlings, she felt most spiritually alive in nature, not in a church. One of the items belonging to Glasgow that Rawlings collected for her biography was a foreword by John Galsworthy to W. H. Hudson's *Green Mansions* that focused on its naturalism and how our creation of towns and culture was driving us ever more quickly away from what mattered, the natural world. Galsworthy argued that religion is best experienced in nature, in part because of the destructive qualities of towns and machinery. Rawlings frequently quoted Galsworthy, and admired his stance. When interviewing Glasgow's friends and acquaintances in

Richmond, Rawlings was told by Henry Anderson that Glasgow disliked certain denominations of Christianity more than others.[59] Anderson claimed that Glasgow was "impatient enough with Presbyterians, but the Baptists were too narrow."[60] The Baptist to whom he referred was Douglas Freeman, who gave mixed commentary on Glasgow and his thoughts about her. Freeman told Rawlings that Glasgow was interested in the philosophical aspects of scientific evolution, which is supported by her writings in *A Certain Measure* and elsewhere.[61] After reading *Children of God*, Glasgow described the Mormons as "a most repulsive people," who reminded her of "that other repulsive and primitive race, the Boers" (*PC* 191). *Children of God* gives a historical account of the Latter-Day Saints that has been, at times, praised, but also criticized for its harsh attempt at a realistic portrayal of the early years in that faith. Mormonism clearly made a negative impression on Ellen Glasgow, but so did the practices of many other religious groups. Both Glasgow and Rawlings wrote sympathetically of pastors in their works of fiction. Glasgow's *Vein of Iron* includes an itinerant Presbyterian minister, John Fincastle, whose failure to subscribe to the strict tenets of his denomination's creed results in his being let go from his congregation and forced to move back to his family's homestead in Ironside. Rawlings wrote a stirring short story about an alienated traveling minister in "Jessamyn Springs." In both instances, the two writers exposed the challenges faced by ministers in maintaining the rigidity of a belief system that isolated them from the natural world and society.

Rawlings uncovered many materials related to Glasgow's political views, which heavily influenced her writing. Glasgow became involved with state politics early in her career when doing research for *The Builders*, a novel about the Virginia state legislative body. She was able to sneak onto the floor at a time when women were not permitted access to legislative proceedings. Around this same time, Glasgow began what was to become one of her most significant love affairs, with Henry Anderson, a prominent Republican politician. Anderson was open with Glasgow about his own political views and opinions regarding international policy. When reviewing Anderson's correspondence, Rawlings added a notation that he was ahead of his time in his views about conflicts that had resulted from the First World War. While he blamed isolationism for the war, Anderson did not consider himself an internationalist, because "one must reserve nationalist sentiments, and not partner with a bankrupt nation and finance a peace among parties we cannot control."[62] Anderson recognized that the rights of minorities and individuals had been exposed by the war and "must be recognized over time."[63] Rawlings read these letters from Anderson carefully and included them in her files on Glasgow, even though none of them was addressed to Glasgow or referenced her relationship with Anderson. Rawlings shared Anderson's sentiments about race in the wake of WWI, writing much later, during WWII, that the "American stand on the Negro question to her invalidated the whole war, for it could not be considered a moral or spiritual crusade 'when we set out merely to stop other nations from doing the very thing that we plan to keep on doing to the Negro'" (Silverthorne 231). Like Glasgow, Rawlings appeared to be interested in Anderson's mind and political views, marking in pencil one passage in which he asserted, to his mother, that the United States should do its due diligence in international affairs, but that it should not "bind [itself] with treaties into leagues and events over which we have no control," specifically in assuming political responsibility for Armenia.[64] Anderson was remarkably personally progressive for the state of Virginia and, as a Republican in the 1920s, not very successful in achieving much political progress. His address upon accepting the nomination by the Republican party to run for governor of Virginia in 1921 focused on how loyalty to state and nation should supersede loyalty to any political party, and tried to emphasize the "huge political machine" that was largely running the Democratic party at the time with the aim of power, rather than the good of the nation or state.[65]

During the years following her move to Florida, Rawlings found her voice and blossomed as a novelist and author of short fiction, but she also discovered what it was that most inspired her compassion. In a letter to the *Ocala Evening Star* defending "Cracker Chidlings" against a negative review, Rawlings stood up for the poorer, rural residents of Florida, who she felt had been misunderstood and misrepresented by the paper. The article she criticized derided local cattlemen, Cracker dialect, and even the penitentiary chaplain appearing in Rawlings's work (Tarr and Kinser

254–255). Her response lent support to the people she represented, and defended her representation of them.

Her decision to move to and write about Florida was inspired by Rawlings's childhood memories of her father's farm in Maryland, and also by her memories of her grandparents' farm in Michigan. These early experiences cultivated her devotion to farming. In an article for the Centennial Anniversary Edition of the *Holly Herald*, a Michigan publication, Rawlings submitted a piece about her grandfather's farm, titled "Abe Traphagen's Farm." She regretted the dissolution of the beautiful way of life she witnessed on the farm, and later wrote her own novel, *The Sojourner*, in homage to it. Rawlings appreciated the relationship between the farmer and the land, which she perceived as a completely symbiotic one requiring hard work, perseverance, and the acceptance of natural setbacks. What was most fascinating to Rawlings in this article was her memory of abundance on the farm, from the kitchen stocked with dozens of treats to the hearty meals provided three times a day to the richness of the land and groves (Tarr and Kinser 265–267).

The abundance of food served at her grandparents' farm and their hospitality instilled a respect for the culinary arts, as well. Glasgow enjoyed entertaining, but was more engaged in planning the menu rather than cooking, another example of how Rawlings differed in personality from the more refined and less resourceful Glasgow. Rawlings immersed herself in understanding and consuming Florida cuisine. One of her earlier pieces on Florida touted the delectable dishes that could be made in a Dutch oven. Rawlings chronicled many of these recipes in "Hyacinth Drift," the chapter of *Cross Creek* that describes her trip with Dessie Smith Vinson on the St. Johns River (Tarr and Kinser 256). She preferred using local ingredients in her cooking. In "I Sing While I Cook," Rawlings explained how she replaced the asparagus that had to be imported from Colorado, California, or New York with fresh okra, boiled and served with Hollandaise (Tarr and Kinser 268). Here, and in *Cross Creek Cookery*, Rawlings paid tribute to Dora, her Jersey cow, "who has the rottenest disposition and gives the richest cream in the world" (Tarr and Kinser 269). Unaware that they were a protected species at the time, Rawlings used local red-winged blackbirds in her blackbird pie (Tarr and

Kinser 279). The incorporation of local produce and game in her dishes helped Rawlings to educate the world outside of Florida about its people and way of life.

Rawlings ultimately recognized in Glasgow a need similar to hers to protect the defenseless—in spite of, or perhaps because of, Glasgow's own weakened state. In one of the last things read by Glasgow before her death that was shared with Rawlings by Bennett, a newspaper columnist responded to the killing of a deer with the poem "Little Things," by James Stephens. In the poem, Stephens wrote:

> Little things that run and quail
> And die in silence and despair;
>
> Little things that fight and fail
> And fall on earth and sea and air;
>
> All trapped and frightened little things,
> The mouse, the coney, hear our prayer.
>
> As we forgive those done to us,
> The lamb, the linnet, and the hare,
>
> Forgive us all our trespasses,
> Little creatures everywhere.[66]

The poem beautifully summarized Glasgow's sympathies and activism for the eradication of cruelty.

Rawlings also valued the raising up of the overlooked in society, like the Florida Crackers, and lauded the individual over the collective mindset of a nation, yet her approach came from living among people she wanted to help as a neighbor and friend. Rawlings immersed herself daily in the natural world, away from social circles and urban busyness. This vision was best described by her 1935 poem, published in *Scribner's Magazine*, titled "Having Left Cities behind Me":

> Now, having left cities behind me, turned
> Away forever from the strange, gregarious
> Huddling of men by stones, I find those various
> Great towns I knew fused into one, burned

Together in the fire of my despising.
And I recall of them only those things
Irrelevant to cities; murmurings
Of rain and wind; moons setting and suns rising.

There was a church spire on a distant hill
Clamorous with birds by day and stars by night,
Devout and singing. I have forgot its site—
Boston, or Rochester, or Louisville—
Of a certain city all I can remember
Is wild ducks flying southward in November. (Tarr and Kinser 260)[67]

The poem speaks to the connection felt by both Rawlings and Glasgow to the natural world, with its changing seasons and birds that exist in spite of our collective attempt to tame them with our "church spires" and "huddling by stones."

Rawlings found common ground with Glasgow in her love for the land and animals. Rawlings was desperate to preserve her Florida home. She wrote in support of conservationism, the troops defending her country, and the Cracker culture around her that was frequently degraded. Both Rawlings and Glasgow used their work to advance the causes they supported. From Rawlings's detailed depictions of life in Florida to the violations of the weakest members of society, human or animal, that could be seen as a trademark of Glasgow's novels, these writers wielded their pens to produce art that was an instrument of revelation and social change.

5

In Search of Truth, Not Sensation

There is an affinity between men and places.

Marjorie Kinnan Rawlings

AS MARJORIE KINNAN RAWLINGS collected materials toward her biography of Ellen Glasgow, she highlighted critics' misreading of Glasgow and the many ways in which she was being overlooked, especially toward the end of her life, in spite of such a prolific and well-respected literary career. Recall the letter to Norman Berg referenced earlier in which Rawlings conveyed with some measure of indignation her Aunt Wilmer's negative response to her decision to write a biography of Ellen Glasgow, "some obscure person," rather than simply resting and having a good time (Bigelow and Monti 390). Ellen Glasgow, who broke into the literary world with the publication of her first novel at the young age of twenty-four, produced many best-selling novels and received both awards and admission into the most prestigious literary circles and organizations of her time, but was somehow relegated to near-obsolescence after her death, except to the elite Richmond society that still held her in high esteem as one of its own.

Rawlings remained determined to tell Ellen Glasgow's story, in spite of these oversights, or perhaps because of them. The two writers may have selected markedly different themes and styles for their major novels, but Rawlings could still see parts of herself in the older writer as Glasgow neared the end of her life, and felt a connection to her that likely made her consider her own mortality, as well as the lifespan of her literary works. Included in Rawlings's folder of collected criticism on Glasgow was a 1936 short list from the *New York Herald Tribune Books* of "What America is Reading" that listed *Vein of Iron*, which helped establish Glasgow's novel as one of the most frequently read books then in circulation.[1] In a 1943 letter to Henry Seidel Canby on the candidates proposed for the Gold Medal of the Institute of Fiction, Rawlings stated that Dreiser's work would not stand the test of time as well as Willa Cather, Ellen Glasgow, or Sinclair Lewis. She went on to label Lewis a satirist, rather than a creative writer. While Rawlings felt that Glasgow and Cather were equally qualified, she selected Ellen Glasgow from the list as her top choice due to "the greater body" of her work that she found to be "of [a] consistently, almost classically high standard" (Bigelow and Monti 244). Rawlings would have ranked Glasgow above Willa Cather and Sinclair Lewis, though both of those authors seem to have achieved more lasting literary influence than Ellen Glasgow.

Rawlings's collection of criticism on Glasgow also emphasized the ways in which Ellen Glasgow produced more sophisticated literature than she was generally credited for, a point that Rawlings would have doubtless made had she been able to complete her biography. One such critical collection, *Lucifer at Large* (1937), by John McCole, claimed "the richly textured and superbly ironic style . . . should have brought Ellen Glasgow the Nobel Prize" (294). Rawlings added her own footnote to this section: "Stimulating book of criticism on 20th century American fiction."[2] She included many other examples of articles in which Glasgow was heralded as a critic of Southern idealism, a woman writing texts of female disillusionment, and a literary revolutionary. Each of these carefully preserved articles indicated the ways in which Rawlings intended to portray Glasgow in her biography, as one of America's greatest writers and a game-changer in the literary movements of her day. More importantly, these notes and clippings helped to create a collage of Rawlings's own views about Glasgow's works. Familiar with criticism of her own work, Rawlings was intent on locating those reviews that best understood Glasgow's complex narratives and her attempts to reveal truth through her novels.

Many of the articles Rawlings collected noted specific ways in which Glasgow affronted the Southern literary regime through her rejection of its normative tropes. This subset of articles must have had an impact on Rawlings as well, due to her similar position as a writer often characterized by her devotion to a particular region. Rawlings, however, used Florida to explore the dark recesses of our shared consciousness, by removing those comforts and limitations provided by urban landscapes. Glasgow's writing of Virginia attempted to expose the artificiality of affluence and the Victorian nature of Southern culture from within by steeping her novels in irony. In one of the articles from Rawlings's collection, "The Last Cry of Romance," James Branch Cabell said of the conclusion of *Barren Ground* that "The things which ought, by every rule of tradition, to have mattered most poignantly have in reality meant nothing" (29). He lugubriously detailed the optimism he found in the face of her characters' many flaws, and wrote that "her punctilious oblation before the fetish of the happy ending . . . I elect to see . . . as the ironist dismiss[ing] her sport" (31). Joseph Collins wrote in "Realism in a Southern Novel" that Glasgow's *Barren Ground* was indicative of the reality behind the romantic tradition, and that it was "the first honest realistic novel of the South" (34). In both critical responses, Glasgow emerged as a capable author of realism, employing irony to denigrate the expected form her work should take and writing instead the narrative she believed would get at the truth of human experience. Glasgow may have written about the South from within its borders, but she was ultimately trying to use those experiences to reveal a universal truth beneath the performances and pretenses of the region. Throughout her collection of essays and articles on Glasgow's works, Rawlings brought attention, through handwritten footnotes and subsets of materials, to the larger problem with Glasgow's reception that Rawlings feared could foreshadow her own fate: dismissal by a pretentious literary canon and the critics responsible for its establishment because her writing was neither gratuitous enough to be considered bohemian by those outside of the South, nor romanticized enough to be lauded by those within.

Ellen Glasgow challenged her categorization as a regional writer throughout her career. In her 1931 address to the Southern Writers Conference, she proudly asserted that those in attendance were "proving beyond argument [that the] South is in the world and Southerners are people" (Raper 95). During the years following the Civil War, writers in the South struggled with the categorization of their literature as Southern literature. Glasgow disparaged many examples of Southern literature as overly idealized in their portrayals of the South before and after the war. In some respects, Southerners felt the need to justify their lifestyle by exaggerating traditions they felt were being threatened by their loss in the Civil War. Glasgow cited Caruthers's *Cavaliers of Virginia* and *Knights of the Horse-shoe*, two historical romances about the Old Dominion, when she criticized sentimental Southern prose in her 1928 essay, "The Novel in the South." She explained sentimentalism by describing "the dark furies of Reconstruction" as being responsible for afflicting "the mind of the South . . . with a bitter nostalgia" (Raper 72). She concluded: "It is only with the loss of this charm and the ebbing of this sentiment that [the creative writer] has been able to rest apart and brood over the fragmentary world he has called into being" (Raper 83). Glasgow faced the daunting task of writing about Virginia at a time when the region was still licking its wounds over defeat in the Civil War. To criticize the region when it was at its most defeated would be akin to treason, yet to glorify it after so many misguided acts would be dishonest. Glasgow chose to walk a fine line between these two impulses, and portray with honesty and sympathy the individuals whose lives emerged from Reconstruction efforts, the impact on social interactions of those efforts, and the strivings of individuals toward their own shifting sense of a fulfilled life.

Rawlings wondered why Glasgow did not receive the same recognition she herself enjoyed. In part, Glasgow's reputation suffered because her refutation of the sentimental tradition during such a controversial time became emblematic of what is now considered canonical Southern writing. As Susan Goodman wrote at the beginning of her biography of Ellen Glasgow, Glasgow's fiction "defined many of the elements we now associate with a larger pattern of Southern literature: a tragic sense of life, a deep-rooted pessimism, a recognition of human capacity for evil, and the decrees of history and place" (1). The revolt against Southern literature became the Southern literature that survived the Reconstruction.

Glasgow had to contend with her contemporaries in her defense of writing that was considered too controversial, and with later readers who would not view her writing as controversial enough.

Rawlings was first drawn to Glasgow through her reading of the prefaces written by Glasgow to clarify the purpose of her writing, because Glasgow's experiences closely resembled Rawlings's own research and writing process. It is in these essays that a reader may best understand Glasgow's reactions to regionalist criticisms of her work. In her chapter on *The Sheltered Life*, Glasgow explained how her best-read family members "all despised what they called 'local talent'" (*CM* 195). Out of fear, she admitted to having "written in secret to escape ridicule, alert, pointed, and not the less destructive because it was playful" (*CM* 195). When writing about *The Battle-Ground*, she described how she came to the realization "in 1897, that [she] did not belong in the South, that [she] did not belong in the North, that [she] did not belong in any place or period [she] had so far discovered" (*CM* 10). In spite of these bold statements, nearly all of Glasgow's novels take place exclusively in the South, the setting that best enabled her to discover those universal truths she aspired to locate through literature.

To defend herself from regional categorizations in overly generalized accounts of her works, Glasgow explained in these prefaces her outrage over a critic "politely" classifying her first books as part of "the Southern school of local colour," calling this classification "both casual and inaccurate" because her "first immature novels were conceived and written in an impassioned revolt, not only from the school of local colour, but from the current Victorian tradition in letters, and, more especially, from the sentimental elegiac tone this tradition has assumed in Virginia" (*CM* 49). Her insistence on correcting the regionalism ascribed to her literature came from her concern that her work was being misread as supporting a Southern status quo, rather than exposing its flaws through realistic and ironic depictions of characters.

Despite the eventual acceptance of Southern literature as worthy of inclusion in academic discourse, regional writers have historically struggled against such branding and the common dismissal that accompanies a regional label. Marjorie Kinnan Rawlings was similarly frustrated over critical response to her writing about the Florida scrub. She was immediately branded a Florida writer, and was expected to produce more regional stories and novels for an audience that, at times, used the stories to solidify misconceptions and stereotypes regarding the people she characterized.

Like Glasgow, Rawlings attempted to overcome regional stereotypes while still focusing her efforts on the area of the country and the people she knew best. Ellen Glasgow felt the need to construct with care novels that were neither steeped in sentimentality nor overly exaggerated, picaresque works meant to shock readers, but that instead spoke of true experience. Marjorie Kinnan Rawlings struggled with a conflict between her desire to represent accurately the Florida scrub and its Cracker population, and her fear that these representations were being read prejudicially by a condescending audience. Both women were challenged by the expectation that they would write certain types of fiction "as women." To complicate matters, Rawlings also worried over being labeled a writer of "juvenilia." As a result of parochial literature and familial criticism at different points in their careers, Glasgow and Rawlings both felt compelled to write novels set outside the regions for which they gained literary fame, even though such projects were not overly successful. Their shared reactions to readership and the categorizations meant to limit the scope of their artistry reveal how editors, critics, and readers in the general populace play a key role in any writer's attempts to create some measure of truth within fiction. Rawlings may have hoped to expose these challenges in her biography of Glasgow.

One of the reasons Glasgow was misread by her contemporaries was that she failed to fit into the two categories open to Southern writers in the late 19th and early 20th centuries. Such writers were assumed either to support the status quo with nostalgic novels about the sentimentalized old South before and during the war, or to repudiate the status quo in gratuitous and experimental narratives of a gothic or Faulknerian style. Glasgow claimed that critics in the South at the turn of the 20th century "would have repudiated any novelist who had attempted to pierce, or even to prick, the sentimental fallacy" (*CM* 11). In part, she felt that her own successful rejection of this fallacy meant that she could confidently claim a space outside the limited scope of Southern literature and the post–Civil War period in which she composed her fiction. At the beginning of her career, Glasgow faced immense pressure to write literature that was steeped in sentimentality, as representatives of the South were still grossly sensitive about their reputation. Throughout her literary career, Glasgow was encouraged to write the kinds of books that it was felt a woman in her position should write, with fewer bastards and more love stories—a pressure that had lessened somewhat by Rawlings's time, but that was still obviously present, as made clear by the fact that she was sued over her less-than-flattering representation of a woman in *Cross Creek*.

In her posthumously published autobiography, which Rawlings was able to review in advance, Glasgow explained the distinction between what she wanted to write about and the expected norm:

> I would write, I resolved, as no Southerner had ever written, of the universal human chords beneath the superficial variations of scene and character. I would write of all the harsher realities beneath manners, beneath social customs, beneath the poetry of the past, and the romantic nostalgia of the present. I would write of an outcast, of an illegitimate "poor white," of a thinker and of a radical socialist. I would take as my theme those ugly aspects of life the sentimentalists passed over. (*WW* 98)

She longed to break free of regional tropes in setting and character development by depicting what she here calls "harsher realities" and elsewhere calls "universal blood and irony" which emerge when a society loses its past. Glasgow was most dissatisfied with novels categorized as "romance," in which "Everybody was happy. Nobody wished to be different" (*WW* 103–104). She could not understand the popularity of these literary forms, and they frustrated her because she knew "Life never was and never will be like this" (*WW* 104). While Glasgow wrote regional literature, insofar as her novels were set in Virginia, she did not ascribe to the formulaic tropes of other works that were similarly categorized, making her not quite fit into any category with defined narrative expectations. Her love of realism also drew her to the harsher, but not sensationalized, telling of *The Yearling* by Rawlings.

Critics often decided that Glasgow's works, in spite of their ironic twists, were sentimental because novels like *The Sheltered Life* and *Virginia* celebrated or sympathized with certain elements of tradition while critiquing others. General Archbald's reverence for Eva Birdsong as an emblem of the ideal Southern lady is to be admired, even though Eva is pitied by the other characters in the novel for so blindly clinging to a false image of her husband and marriage. Glasgow admitted that in her own mind, General Archbald, not Jenny Blair Archbald, was the true protagonist of the novel. In the same way, she modeled the titular character of *Virginia* after her own mother, creating a woman whom no one would wish to emulate, but for whom the reader cannot help but feel compassion. Glasgow acknowledged the difficulty she had in outgrowing this "insidious sentimental tradition" because she "had been brought up in the midst of it" (*WW* 104). She writes, "I was a part of it or it was a part of me; I had been born with an intimate feeling for the spirit of the past, and the lingering poetry of time and place" (*WW* 104). In the same way, Marjorie Kinnan Rawlings chose for the subject of her writing a lifestyle from her own past, the impoverished struggles with farming experienced by her grandparents out of necessity and by her father out of choice. Their love for the land was the inheritance she embraced in her move to Florida; however, like Glasgow, she chose to portray these experiences realistically, without overly romanticizing their struggles.

Glasgow's major stylistic difference from Rawlings's writing was that she chose to pit her protagonists against social challenges, rather than trials in nature. In Glasgow's novels, characters struggled with one another. With the death of the Old South that so many of her characters had championed came a remarkable shift toward trying to preserve the image of the South in the same way that stories of the dead are embellished to build up their good qualities while forgetting the bad. Glasgow's characters must parse the real from the fictive representations of the world around them to try to understand what is true. Glasgow described post–Civil War sentimental fiction, meant "to defend the lost . . . while a living tradition decayed with the passage of years into a sentimental infirmity," as "lack[ing] creative passion and the courage to offend which is the essential note of great fiction" (Raper 72). To embrace fully the kind of realism that she wanted to portray regarding the South, Glasgow felt that she needed to divorce herself from any attachments she might feel to the setting or characters she portrayed. She supported the modern technique of removing the author from the narrative, claiming that "it is essential that the look within should be that of the artist, not of the lover" (Raper 83). Rawlings had identical issues with her own writing, proudly declaring her love for the Cracker communities of Florida through *Cross Creek*, while later finding that her realistic sketches could offend those same communities and alienate her from their midst.

While both Rawlings and Glasgow refused to write the kind of literature that would be completely inoffensive to the regions in which they lived, Glasgow, as a more established author, struggled against another offensive sect of Southern regional writing that came to be known as the grotesque. Her criticism of the grotesque was that it had devolved into "literary ruffianism" that she found to be "more sensationalist than real" (*CM* 15). What Glasgow wanted to achieve was a realism that was neither sensationalist nor sentimental by maintaining an objective point of view. Those writers Glasgow would have considered to be lovers of their subject matter would either idealize their subject matter or sensationalize it to make it appear more desirable to the audience. As referenced earlier, Douglas Southall Freeman pointed out in his 1935 *Saturday Evening Post* essay "The Idealist" that Glasgow would go through "the muck" if she had to, but would not intentionally seek it out.[3] Irita Van Doren told Rawlings that Glasgow had "very little use for the school of the Southern novel (Welty-Faulkner-Caldwell, etc.)," claiming that it was not that her "morals" were "offended" by them, but rather that her "character [was] strong; but [her] stomach [was] weak."[4] She begged such writers "please to spare [her] appetite."[5] Sensationalist Southern writing was physically nauseating to Glasgow, and though it had cemented Faulkner's reputation as a renowned writer of the Southern gothic and led to the highly recognized grotesque writings of Flannery O'Connor, Glasgow refused to compromise her instincts, and as a result, she has typically been overlooked in canonical studies of Southern literature. This serves up another parallel with Rawlings, who also preferred the "real" over the "sensational" and would have explained the reasons for such a preference in her biographical work on Glasgow.

Despite Glasgow's current absence from contemporary studies on early 20th century Southern literature, she was very much a notable figure during her lifetime. She won a Pulitzer when her last novel, *In This Our Life*, was published a year before her death, and many of her contemporaries felt she had previously been repeatedly overlooked for that award, including Rawlings.[6] Glasgow was a featured speaker at the Southern Writers Conference and the Modern Language Association, and was a regular contributor to the *New York Herald Tribune Books* and the *Saturday Evening Post*, achievements that further established her as a renowned writer among her peers.

Glasgow's work achieved a precarious balance between the modern and the antiquated by recognizing the value of each and refusing to dismiss either. In her fiction, critics found seemingly modern critiques of established literary forms when, for example, she rewrote the "fallen woman" narrative of Thomas Hardy into the "victim becomes victor" narrative of her own *Barren Ground*. However, she also consistently aligned herself with characters like General Archibald from *The Sheltered Life* and the title character from *Virginia*, for whom traditions are worth martyrdom, even when it becomes apparent that all the other characters recognize such traditions as a weak façade.

Rawlings's insistence that Glasgow's sterling literary reputation should have been sufficient to carry her beyond the confines of Southern literature belies her own struggles with being characterized as a regional writer of Florida literature, something that Rawlings desperately wished to overcome. The character sketches of life among the Florida Cracker community that cemented her literary career also caused her a great deal of internal conflict. For years, Rawlings struggled to write *The Sojourner* in order to distance herself from the Florida landscape. Her refusal to portray Florida culture with any level of sentimentality, though she did clearly care for and sympathize with her characters, led to a lengthy trial when Zelma Cason sued Rawlings for invasion of privacy. Zelma Cason was one of the many local residents described in Rawlings's autobiographical *Cross Creek*. Though most townspeople supported Rawlings as an author, Cason felt so strongly that her characterization in the book damaged her reputation and deserved monetary reparations that she took legal action, suing Rawlings for invasion of privacy (Silverthorne 215–218). The trial was emotionally draining, and left Rawlings feeling disconnected from the culture that had once embraced her.

One of the reasons her connection with local Floridians was so important to Rawlings was that she did not have the same ties through heritage to Florida that Glasgow had to Virginia and its dark past. Perhaps this lack of strong familial heritage, and even mythology, led Rawlings to move from one journalistic job to the next with her first husband, Charles "Chuck" Rawlings, after college. Rawlings grew up in Washington, D.C., but her parents did not have roots there, having moved there not long before her birth to facilitate her father's position with the U.S. Patent office (Bigelow 5). After her father's death, her mother saw Rawlings through school, and then moved herself and Rawlings's younger brother to Madison to help support Rawlings through her undergraduate studies at the University of Wisconsin (Silverthorne 27). The only loyalties Rawlings had felt to any region before Florida were to the farmland her mother's family maintained in Michigan and the farm her father had purchased and developed in Virginia at the same time he was working for the Patent Office. Although she had a clear passion for farming as a lifestyle, before she moved to Florida with Charles, Rawlings had had no practical experience on a farm, aside from observing her father, whom she idolized when she was a child.

Unlike Glasgow, who was writing her way out of a morass of Southern heritage and sentimentality, Rawlings became a pioneer in the Florida scrub. She intentionally chose the location to escape all ties to her past and begin life anew. Her experiment worked. After Rawlings had received rejection letters for more than a decade, *Scribner's Magazine*, the preeminent publisher in the country at that time, published her first collection of short character sketches about life in Florida. She explained her choice of Florida as a theme in her letter to Alfred S. Dashiell, the *Scribner's* editor who accepted "Cracker Chidlings" for publication:

Two years ago my husband, a newspaperman, and I deliberately cut our civilized ties in Rochester and migrated to this firmly entrenched outpost of the vanishing frontier. We do not expect ever to regret the move. We have a profitable orange grove on the jungle edge of Cross Creek, between two lakes, where life has as many elements of the idyllic as is quite reasonable. You ask how I happened to become interested in this material and how I gathered my facts. This wild, beautiful country, tucked off the tourists' highways by no large number of actual miles, is in itself a challenge to the imagination. I had met only two or three of the neighboring Crackers when I realized that isolation had done something to these people. Rather, perhaps, civilization had remained too remote, physically and spiritually, to take something from them, something vital. They have a primal quality against their background of jungle hammock, moss-hung, against the tremendous silence of the scrub country. The only ingredients of their lives are the elemental things. They are a people of dignity, speaking often in Chaucerian phrases, aloof; but friendly and neighborly once even a Yankee has proved himself not too hopelessly alien. (Bigelow and Monti 36–37)

Some of Rawlings's critics found these initial characterizations of the Cracker lifestyle to be condescending (Silverthorne 62). However, that condescension evaporated as she immersed herself more fully in the culture and lifestyle that she chose, complete with its hardships as well as physical and emotional tolls.

Rawlings found in Florida a wilderness of mysterious growth and people untouched by the corrupting forces of society. When writing on Florry, a character featured in both "Jacob's Ladder" and in the chapter "Antses in Tim's Breakfast" from *Cross Creek*, Alison Graham-Bertolini contends, "Much of Rawlings' writing is inspired by the intersection of the two very different ideologies of Cracker culture and modern culture" (51). The Crackers represented, to her, a kind of noble savagery that had not yet been explored in literature. These revelations, however, seemed to rely on those characters intersecting with the modern world and its trappings. Rawlings described an episode in which she was lost in the scrub on the first day of hunting season as the day she "encountered for the first time the palpability of silence" (Bigelow and Monti 43). Such experiences led her to write her first novel, *South Moon Under*, on the experiences of a fugitive moonshiner and his family in the lawless wilderness of central Florida.

Ironically, Rawlings experienced pressure to publish a certain type of fiction only after she decided that she wanted to write literature outside of the Florida setting to keep from being branded a regional writer. Following the success of *South Moon Under*, she worried that literary critics would pigeonhole her if she continued to focus solely on the Florida wilderness. Maxwell Perkins at Scribner's encouraged her to write a boys' book, which eventually became *The Yearling*. After an initial, favorable response to his request, Rawlings considered it more closely and wrote:

> I think we must come to a much clearer understanding of what you are expecting of me as to the boys' book... You say "The book would probably be one anyhow that men would read as well as boys,"... Do you by any wild chance think that once I get into it, I will automatically find myself doing another Cracker book for mature consumption?... I can't say too emphatically that that is not the case. In the first place, the material simply is not there. And in the second place, if it were, or if it could be induced, I have neither the taste nor the heart for such a book.... The principal reason... is that for the present at least I have nothing to say for mature people along the *South-Moon-Under* line. A book in the same general locale could only be compared with the first book, could only be called its sequel or successor at best, and, at worst, would be considered an attempt to capitalize on what earlier interest there was in such characters in such a setting. It would be ruinous. (Bigelow and Monti 76–77)

Rawlings later insisted on completing her second novel, *Golden Apples*, before beginning work on what she claimed Perkins wanted to be a "classic boys' novel" (Bigelow and Monti 81). However, *Golden Apples* shared the same setting as *South Moon Under* and *The Yearling*. Its only distinctive quality was the intrusion of a British landowner who came to understand the foreign landscape and its people while visiting a property he owned but had not yet seen. Adding to her publication pressures, her agent, Carl Brandt, convinced her to have the novel released as a serialization in Hearst's *Cosmopolitan*, a format she felt only degraded the work more (Bigelow 18). While, in some respects, the pressures Rawlings received from Perkins, Brandt, and Scribner's solidified her position as an important American writer and helped to pay her bills, they also consistently took her away from the kinds of fiction she would have chosen to write in order to write juvenilia and Florida scrub stories instead. The pressure to publish and sell literature, in her case, coincided with the writing of what many consider to be Rawlings's best work, but the constraints of writing to appease agents, editors, and publishing companies should not be overlooked for either Glasgow or Rawlings.

Rawlings addressed the concept of regionalism in several articles written after she became an established novelist. She had mixed feelings. On the one hand, she loathed bad writing that capitalized upon the categorization of "regionalism." On the other hand, she strongly believed "the best writing is implicit with a profound harmony between the writer and his material, so that many of the greatest books of all time are regional books, in which the author has used, for his own artistic purpose, a background that he loved and deeply understood" (Tarr and Kinser 276). For this reason, Rawlings had significant difficulty writing *The Sojourner* without completely immersing herself in Michigan culture. She only successfully completed the book after spending time at her Van Hornesville, New York, home following WWII.

In 1939, Rawlings was asked to address the National Council of Teachers of English in New York. Her paper, "Regional Literature of the South," later published in both *College English* and *English Journal*, made several arguments about writing that, at the time, was being demarcated as "regional literature" to explain why authors like herself and Ellen Glasgow fought against this terminology. She first pointed out that books being given this classification were almost always rural, and could nearly all fit into two specific regions, the American Midwest and the American South. (While a British author like Thomas Hardy clearly situated his writing in a landscape he knew and loved, his works are never called "regional.") Because this regional literature was also being published and marketed in the wealthy urban areas far removed from the locations in which the books were set, the category also implied a type of urban interest in quaint stories of rural Americana. This, however, is not to suggest that residents of the representative regions turned a blind eye to their own regional literature. As Rawlings wrote, "The South also reads books about the South. That is because, while not too much concerned with what outsiders say about us, we are all agog to know what we say about one another" (Tarr and Kinser 275). Furthermore, the popularity of such fiction led to "regional writing done because the author thinks it will be salable," an act that Rawlings called a complete "betrayal of the people of that region," whose lives are "turned inside out for the gaze of the curious . . . not as human beings, but as literary specimens" (Tarr and Kinser 275). Her fear, one that Glasgow shared when she worried what her relatives would think of her Virginia novels, was that she would be dismissed because her choice of region was considered a literary novelty of the dime-novel variety.

More importantly, Rawlings emphasized Ellen Glasgow's influence in this paper by naming her the sole writer of what Rawlings considered regional *literature* of the South, as opposed to the vast amount of regional writing without merit. Rawlings compared Glasgow to Hardy, "for while she would have written with great art of whatever people came into the ken of her interest, she is so steeped in the Virginia which she knows that it is an inextricable part of her work, like the colors of a painting or the dye of the wool of a tapestry. But she is first an artist and then a Virginian" (Tarr and Kinser 277). While she did not omit Faulkner from her discussion of regional literature, Rawlings argued that he could not be classified as regional because the "storm-swept realm of the libido knows no geography" (Tarr and Kinser 279). She hoped, with time, *Gone with the Wind* would be read as regional literature, in spite of its stylistic limitations. Rawlings was convinced that Glasgow would be heralded as one of the greatest writers of their time after they were both long dead. Instead, Rawlings would be the one to gain more lasting fame after their deaths.

Rawlings was also concerned with the misrepresentation of Glasgow by literary critics and the ways in which that misrepresentation frustrated Glasgow. In her biography of Ellen Glasgow, Susan Goodman addressed the difficulty that critics found in reading Glasgow after learning that the author of *The Descendant*, a book first noted as "distinctly, almost audaciously, virile and vigorous" (*Reviews* qtd. in Goodman 60), was in fact a genteel Southern woman. Glasgow went so far as to use her more feminine qualities as marketing tools to promote *The Descendant*, releasing the second edition of her first novel with her own portrait printed in the front. She seemed to enjoy the shocked critics and interviewers who would repeat in their reviews such sentiments as "'This bright-looking young girl, with keen brown eyes and chestnut hair and the very daintiest of feet,' had renounced society for 'her own chosen pursuits'" (*Reviews* qtd in Goodman 61). Keep in mind that these reviews were coming out around the time Rawlings was born. The generation gap between Glasgow, who published her first novel in 1897 at the age of twenty-four, and Rawlings, who was born in 1896, is immense in terms of women's representation in literature.

In the same way in which Rawlings contended with editorial advice to write a certain kind of novel, Glasgow's publisher once insisted that she "write historical romances" in order "to be popular" (*CM* 29). Glasgow rejected these "Colonial pieces in fiction," finding that "the literary woods were filled with stalking savages and captive damsels in fancy dress" (*CM* 29). This advice was emphasized to Glasgow because her gender and regional identity paralleled those of writers who had gained professional success by writing that very type of fiction. When Glasgow's work achieved the popularity that she condemned, she worried that she had "taken the wrong turn" and was "moving steadily in the wrong direction" (*CM* 30). Yet the reason Glasgow felt frustrated by her popular literary achievement stemmed directly from her rejection of the forms she used and subverted.

Glasgow realized that her work was not been yet considered to have the literary relevancy she desired. Instead, she was categorized as a writer of the very type of literature she detested. In the same way as Rawlings feared being guilty of writing the kind of regional novels that could be considered "trash" at best, and exploitative of the people being represented at worst, so did Glasgow fear that she would be read as a stereotypical novelist of manners, like Edith Wharton. As she explained in an essay on *Vein of Iron*, "Although I have had my loyal friends and critics, few persistent novelists, I suppose, have ever received in one lifetime so generous a measure of benevolent neglect" (*CM* 177). She recognized that her critics and reviewers, though responsible in part for her popularity and financial success as a writer, neglected to understand the important contributions of her craft to the greater canonical works of American fiction. Glasgow claimed to have overcome this neglect when she wrote,

"It is true that I have seldom received prizes, but it is true also that I have seldom been obliged to return thanks" (*CM* 178).

In reckoning with this misperception of her work, Glasgow sought solace in the very privilege of her writing life. She quoted Virginia Woolf's famous essay, "A Room of One's Own," in writing: "I wanted 'a room of my own,' and it was granted me. I wanted a pursuit that I might follow with interest between the cradle and the grave, and that too was allowed" (*CM* 178). These sentiments follow Glasgow's contention that she had not been accurately received or represented in critical writings on her work. She still achieved, however, a few narrative successes that could not be denied or misrepresented, and she was proud of those few critical achievements. The most impressive of these acknowledged successes was the creation of Dorinda Oakley in *Barren Ground*, a novel in which Glasgow proudly claimed to have offered "a complete reversal of a classic situation," in which "the betrayed woman would become the victor instead of the victim" (*CM* 160). Glasgow's success with *Barren Ground* proved in part that "single aim" she spent "forty years of endeavour" trying to reach (*CM* 178). Glasgow exposed the illusive qualities of sentimental idealism, especially those so prevalent in Southern literature, and the oppressive forces that such ideologies mask.

By virtue of a generation's worth of societal progress, Marjorie Kinnan Rawlings did not experience the degree of sexism faced by Ellen Glasgow. However, she was aware that being a female writer came with a degree of literary misrepresentation and unique challenges. Most telling are the many articles she collected for her biography of Ellen Glasgow that focused on her gender. In a 1928 essay on Glasgow from this collection, Dorothea Lawrance Mann qualified her literature of revolt by writing how, even though Glasgow was "very easy to look at" and in some ways similar to those she critiqued in her literature, she was able to examine the sentimental tradition harshly for the truth beneath its façade, especially when it came to plantation life (3–4). Clearly focused on Glasgow's appeal as a feminist writer, Mann told the story of how Glasgow and her sister had themselves "smuggled into the state convention" in Virginia to gather notes toward *Voice of the People* at a time when women were not permitted there (14). She concluded the story by offering her own suspicions "that it was because she was so very feminine and

Virginia gentlemen were so notably gallant that she was able to obtain so many facts about politics and battles" (14). No matter how revolutionary Mann considered Glasgow, she still pointed out that "writing and teaching were the two professions in which it was admitted that a Southern lady might engage without loss of caste" (15). By collecting articles like this one in her research on Ellen Glasgow, Rawlings revealed her own interest in the ways in which Glasgow liberated women in her fiction by characterizing them as capable of breaking the exaggerated gender boundaries and Victorian sensibilities of the post–Civil War South.

Understanding pressures Rawlings may have felt as a woman writer is difficult when observing the content of her fiction. Rather than correcting for women's dependence on romantic entanglements, Rawlings chose to focus her novels on the survival of characters in the Florida scrub, concentrating her narratives on young male characters with whom she shared a stronger connection than the women she wrote into her stories. One of her more intensely gendered stories, "Gal Young Un," was initially rejected for consideration by a film company because, in part, of the impurity of the young title character in the story. "Gal Young Un" tells the story of a spinster who is finally married to a younger man. The younger man uses her for her property and, in time, brings his younger mistress home and leaves the two of them alone while he is off pursuing his own business. In this story, Rawlings demonstrated her awareness of gender as a crucial and even debilitating factor for certain characters, while maintaining her separateness from such characters. Rawlings demurred to Charles Rawlings's opinions at times by taking his criticism of her work to heart, but she fought him capably when she felt he was wronging her, and divorced him before she allowed her life to be overrun by his jealousy or anger. After a car wreck that left one side of her face bruised and battered, Norton Baskin told their friends, "The fact that I'm alive proves I didn't lay a hand on her" (Silverthorne 277). While Rawlings occasionally admitted being distracted by her relationship with Baskin, she never considered herself to be "damaged goods" as a divorced woman seeking a second marriage, as many of Glasgow's characters did. Whereas Glasgow may have had some difficulty in relationships because her lovers viewed her as a professional writer, not a wife and mother, and she never married, Rawlings married twice and maintained a strong literary reputation through both relationships, despite the fact that she did not resemble a maternal figure or housewife in the least. The success of her second marriage came, to some extent, from her mutual understanding with Baskin that they would spend lengthy periods apart while she completed her work and he managed his restaurants. Her ability to remain independent within the relationship was what made it so successful.

If anything, Rawlings embraced a more masculine identity in both her writing career and personal relationships. Her novels focused primarily on male protagonists, often portraying women characters as strict to the point of cruelty, self-absorbed, or pitiful. When writing to Max Perkins on the reception of *Golden Apples*, Rawlings admitted, "I never got inside Camilla; never even tried to. I presented her as she appeared to other people. Why Tordell is not completely successful, I do not know. I understood him thoroughly" (Bigelow and Monti 101). Rawlings could only understand the women in her novels through their appearance to others, and clearly preferred to inhabit the male gaze when writing about women. This desire to inhabit the masculine writing space led her initially to request that Perkins not publish *The Yearling* under her name, but under "a pseudonym, at least some variation of my name that would keep them from realizing the writer was a woman" (Bigelow and Monti 77). She was concerned that boys, especially teenagers, would not read a novel directed at their demographic if it had been written by a woman.

While Rawlings was not pressured to write certain types of fiction that could stereotypically be called "women's literature," she faced some humorous misconceptions from an audience that was not entirely familiar with her work. At one point, Rawlings was contacted by the editor of *Cosmopolitan* with a request that she write a second serial for the magazine. The editor was most interested in the work she was completing on *The Yearling*. In a letter to F. Scott Fitzgerald, Rawlings shared her response, "I wired back there was no use in anyone looking at the manuscript—the story was about a twelve-year-old boy in the scrub—there was no love interest. In desperation I finished, 'All women characters past the menopause'" (Bigelow and Monti 137). If anything, Rawlings was amused by the request. Another similarly odd response, this time from her readership, occurred when Rawlings received a letter from a Filipino man that read, "I am lonesome orphan boy 25 years old in American Navy. I read your book and you seem like a kind mother lady. Will you adopt me please for son?" (Bigelow and Monti 362). Anyone familiar with Rawlings's literature would be shocked to hear that she came across as maternal to this young soldier. Perhaps he was, like many of the soldiers who wrote to Rawlings, enamored of her descriptions of food, which led to the publication of *Cross Creek Cookery*. Rawlings responded to the young man that she was "fortunate enough to be free of any race prejudice, but that, alas, 25 did seem too advanced an age for an adopted son" (Bigelow and Monti 362). Aside from these comedic sketches of gross misunderstandings, Rawlings did not suffer through the misrepresentation that Glasgow faced as a woman. She was never pressured by Perkins or any other editor to write women's literature. Instead, she was strongly encouraged to continue producing the literature of the Florida scrub and its people, with themes ranging from running moonshine to hunting bears, atypical writing for women. In one short generation, the publishing world had grown to accept women as writers and promote them based on the quality of their prose.

Despite this greater acceptance, Marjorie Kinnan Rawlings felt the need to respond to critics of her work, many of whom called for the type of sentimentalism and traditionalism that Glasgow railed against. Her first *Scribner's Magazine* publication, "Cracker Chidlings," met with a scathing review in the local *Ocala Evening Star*, mostly due to the editor's insistence that Rawlings was confusing the Florida Crackers with what he assumed was most likely a trip to the Cumberlands. In her response, Rawlings echoed Glasgow's critique of sentimentality by quoting an article by H. L. Mencken from the *Forum*, in which he writes:

> There are men in the world, and some of them not unintelligent men, who have a natural appetite for the untrue, just as there are others who have a natural appetite for the ugly. A bald fact somehow affrights them; they long to swathe it in comforting illusions. Thus one hears from them that it is somehow immoral for an artist to depict human life as it actually is: the spectacle of the real must

be ameliorated by an evocation of the ideal, which is to say of the *un*-real. So Thomas Hardy becomes a bad artist, and the author of *Pollyanna* a good one. (Bigelow and Monti 39)

After the success of the novel, Rawlings had mixed feelings toward her readership. While the local Floridian families on whom she based the novel reveled in its accuracy, telling her "You done a damn good job for a Yankee" (Bigelow and Monti 67), critical reviewers' comments on the characters and the Florida Crackers in general left Rawlings feeling like a traitor. She wrote to Perkins at one point that she feared "she has delivered the Crackers to the Philistines" (Bigelow and Monti 61). Her characterizations, though deeply meaningful to her own mind, seemed not to translate in the way she had hoped to readers who were unfamiliar with rural Florida and its inhabitants.

Although Rawlings had a fiery temperament, she never rejected criticism over her work out of hand. Take, for instance, her own self-effacing remarks on what she considered her weakest novel, *Golden Apples*. She predicted negative reviews when writing to Max Perkins, "I don't blame anyone but myself for 'Golden Apples' being interesting trash instead of literature. But you should have bullied me and shamed me further. I can do better than that and you know it" (Bigelow and Monti 99). When the reviews arrived, she was "astonished at their generosity" (Bigelow and Monti 100). Rawlings decided after the initial batch that she did not wish to see any additional reviews because she knew what they would say and was simply pleased by the interest, in spite of the novel's shortcomings. Later, she was convinced that the book had been so negatively received that Scribner's stopped advertising it altogether, writing to Perkins that she was upset by its absence from the *New York Herald Tribune* list, in part because of her anxieties about the quality of the novel (*MM* 233). Perkins wrote her a lengthy response on the publisher's formulae for advertising times based on book release dates and prices to convince her that she was not being overlooked (*MM* 235). His concern, which Rawlings shared, was that she did not have the same degree of familiarity with the English that she did with the Florida Crackers, and would therefore struggle to write the strange English nobleman into the Florida scrub. Despite the fact that Rawlings had a real-life Englishman in Florida to serve as a model for that character, Tordell remained a largely unsuccessful character, even by Rawlings's own estimation.

Because Rawlings was portraying real individuals, she most valued letters in response to *South Moon Under* from those who had some measure of familiarity with Florida and approved of her characterizations of the land and its people. She asked Perkins to return those letters for her to respond to personally after she sent them to him with the following introduction: "I am sending on three letters of favorable comment that may interest you as they did me, for they are from three of the comparatively rare souls who have seen the Florida I see" (Bigelow and Monti 44). Rawlings regarded the approval she received of her work from the Cracker community most highly.

From those not familiar with Florida, she hoped for recognition of the universality of her stories, rather than just curiosity about the exotic people and places she described. Her favorite review of *South Moon Under* came in the *London Times Literary Supplement* from a reviewer who "emphasized the cosmic pattern I had in mind, and which I felt I had failed to 'put over,' because the American reviewers weren't particularly conscious of it" (Bigelow and Monti 76). Like Glasgow before her, Rawlings loved where she lived, but she wanted to write about it as an artist, not an entertainer sharing a joke at the expense of uneducated Crackers.

If anything, Rawlings protected the Crackers about whom she wrote. She refused to let Max Perkins include anecdotal praise for *South Moon Under* from her local community because she feared "it would be a matter of actually getting a definite family in trouble with the law by identifying them too publicly with [her] book characters" (Bigelow and Monti 68). Rawlings wrote realistically of the Cracker community, and knew that many of the illegal activities she described, from hunting out of season or in restricted areas to running moonshine, could result in serious repercussions for her neighbors. As she explained to Perkins, "'one of them Christian-hearted sons of bitches' would raise a great row about moonshining in Marion County being so common and public that a Yankee writer could make a book about it" (Bigelow and Monti 70). The worst infraction Rawlings could imagine would be to represent the real people she was describing "not as human beings, but as literary specimens" (Tarr and Kinser 275). She wrote to Perkins about the suspicious son of

Barney Dillard, who was helping her understand the local herbs used for medicines and "remedies." The son began following her around because he was certain she was going to tell all his father's stories, but Barney corrected his son by explaining that Rawlings "is interested in the old days and the old ways," not like his son, whom he described as a "sorry, no account thing" (Bigelow and Monti 120). The son was so impressed, he gave Rawlings a beautiful ram's horn before she left their home. The story illustrates Rawlings's life among the rural inhabitants of the Florida scrub. She respected people and their ways of life in her writing, going so far as to review the proof of *South Moon Under* with Leonard, upon whose life the novel was based, before publishing it.

Rawlings could have viewed Ellen Glasgow as less-involved with her subject matter because of her choice of more abstract characters and imagined social crises, but she did not. Instead, Rawlings wondered whether she was taking an easier approach herself by writing on the simplicity of the Florida life she had adopted. In a letter to F. Scott Fitzgerald, whose writing would have more closely aligned with Glasgow's than hers, Rawlings admitted:

> You have what must actually be a painful insight into people, especially complicated people. I don't understand people like us—and what little I do understand terrifies me. That's why I write, gratefully, of the very simple people whose problems are only the fundamental and primitive ones. I have probably been more cowardly than I'd admit in sinking my interest in the Florida backwoods, for the peace and beauty I've found there have been definitely an escape from the confusion of our generation. (Bigelow and Monti 122)

For Rawlings, the Florida Crackers, with their celebration of life and basic survival, were the most understandable of characters, certainly more understandable than the melodramatic malaise afflicting upper-class circles in the cities of Glasgow's and Fitzgerald's imaginations.

After reviews sparked recommendations that she should change her writing's focus, Glasgow doubled down on her choice of themes for her novels by writing stories that were even more political, with tragic social commentary. Rawlings, for her part, actually did consider completely changing her approach to writing about Florida after the first reviews of *South Moon Under* left her with "the feeling that [she] [has] written a wild animal book" (Bigelow and Monti 62). She emphatically wrote to Perkins, "No more Crackers. I have two or three humorous short things in mind, but no more Cracker novels" (Bigelow and Monti 62). Fortunately, she found that she simply had to write about Florida, because the land was a part of her and it was through the people of Florida that she had come to understand herself and humanity as a whole. After the mixed reviews of *Golden Apples*, Rawlings explained this decision to continue writing about Florida:

> I believe, from the reaction, I should go on with the Florida vein in one form or another, a little longer. One hates to be localized. Yet there is still much fascinating material here. And if real and true and honest characters can be made to move across a little-known setting, I suppose it is foolish for me to long for wider worlds to conquer. And I still think I shall write a good book some day. (Bigelow and Monti 100)

Rawlings could not leave Florida behind because, to her, it was not a convenient, "localized" setting for fiction. The landscape and rich culture moved her to find within herself a life of such meaning that she admitted she could call no other place home.

Ellen Glasgow never experienced a dramatic discovery of place; rather, she experienced a rediscovery of place with novels that bounce back and forth between New York and her lifelong home in Virginia. In her first novel, *The Descendant*, Glasgow escaped from the South by having her protagonist, Michael Akershem, immigrate from Virginia to New York. The novel served the dual purpose of proving that she could write capably of places other than the South, while also giving her an opportunity to critique southern culture more incisively. Glasgow explained such novels as *The Descendant* in her autobiography, *The Woman Within*: "I hated—I had always hated—the inherent falseness in much Southern tradition. . . . Those superficial critics who classify me as 'beginning in the local color school' can have read none of my earliest novels" (*WW* 97). She chose New York as the novel's setting because, as she writes, "I needed a big city, and New York was the only one in which I had stayed as long as two weeks—or even two days" (*WW* 98). New York enabled Michael Akershem to grow in intelligence and complexity without the stifling conservatism of Virginia, but it was also a location of extreme isolation that resulted in Michael losing sight of his own identity, which was grounded in the heritage he had escaped.

Michael Akershem lives most of his life in New York, where he is able to escape from poverty and the "bastard" label he had in Virginia. He becomes a writer and editor of a socialist publication, the *Iconoclast*. Eventually, he becomes alienated from his heritage and adopts a style of writing on class issues that is completely hypocritical. Michael grows so disgusted by the poor that he cannot stand to be around poverty, yet he continues to incite labor protests, endangering lives and costing some individuals their jobs. Michael's moment of disillusionment occurs when "he realized the emptiness of ambition, the futility of reward. Was he who loathed pain the one to close the gaping wound? He who shrank from filth the one to purge from uncleanliness?" (187). He gains a new identity in New York and finds himself wandering the streets, "pursued by his self-distrust" after he realizes that he has "fought for the sake of fighting, not for the sake of the cause" (187). Michael's downfall in New York occurs when he realizes his success has been based on his own ambition to have people see him differently from the way they did when he was a bastard orphan in Virginia. Despite his efforts to the contrary, he is serving the Southern tradition that so reviled him as a child. Michael Akershem's conflict mirrored Glasgow's own struggles with her identity as a Southerner who did not want to espouse the doctrines of the South blindly in her writing. Rawlings never experienced this kind of conflict because she did not grow up with this same attachment to place. By the time she had adopted Florida as her home, Rawlings was an adult who wanted to promote her new home, not a native attempting to critique it.

In another example of Glasgow's torn allegiance, Dorinda Oakley of *Barren Ground* (1925), written much later in Glasgow's career, boards the first train to New York with seventy dollars pinned inside her dress after she discovers that she is pregnant and that her fiancé has married another woman. Just as Michael Akershem escapes the prejudices of being a bastard, so Dorinda Oakley hopes to escape the stigma of being unmarried and pregnant. In the same way that Michael Akershem is shown mercy by the editor of the *Iconoclast*, a physician takes pity on Dorinda and treats her after she is struck by a carriage and miscarries. The physician and his wife hire her as a nanny and provide her with access to educational opportunities in New York, including, fortuitously, lectures on dairy farming. Ultimately, Dorinda becomes a successful farmer after inheriting her father's land. Michael Akershem's alienation lands him in prison after he shoots a man and, later, puts him at the mercy of his former lover as his nurse and caretaker when he is diagnosed with a terminal illness. Dorinda Oakley, on the other hand, uses her time away from the South carefully to construct a wall that protects her against romantic encounters and enables her to reconstruct an independent life for herself. In an emotionally distant scene, Dorinda ends up caring for her ailing former lover. In Dorinda's case, the time away from the South has given her the strength to return with a renewed sense of heritage and her own identity, one that has overcome the ugliness of that heritage. As Dorinda reflects toward the end of *Barren Ground*, "The difference was that at twenty her happiness had depended upon love, and at fifty it depended upon nothing but herself and the land" (470). Glasgow showed that the sentimental tradition should not be dismissed out of hand, but that it should be critiqued for its superficial qualities. The core of tradition, however, provides Dorinda with a fortitude that she attributes to her ancestors. Glasgow shared this worldview with Rawlings, who constructed her writing life on the foundation of the experiences of family members with similar connections to the land and farming.

Each time Glasgow wrote of a character traveling to New York, she emphasized a Southerner's perception of the Big Apple. Glasgow did not want to be considered a New York writer, even though she visited the city frequently. As she explained, "In New York, all that I could strive for would be Cezanne's 'little sensation' in art, and I had even less ambition to provide 'the little sensation' in my work than I had the need to display it in my own person" (*CM* 10). Nevertheless, Glasgow saw the need to establish herself with a Northern audience to be respected as an author:

> There is more truth than wit in the gibe that every Southern novelist must first make his reputation in the North. Perhaps this is why

so many Southern novelists write of the South as if it were a fabulous country ... Had I entered the world by way of Oxford, or even by way of Bloomsbury, I might now be able to speak or write of my books without a feeling of outraged reserve. (*CM* 195)

At the turn of the century, writers from the South experienced the same degree of prejudice as citizens of the South. While many Northern writers felt this same prejudice when being read by their British counterparts, they did not extend any sympathy toward the Southerners they excluded from elite literary circles and the publications they maintained. Glasgow had to walk a fine line between writing novels that were sophisticated enough to be accepted by these groups and maintaining her own sense of realism in her narratives, just as Rawlings would later try to write realistic novels of Florida that did more than entertain a Northern audience with humorous anecdotes.

Glasgow's attempts at realism were complicated by the fact that most novels being branded as realistic were coming out of the North and had their own overly regimented structures. When explaining why she did not subscribe to the strict tenets of realism espoused by Howells, Glasgow wrote, "I had not revolted from the Southern sentimental fallacy in order to submit myself to the tyranny of the Northern genteel tradition" (*CM* 14). Glasgow insisted that her "quarrel, alike with Southern romance and Northern realism, was simply the old resentment against fixed patterns of work and the rule of averages in general" (*CM* 15). These were structures with which Rawlings never had to contend. Instead, Rawlings elected to write through the seasons with a natural cadence that accompanied characters who live off the land.

Even when Glasgow chose to situate a novel entirely in New York, as she did with *Life and Gabriella*, she was "careful to deal only with Virginians, and with their transplanted loyalty to their native culture" (*CM* 99). In this way, Glasgow maintained an authentic perspective within the New York sections of her novels. Her description of characters could as easily describe Glasgow herself: "Wherever they may settle, it is typical of Virginians that they should remain parochial in sentiment" (*CM* 99). To illustrate how she would write a character into this setting, Glasgow gave a detailed description of *Life and Gabriella*:

It follows, therefore, that the circle Gabriella enters in New York is quite as provincial, and even more clannish at heart, than the family circle in Richmond. . . . And, meanwhile, from her earliest revolt, in the deep Victorian gloom of the front parlour in Hill Street, to the moment, some eighteen years later, when she follows O'Hara to the Pennsylvania Station in New York, the whole train of events is observed entirely through the eyes and the consciousness of Gabriella. (*CM* 99)

Glasgow was known for constructing narratives with shifting points of view, focalizing a story through the narrative lens of multiple characters, yet she pointed out that her use of such shifting perspectives did not allow for a view of New York by any character other than a Virginian, like herself. Looking back on the novel, Glasgow was able to relive her experiences while writing the book from her New York apartment: "I see again the lights blooming out of the trees in Central Park, and the flushed outlines of the towers on the horizon" (*CM* 100). She constructed the Fowlers' brownstone and Gabriella's "dreary apartment-house" from places she resided on different trips to the city. Glasgow effectively remained tied to places she knew well in her narratives, just as Rawlings did when choosing to partly base *The Sojourner*, her one novel to take place outside of Florida, on her grandparents' Michigan farm.

From her first trip to New York in search of a publisher to the many years in which she visited there off-and-on throughout the year, Glasgow found that traveling away from One West Main, the Richmond address where she lived from childhood to her death, enabled her to write more clearly about her home state of Virginia. Describing her time in New York, Glasgow explained, "Even at the time I worked altogether there . . . I did not write the things immediately about me. One really must get at some distance and obtain a perspective, especially for realistic writing" (Raper 119). Glasgow gained perspective by traveling to New York in the same way that her characters did in some of her best-known works, *The Descendant, Barren Ground, Virginia*, and *Life and Gabriella*. Those characters, like Glasgow, used New York to understand Virginia better while remaining citizens of the South and observing New York through a Southern eye.

Marjorie Kinnan Rawlings's struggle to escape from Florida in her fiction was not as successful as Glasgow's from Virginia. *Golden Apples* attempted to bring the outside world into Florida with Richard Tordell, an Englishman who moves onto property he owns in Florida only to find homeless youths already living there. However, Rawlings's most successful venture outside the Florida scrub was with *The Sojourner*, her last novel. Rawlings worked diligently on *The Sojourner* throughout her final years, despite the fact that she had lost the aid and comfort of her talented editor, Max Perkins, who helped her tremendously with her major literary works. His death affected her deeply. *The Sojourner* was set in the farmland of the North, based partly on her grandparents' farm in Michigan and partly on the area around Van Hornesville, New York, where Rawlings escaped to complete the novel, and included characters resembling members of her own family.

In many respects, *The Sojourner* was less of an escape from Florida than a return to a heritage that Rawlings carried with her throughout her career, similar to Glasgow's Southern heritage. Her memoir and first book, *Blood of My Blood*, though not published during her lifetime, included many of the same characters as *The Sojourner*, based on her mother's family in Michigan. That first work of pseudo-nonfiction was both a scathing critique of her mother's overbearing personality and a direct assault on Rawlings herself as a spoiled and egotistical young woman. Rawlings hoped to understand her relationship with her mother better through the writing of *Blood of My Blood*, in the same way as she anticipated *The Sojourner* would allow her to understand the qualities of her mother's family that led to their conflicts. By returning to her mother's home for the novel, Rawlings was able to grapple with the complex relationships that reconcile the prodigal son and his dutiful brother with the land they share. In *The Sojourner*, Rawlings did not so much escape her label as a regionalist writer as adopt a new region with which she was still intimately connected.

Rawlings felt more connected to her father than to her mother. She also had an abiding love and respect for her maternal grandfather, Abe Traphagen, more so than for his wife Fanny. More than the man, she admired the lifestyle he embodied, however much she may have romanticized it. Rawlings wrote of his farm, "I think of a way of life that was beautiful, and that is gone. . . . I, too, should have written such a book about those Michigan acres I knew, but I understood too late their meaning" (Tarr and Kinser 264). She lamented that Abe Traphagen passed away before she could take from him the memories she felt would help her to write an accurate account of his life. One of the reasons Rawlings prolonged her work on *The Sojourner* for so many years was because of how challenging it was to create a historical family truth from scraps of memories. She idealized Abe and Fanny Traphagen's life to the point where she wrote, "I think perhaps men and women are no longer willing to work as hard. . . . We talk now of hours and wages, and do not give ourselves with quite the uncalculating fervor to living" (Tarr and Kinser 264). Their lives, like her life with her father on their Maryland farm, inspired Rawlings's own grand Floridian adventure.

Indeed, Rawlings brought to life all the elements she most treasured about the Traphagen farm from her memories. When writing about the farm, she consistently emphasized an improbable abundance of resources, given that the family consumed most of what it produced. She recounted that "a farm that did not provide lavishly was, simply, a poor or shiftless farm" (Tarr and Kinser 265). The description of food stores and baked goods in the Traphagen home perfectly paralleled the elaborate descriptions of food from *Cross Creek* and *Cross Creek Cookery*, indicating where Rawlings's love of food preparation originated.

For Rawlings, writing about Michigan was far more challenging than writing about Florida, and even more challenging than Glasgow's writings on Virginia, because Rawlings's experience with the state was so underdeveloped. Her grandparents lived and farmed there. She grew up with stories of them and the area. However, she never lived in Michigan for any extensive period, and drew most of her ideas of their lives from piecemeal stories and childhood memories. Despite this sparse foundation, Rawlings felt indebted to her grandparents and their land while writing *The Sojourner*, and was committed to the memory of the place.

Many scenes from *The Sojourner* were replicated in a *Vogue* article written by Rawlings about Fanny Traphagen. Not only did she describe Fanny as more pretty than beautiful, but she also emphasized Fanny's "foolishness," a foolishness embodied by Nellie Linden, Ase's wife in *The Sojourner*. Just as Nellie dressed as a tramp to fool Ase, so did Rawlings describe how Fanny once showed up at the farmhouse "disguised as a tramp" (Tarr and Kinser 282). Rawlings also imagined Fanny going to Abe in the fields and letting the pins out of her hair in the same way Nellie does with Ase in the novel. While Rawlings did not admire Fanny as much as Abe, she respected her a great deal more than her own mother. She concluded the *Vogue* article by writing of her grandmother, "But she quite simply went her own way, saucy, ribald—and took admiration for granted. . . . The point of view is natural to a beautiful woman. I recommend it as well to the merely pretty and to the plain" (Tarr and Kinser 284). Rawlings commiserated more with her serious grandfather struggling to understand his wife's sense of humor, but, in fact, her own life rather resembled Fanny's. Rawlings was known to have a temper, and made her fair share of humorous jabs at friends and loved ones in her letters, a trait shared by Glasgow, who could also be very direct in her correspondence.

Writing about Abe and Fanny Traphagen's life permitted Rawlings not only an escape from Florida, but also an understanding of a heritage for which she longed but with which she could not quite identify. She explained this need most clearly: "I wrote 'The Sojourner' because I was haunted by a grandfather I had not known. I was never to know him, and I was obliged to create another man and another life, that may or may not have resembled his own, but which I came to know as well as I know myself" (Tarr and Kinser 346). Rawlings felt cheated by a life that intrinsically linked her most closely to the one relative, her mother, with whom she felt she had the least in common. She never had the luxury that Glasgow did of growing up surrounded by her extended family. While finishing *The Sojourner*, Rawlings remarked, "I was so identified with Ase that I felt the same soaring release that came to him. I realize now that subconsciously this was what I had always intended" (Tarr and Kinser 347). Concluding the novel just before her own premature death allowed Rawlings to come full circle by embracing the heritage denied to her in her younger years.

Although most struggles faced by Glasgow and Rawlings in their critical reception had to do with their categorization as regional writers, Rawlings faced an additional and unique challenge in being pressured to write juvenile fiction to make her regional literature of Florida marketable to the large audience of adolescent boys who enjoyed reading wilderness stories that appealed to their sense of adventure. The first person to push her in this direction was Rawlings's then-husband, when she was working on her first novel. After reading chapters from *South Moon Under*, Charles Rawlings was so sure that the book was more likely to sell as juvenile fiction that he implored her to remove Lant's profanity throughout the book. When writing of the exchange to Perkins, Rawlings claimed she "was as shocked as if he'd suggested that I sell myself into slavery . . . remarking caustically that possibly the book could become the first of a series, 'The Rover Boys in Florida'" (Bigelow and Monti 57). She comforted herself with "copious draughts of native rye" and then listened to Chuck explain further how the book could be like Twain's *Huckleberry Finn* or Kipling's *Treasure Island* (Bigelow and Monti 57). She did not claim to care whether the book sold, just that it be good, but she did begin questioning whether Chuck was correct in his assessment of her work.

In spite of his assurances to Rawlings that she should retain Lant's profanity in *South Moon Under*, Perkins agreed with Charles Rawlings's assertions that her themes would work well for a younger audience. Rawlings seemed at first put out by his suggestions, responding, "I really didn't intend to bait you into telling me about your plan for me 'in connection with' writing—which, incidentally, is an entirely accurate phrase for what you have in mind! Such a book had never occurred to me" (Bigelow and Monti 73). She quickly warmed to the idea for the same reason as the Florida landscape appealed to her: it reminded her of her childhood. Rawlings moved to Florida, in a sense, to live out the farming life she had idealized from her childhood. Those childhood memories included the types of juvenile adventures she imagined for this new novel. Her initial impulse was to write a story about wolves. She then decided she wanted to use material from *South Moon Under* as part of the text. Finally, she created a bear hunt as the central theme. She so successfully captured the perspective of Jody Baxter in *The Yearling* that MGM asked her to write a script for a *Lassie* film to star Claude Jarman, the same actor who played Jody in the film adaptation of *The Yearling*. The *Lassie* film ended up being an adaptation of "A Mother in Mannville," titled "A Family for Jock," and was so popular that MGM wanted her to write more. Unfortunately, her second attempt, involving WWII K-9 dogs, was rejected (Silverthorne 270, 291). Nevertheless, Rawlings proved that she could write for and about a younger audience, which was a financial boon but not necessarily in line with her expectations for her writing career.

Rawlings repeatedly altered her plans for the book that would become *The Yearling*, until at some point, Perkins clarified that he did not simply want a juvenile book, but a "boy's *classic*," a request that completely changed Rawlings's concept (Bigelow and Monti 81). Rather than writing a book for boys, Rawlings decided, "It will not be a story for boys, though some of them might enjoy it. It will be a story *about* a boy—a brief and tragic idyll of boyhood. I think it cannot help but be very beautiful" (Bigelow and Monti 107). By the time Rawlings neared completion of the book, she no longer wanted it to be considered juvenile in any way, writing to Perkins:

> What I am concerned about is that the forthcoming book should not be labeled a "juvenile," because I think it will only incidentally be a book *for* boys. I hope there will be nostalgic implications for mature people for we never *feel* more sensitively than in extreme youth, and the color and drama of the scrub can be well conveyed through the eyes and mind of a boy. I believe, I hope, that the book will be able to stand on its own feet. The only thing different I am doing with the market, or appeal for boys, in mind, is avoiding the psychological (usually sexual) involvements of maturity. But a boy's reaction to the mature world is a valid one, and has value for anyone. The adventure and simplicity, will carry it, quite secondarily, for boys' use. But it is important that no announcement ever be made, anywhere, that the book is a "juvenile." (Bigelow and Monti 128)

Rawlings felt a mixture of pride and pressure to produce juvenilia after writing *South Moon Under*, and, indeed, *The Yearling* may be said to contain a juvenile appeal. However, she reclaimed the novel from the suggestions and recommendations she felt would pigeonhole her into that category of writing and made the book into a tragic *Bildungsroman*, a novel with universal appeal. Many younger readers could not fully appreciate the choices Jody must face. In this case, the advice of an editor directed

Rawlings into the work that best served her career as an author, rather than steering her into what Glasgow feared most—a field of popular fiction with little lasting merit.

Both Glasgow and Rawlings suffered feelings of isolation brought about by their compulsion to perfect their literary craft. They secured their careers through regional novels, but they were also limited by being categorized as regional writers. In her last letter to Glasgow before Glasgow's death, Rawlings begged her to complete her autobiography because she felt that "posterity" would benefit from learning more about how her "mind and emotions have functioned" (Bigelow and Monti 275). She wanted to know more about what Glasgow intended to accomplish through her fiction, because Rawlings recognized that the critics were so often wrong. While both writers struggled with critics who were quick to dismiss their writing as stereotypical of a certain place or genre, Rawlings and Glasgow desperately sought to continue writing fiction with the hope that the universal truths they wanted to share would yet come across. Their letters echo this desire for culturally transcendent literature. When Rawlings reminded Glasgow of the dream they once shared, she appended the memory by asking her to visit Florida: "I feel somehow that I, we, can give you some warmth—and you, of course, can always let us warm our hands at your fire" (Bigelow and Monti 276).

6

The Sheltered Life

Yes, I have had my life. I have known ecstasy. I have known anguish. I have loved, and I have been loved. With one I loved, I have watched the light breaking over the Alps. If I have passed through "the dark night of the soul," I have had a far-off glimpse of the illumination beyond. For an infinitesimal point of time or eternity, I have caught a gleam, or imagined I caught a gleam, of the mystic vision.... It was enough, and it is now over.

The Woman Within: An Autobiography, by Ellen Glasgow

WHEN MARJORIE KINNAN RAWLINGS committed to her biography of Ellen Glasgow, one area of Glasgow's life, in particular, fascinated her more than any other, and led to a series of interviews with and private commentaries on Glasgow: her love life. Superficially, Glasgow epitomized the stereotype of a spinster. Echoing the title and theme of her 1932 novel, Ellen Glasgow lived *The Sheltered Life*, too frail to attend school, coming of age before women were permitted at the University of Virginia, and with a hearing impairment that meant she required relatives or close friends to accompany her when she traveled. Glasgow never married. However, Rawlings discovered that Glasgow had been engaged twice, and seemed to have a more complex romantic past than one would have thought. These details interested Rawlings, who had an active dating life from her high school days, attended the University of Wisconsin, and maintained an active social life with her sorority, then was married, divorced, and married for a second time. She was known, even in her later years, as the kind of woman who appealed to men with her quick wit and easy camaraderie. She also left a trail of letters leading to her past and present lovers, and spoke openly about her experiences. Rawlings struggled to learn the details of Glasgow's love life, however, because the latter had deliberately destroyed any letters that could provide details about her romantic trysts, used pseudonyms for her lovers in her autobiography, and left the impression, at least with her literary executors, that she did not want her autobiography published before the death of her former fiancé, Henry Anderson, who might be hurt or offended by her portrayal of him. From what she was able to uncover about Glasgow, Rawlings learned that she had endured a struggle similar to Rawlings's own to maintain her independence and professional success within the framework of a romantic relationship. They both felt that their writing suffered from the time commitment and emotional drain of a relationship. Rawlings confided openly in Glasgow about her romantic past and present, but Glasgow maintained her own privacy, ultimately leaving Rawlings to make assumptions about her past from her published writings. Rawlings was determined to learn the secrets of Glasgow's past, even though she was reticent about including the material in her biography of Glasgow.

In her 1932 novel *The Sheltered Life*, Glasgow wrote about two generations of women, and men if you count General Archbald, suffering from what she called "the sheltered life." This sheltering prevented characters from discussing immoral acts or admitting to particular types of character flaws openly, even though everyone knew about them. For the older generation made up of men like General Archbald, Eva Birdsong is a romantic ideal, a beautiful "songbird" who had foregone her career in music to marry the ne'er-do-well George Birdsong, a womanizer who makes little effort to hide his affairs while Eva works overtime not to notice them. To give a younger generation's perspective, Glasgow narrated much of the novel through the character of Jenny Blair Archbald, which helped her offer a strong critique of the kinds of subterfuge frequently seen in these so-called prestigious social groups. Jenny Blair, the precocious granddaughter of General Archbald, easily dissects the hidden meanings and realities beneath the surface of things, and decides, somewhat callously, to play her own game with these characters and their façades by starting a flirtation with George Birdsong. This act becomes a final breach of trust Eva cannot bear, and leads her to murder George in cold blood. Through the novel, Glasgow revealed many of her own conflicting experiences with a dying Victorian age that she respected aesthetically, but ultimately recognized as a conceit that was both lacking in sincerity and potentially harmful. Her approach to romantic attachments was informed largely by her conflicting desires for discretion and passion, with the added obstacle of her career, which she valued above all relationships.

Rawlings, who was more open about her own sexuality, either omitted the topic from her writing altogether, as in many of her short stories and *The Yearling*, or wrote about it organically, as part of the natural landscape, barely distinguishing human sexual experiences from animal. When Mart approaches Florry at her home in "Jacob's Ladder," he simply asks, "You want to go off with me?" (Tarr 50). His reason for approaching her is that they both seem lonely in the same way. They agree to start their life together with no need for a marriage certificate, which they would not have been able to afford anyway. Florry tells Mart, "I ain't too pertickler about standin' up in front of a parson" (Tarr 52). Their nomadic life together evades the provincial laws that would normally insist upon marriage licenses, home ownership, and even hunting and fishing rights. In this way, Rawlings created characters who never experienced the comforts or trappings of any "shelter," and instead lived, physically and emotionally, in a struggle with nature for their very survival.

Much of what Rawlings learned about Glasgow's romantic past initially came from her review of Glasgow's autobiography, *The Woman Within*. Glasgow began spending more time in New York and abroad in her twenties, giving her a reprieve from the stifling community of Richmond, which bore too much Southern nosiness about people's goings-on. During this time, Glasgow was able to indulge in her first serious flirtations. She unintentionally jilted the first man to take a serious interest in her because of her hearing impairment and inability to acknowledge that impairment, even after he pressed her to let him know whether she had trouble hearing. Even as a young woman of twenty-two, Glasgow wrote, "I told myself that marriage was not for me, and I meant it more firmly every year that I lived" (*WW* 138). Such a statement would have been audacious for a woman of Glasgow's age at the time she uttered these words in the 1890s.

When writing about her first love in her autobiography, Glasgow explained her thoughts about marriage more fully: "I felt that I could not surrender myself to constant companionship, that I could not ever be completely possessed" (*WW* 153). She recognized that she had no "maternal instinct," but she also felt that her temperament and hearing disability made her ill-suited for a relationship. This first love, whom Glasgow referred to as Gerald B—, came about when Glasgow was in her mid-twenties. In her own narrative of events, she described him as a Wall Street man with two grown sons and a wife from whom he was estranged, but Rawlings and others questioned how much of this description had been fabricated to disguise his identity. Glasgow claimed that the relationship lasted seven years, until Gerald's death, and that it helped her to emerge from the mourning clothes and attitude she had assumed since the deaths of her mother and brother-in-law. Her hearing disability was never a challenge with Gerald, because he spoke in tonalities she could usually pick up, and responded to her occasional needs for repetition in so natural a way as not to make her self-conscious about them. Glasgow recalled their time together at length in *The Woman Within*:

> There were dozens of small, foreign restaurants he had known of, or we had stumbled upon almost by accident. Sometimes, in summer or on mild spring evenings, we would take a boat to Coney Island, where we could lose ourselves completely among the four elements. Yet a few memories start out more vividly. Going out with him the first time he drove his small racing car. An evening in the country, when we sat on a bench before a tiny tavern, waiting for the car to be mended, and wondered what would happen if we never went back. (*WW* 161)

One of the memories she shared was of a Hungarian restaurant where they heard a violin playing a melody that she would later compare with Proust's idea of the "little phrase"; it wound its way through many of her memories of their time together. She found it ironic that such a phrase would occur in music for her, given her hearing difficulties. Glasgow had other love affairs and even engagements, but she admitted that after Gerald B—, "never again could I feel ecstasy, never again the rush of wings in my heart" (*WW* 162). After recounting a time spent walking together in the Alps, Glasgow gave the final memories of his death, a moment in time that led to what she considered a transformative mystical experience that brought her much closer to God than had any religion. She was traveling abroad and received a letter from him after he was hospitalized, telling her that he was dying and lamenting that "it meant giving you up" (*WW* 165). She learned of his actual death from a newspaper before sailing home. In the meantime, she went on a solitary walk and lay in the grass, writing, "I thought of the mystics, who had attained Divine consciousness through a surrender of the agonized self. By giving up, by yielding the sense of separateness, by extinguishing the innermost core of identity" (*WW* 165). In this sublime moment, Glasgow found "ecstasy born out of agony . . . as fleeting as the old delusions of mind or of heart" (*WW* 166). Once again, she had to cope with the death of her most intimate companion. Having lost her mother and the brother-in-law who had helped kick-start her career before she met Gerald B—, she would come to lose both her brother Frank and her closest sister Cary within six years of Gerald's death.

Biographers and Glasgow scholars, it should be noted, have questioned the existence of this man—and theorized about the construction of this romance, or exaggeration of it, in Glasgow's autobiography. Pamela Matthews noted in *Perfect Companionship*, "If Glasgow had a romantic relationship from 1899 to 1905 with the 'Gerald B—' of her autobiography, it did not hinder her expressions of affection to other women in her letters from about the same time" (*PC* 17). Matthews went on to question further the existence of Gerald B— in *Glasgow and a Woman's Tradition*, pointing out the observation of another author, Will Brantley, that Glasgow titled this chapter in her autobiography "Miracle—or Illusion?" (*EGWT* 38). James Branch Cabell called her autobiography one of Glasgow's best works of fiction. Her biographer Stanly Godbold stated:

Despite the rampant self-pity, her moments of happiness with Gerald and during her visits in England are sufficiently chronicled that the reader cannot help suspecting that she did not suffer quite so much as she pretended and must have found her extraordinary success in her own lifetime to be at least some consolation for the agonies of her inner conflicts. (210)

Responding to Godbold's assertion, Nancy Walker used Glasgow's study of Joyce's *Portrait of the Artist as a Young Man* to contend that Glasgow was using "the creation of a *persona* large enough to at once carry the burden of the classic suffering artist in the masculine tradition and reinforce the traditionally feminine notion of suffering as metaphor for womanhood itself" (Scura 34). Whether Gerald B— was a real person or a persona created from various experiences in Glasgow's life to present an image of herself she wished others to have, Glasgow's narrative about him in her autobiography revealed her desire to overcome the misconception she frequently faced that she was something of a sexless homebody.

The fact that Glasgow most likely altered critical details to protect the identity of Gerald B—, whom she identified as a married man with children, makes determining his identity challenging. Glasgow's biographer, Susan Goodman, looked extensively into Glasgow's correspondence and potential acquaintances for hints of who could have fit the identity of Gerald B—. Quoting several marginal notes by Glasgow in books she was reading at the time of the affair that seemed to repeat "Thou shalt renounce," Goodman theorized that Glasgow struggled with the "guilt and recriminations, the shifting balances of power and commitment common to such affairs" (Goodman 78). When trying to piece together the affair, she found Rebe's denial of the existence of Gerald B— to be highly suspect, given that she had "barricaded herself in Glasgow's study following her sister's funeral, destroying or removing anything that might damage Glasgow's reputation, including books on the psychology of sex" (Goodman 78). The candidates Goodman included in her list of possibilities for Gerald B— "included Walter Hines Page; Pearce Bailey, a New York doctor; Holbrook Curtis, another doctor; Hewitt Hanson Howland, an advisory editor at Bobbs-Merrill; and, most recently, William Riggin Travers, a wealthy man of leisure" (Goodman 80). Irita Van Doren, Glasgow's literary executor and close friend, named Howland as Glasgow's lover, but Goodman questioned whether any of the men identified could have played that role (Goodman 80). Howland's biographical details did not match those of Gerald B—, even though those could have been largely invented to mask his identity. Goodman explored at length the possibility of Travers being Gerald B—. Pamela Matthews explained the reasoning behind that theory in one of her notes from *Glasgow and a Woman's Tradition,* pointing to an article by Frances W. Saunders that had appeared in the *Ellen Glasgow Newsletter* (221n34). Matthews did not find the evidence convincing. Gerald did fit the description of a wealthy New England man in a troubled marriage whose wife filed for divorce just before his suicide, and his obituary appeared in the Paris edition of the *Herald Tribune* around the time that Glasgow reported reading of it while traveling abroad. Goodman, who was not convinced of the match, pointed out that an attorney named Herbert Valentine could just as easily have fit these parameters, and that he seemed to have more in common with Glasgow, as well as having family connections in Richmond and a history of traveling abroad during the times at which Glasgow claimed to have met with Gerald B— in Switzerland (Goodman 81). The search for Glasgow's mystery man remains unresolved, but Rawlings was not alone in her intensive investigation.

In addition to trying to uncover Gerald B—'s identity, biographers and others have searched for evidence that Glasgow had any other relationships at this point in her life. The only evidence that Goodman found was a letter to "Elaine" from "Gray," dated March 23, 1901, in which Gray wrote passionately of their last "few fast fleeting hours" and the three parting kisses they shared (Goodman 82). While Glasgow and Henry Anderson also used pseudonyms during their courtship, Goodman pointed out that the letter could have just as easily been written to Glasgow by a woman named Gray, with whom she was friends at the time, given the exaggerated romantic nature of her correspondence with women (Goodman 83). Given all these uncertainties, Goodman concluded that the relationship between Glasgow and Gerald should be weighed for its "meaning and its import for her fiction" (Goodman 83). Pamela Matthews cited numerous misrepresentations of key places in Glasgow's correspondence to try to prove that Glasgow's critics were using her affair with Gerald B— to overemphasize the "ostensible sexual fulfillment that presumably brought Glasgow a rare moment of happiness," in a way that caused them to "marginalize female friendship" and privilege normative heterosexual relationships as the ultimate object of satisfaction in Glasgow's life (*EGWT* 51). While the mysterious nature of Gerald B— tantalizes readers of Glasgow, Matthews makes a valid point that much of Glasgow's autobiographical writing and correspondence emphasizes her platonic friendships with other women, like Rawlings, which added more meaning and value to her life than her purported dalliances with a few select men.

Matthews delved into Glasgow's works for scenes resembling those she shared with Gerald B— to try and uncover what the experience, real or imagined, actually meant to Glasgow. She found the Alpine scene Glasgow claimed to have experienced with Gerald B— repeated in her works of fiction, particularly *The Wheel of Life* (1906) and *Vein of Iron* (1935), and in the letters Glasgow exchanged with an older writer, Louise Chandler Moulton, around the time of Gerald B—'s purported death. These connections resulted in Matthews's assertion: "Even Glasgow's saying that he and her love for him existed does not make it so, particularly considering the probable strength of the pressure to *have* had such a man in her life. Her 'truthful' autobiography would have been the perfect place in which to invent him" (*EGWT* 55). Matthews included a quotation from one of Glasgow's novels, *The Miller of Old Church* (1911), in which a female protagonist exclaimed, "Why do you seem to think that the beginning and middle and end of my existence is a man?" (*EGWT* 54). Glasgow never married, but maintained from her love affairs the certainty that "the memory of longing should survive the more fugitive memory of fulfillment" (*WW* 163). Her writing on this affair also hid the nature of her intimacy with Gerald B— or others. Glasgow wrote, "The modern adventurers who imagine they know love because they have known sex may be wiser than our less enlightened generation. But I am not of their period. I should have found wholly inadequate the mere physical sensation, which the youth of today seek so blithely" (*WW* 163). Such obfuscations pose the question, *Did she or didn't she?*

Rawlings's only autobiographical work written before her move to

Florida has many of the same troubling inconsistencies as Glasgow's autobiography. In addition to having been written from a young and impetuous perspective, *Blood of My Blood* was meant never to have been published, and is riddled with exaggerations and biased expositions. Norton Baskin fought against its publication when a copy was discovered in Julia Scribner Bigham's estate. Rawlings had given a copy to Scribner Bigham to encourage the latter's writing. The manuscript was not published until 2002. With the proviso that her portrayals of herself in this work are slanted, *Blood of My Blood* still gives valuable insight into Rawlings's early dating life, and was written at a time when those experiences would have still been fairly fresh in her mind. Ellen Glasgow was brought up in a formal Southern household where girls came out at debutante balls and courtship happened, at least superficially, in public. By Rawlings's teen years, a new era had begun. She attended parties and school events, but she also went out on unsupervised dates with young men from her school. Even in her later years, Glasgow, according to certain of Anderson's letters to her, considered having her time with him "chaperoned," albeit tongue-in-cheek.

In a chapter from *Blood of My Blood* titled "Beaus for Ida's Daughter," Rawlings claimed that her mother began encouraging her to be friendly with boys when she was as young as seven. She was courted by a young neighborhood boy, Jimmy, whose most redeemable trait seemed to be the money he spent on Rawlings, and sometimes her younger brother, when he would take them to the local soda fountain or ply her with gifts (*BB* 81). When Rawlings finally dismissed this suitor, Ida "was delighted" because she thought it proved her daughter's success with the opposite sex and acknowledged her ability to be selective (*BB* 81). Rawlings responded by attempting to demonstrate that she could not have cared less about boys, refusing to compete with other girls for their affections in her adolescence, at which point her mother became concerned, explaining that "you must like them if you expect them to like you" (*BB* 83). Rawlings read articles in her mother's *Ladies Home Journal* meant to instruct mothers and daughters on exactly how young women should behave, what they should be "warned" of, and what kinds of facts they should know about sex and dating. When Rawlings was as young as thirteen, her mother became so concerned that her daughter would get into "trouble" that she spent several days screaming "Shame!" at her for having ridden in a cart at the family farm with the son of a local farmhand on his chore rounds, after which Ida told Rawlings the facts of life in such gratuitous detail that it left the girl sobbing (*BB* 87–88).

During her high school years, Rawlings received weekly flowers from another girl at her school who had developed a friendly crush on Rawlings and who was using her lunch money to purchase the flowers (*BB* 95–96). When Rawlings began dating the respectable and wealthy "Harry," Ida seemed to forget her earlier rules, allowing her daughter to sleep over at the boy's house, under his mother's supervision, and to drink alcohol, which was deemed acceptable when done in such a "cosmopolitan" fashion, as when sitting next to Mary Pickford and David Belasco at the old Raleigh Roof Garden after a night at the theater (*BB* 98). Ida turned into Rawlings's private lady-in-waiting, expending all her time and effort on her daughter's needs and receiving caustic insults in return. Describing her own bad behavior, Rawlings wrote of herself that "what the girl needed was not the urge to glory, but to be thrashed within an inch of her life before it was too late, and sent on her way with a normal outlook" (*BB* 98). She experienced a symbolic thrashing when she found herself torn between a new gentleman caller (a banker) and her father on the night of the latter's death, as she portrayed it in her memoir. Rawlings favored her father over all others, and wrote with painstaking honesty that she had dismissed the severity of his illness until the night of his death, when she was torn between her concern for him and a new beau she had waiting in the sitting room to take her on a date. While admittedly part of a fictionalized and exaggerated account of her life, the scene highlights Rawlings's own self-centeredness and is sympathetic to her mother, who is condemned elsewhere in *Blood of My Blood*.

Rawlings developed a more strategic approach to dating at the University of Wisconsin, accepting invitations and then canceling them if something better came along. Eventually she married a college classmate, Charles "Chuck" Rawlings, against her mother's wishes. Once her mother saw the sorts of men her daughter preferred in college, she pulled back on her initial rush to see the girl paired off, "thought Marjorie too young to marry and had doubts that Chuck would become a husband who could support a wife at the level to which she held ambitions for her daughter" (Silverthorne 35). Rawlings, as rash as ever, could not wait to marry a fellow writer with commensurate anxieties and begin the struggles of such a union that no doubt awaited a pair of aspiring writers. Charles Rawlings stood out by displaying the same brutal honesty that Rawlings appreciated from her college professors, the ones who seemed to be borderline inappropriate in their criticism (*BB* 120). She recalled Chuck turning to her mother in front of the rest of the parents at Marjorie's college graduation and bitterly critiquing the poem she had written and read for the occasion, saying, "I'd rather write a poem that wouldn't even be read until after I was dead, and have it good, than a lifetime of trash that nit-wits would applaud" (*BB* 143). Rawlings announced her decision to marry Chuck a week before the intended nuptials, giving her mother little time to stage a protest, though she did try her best, even recounting to Rawlings an ominous dream she had had as premonitory (*BB* 152). Mother's and daughter's exchange of words about birth control before the wedding caused Rawlings to become violent and slap her mother across the face and then beg her forgiveness. In fact, her mother turned out to be right about Chuck's inadequacy as a husband (*BB* 153).

Rawlings and Chuck seemed to conflict from their earliest correspondence, but their marriage reached its breaking point at the same time as Rawlings's career was taking off. Chuck was not as successful in the pursuit of a writing career as Rawlings was, and he preferred fishing off the Gulf Coast to staying at Cross Creek with her. Their final break occurred just as Rawlings experienced the success of her first novel, *South Moon Under*. When the reviews of the book arrived at their Cross Creek home, "Charles asked if she wanted to be alone. She said yes. He packed and left for the seacoast, and they both understood that he was not coming back" (Bigelow 16). Shortly thereafter, Rawlings embarked on an adventure to help her cope with the end of her marriage. She described the experience in *Cross Creek* in the chapter titled "Hyacinth Drift," in which she traveled down the St. Johns River with her friend Dessie Smith Prescott, a true outdoorswoman who taught Rawlings a great deal. Rawlings and Chuck formally separated shortly after she completed *South Moon Under*, and were divorced several months later, in November of 1933. He left for Tarpon Springs, a Greek fishing community on the Gulf Coast, where he received news of the divorce decree in a startlingly benevolent letter from Rawlings, who was known to fly off the handle at times. After letting him know that the divorce had been granted, Rawlings wrote:

> You're free as the wind, big boy, and I hope you'll make the most of it. Take the women as they come—we're a tough breed, and can stand considerable man-handling. . . . Had a frightfully nice letter from your mother, in answer to mine—glad she and I can go our ways with mutual respect and affection. . . . Let me know when you want your odds & ends. Best of luck—and hope your material is pouring out nicely. (Bigelow and Monti 79)

The rest of the letter described the house and recent repairs to it, made sure he was receiving his forwarded mail (especially manuscript proofs, as he was also in the process of submitting and publishing short fiction), and she also told him a funny anecdote about her liquor stash being accidentally sealed up in her living room closet by a handyman who had no idea she had anything stashed there. The letter was conversational and friendly, and gave no indication of being a somewhat awkward correspondence at the end of a fourteen-year marriage.

Rawlings had to go through the process of informing people in her life that her marriage had ended, a task not required in the dissolution of Glasgow's more private romantic intrigues. In a letter to Max Perkins, Rawlings wrote,

> I was granted a divorce yesterday from my husband. The end, simply—I hope—of fourteen years of Hell—of a fourteen-year struggle to adjust myself to, and accept, a most interesting but difficult—impossible—personality. It was a question, finally of breaking free from the feeling of a vicious hand always at my throat, or of going down in complete physical and mental collapse. . . . I am not riotously happy, not being interested in freedom for its own sake—I could have been a *slave* to a man who could be at least a benevolent despot—but I feel a terrific relief—I can wake up in the morning conscious of the sunshine, and thinking, "How wonderful! Nobody is going to give me Hell today!" (Bigelow and Monti 80)

Rawlings concluded with "enough of such nonsense" and got back to the business of her letter, as if she had to reveal the news in the blithest way possible so she could return to the important discussion of her work.

In spite of her opposition to marriage, Glasgow confessed to two engagements in the autobiography that Rawlings reviewed. The first, and less-serious, of the two occurred just after the purported death of Gerald B—; it was to Frank Paradise, an Episcopal minister who conducted the wedding ceremony for Glasgow's sister Rebe and Carrington Cabell Tutwiler (Goodman 104). Of this initial engagement, Glasgow wrote, "I became engaged, and the engagement, which, on my side, was honestly and frankly experimental, lasted for three chequered years. Everything in me denied it; for it was the wrong moment" (*WW* 178). With Paradise, Glasgow experienced "intellectual congeniality, poetic sympathy, and companionship which was natural and easy, without the slightest sting of suspicion or selfishness. Everything but the sudden light in the heart, the distillation of joy" (*WW* 178). In other words, Glasgow found herself coming out of a passionate and illicit love affair into a tepid engagement that had, as a foundation, a strong friendship. Without offering any details about how the relationship ended, Glasgow wrote simply, "in the end, this experimental engagement was broken, and I turned away from what might have been, or might not have been, happiness" (*WW* 179). She gave the impression that Paradise was brokenhearted at the end of the relationship, sharing a message a friend brought to her after the friend ran into him in Paris, in which Paradise was quoted as saying, "If ever you see Ellen . . . tell her I still love her, and that it is exactly the same love" (*WW* 180). Paradise later married, and wrote to Glasgow with pictures of his new wife and news of his happiness (Goodman 104). Susan Goodman suggests that Glasgow's relationship with Paradise was a way of coping with the trials she was experiencing at home where she was, once again, living with her authoritarian father (Goodman 104). She also points out that Glasgow's response to Louise Willcox's message from Paradise was to send him a copy of *Barren Ground*, her latest novel (Goodman 104). A letter from Willcox to Glasgow indicates that Willcox may have taken it upon herself to send the copy of the book to Paradise with the thought that it would "mean so much to him just to feel he once knew the person who could do it" (*PC* 71). The fact that Frank Paradise was named in so many letters and biographical pieces perhaps proves how harmless and platonic his relationship with Glasgow was, given the extent to which she destroyed letters and used pseudonyms in writing about her other affairs.

Rawlings was intrigued to learn about the liaisons in Glasgow's past. She spent most of her research time trying to pin down Henry Anderson's relationship with Glasgow and the identity of Glasgow's married lover, Gerald B——. Between her marriages to Chuck Rawlings and Norton Baskin, Rawlings also had an illicit affair with a married man, and she was known occasionally to harbor lovers at Cross Creek who were evading their spouses. Rawlings appealed to men with her intellect and humor. She was called "handsome" as she aged and was still sought-after. According to her biographer, Elizabeth Silverthorne, who conducted extensive interviews with Norton Baskin and Rawlings's lifelong friend from her days at the University of Wisconsin, Beatrice Humiston McNeil, Rawlings had a relationship with Otto Lange, a professor of military science at the University of Florida, during the years following her divorce. Robert Herrick warned Rawlings against "too deep an involvement with a lover 'who has a divided soul and who is merely assuaging his thirst at a gushing fountain'" (Silverthorne 110). Lange married a woman who was deaf and had children. His family obligations prevented his relationship with Rawlings from solidifying into anything more than an affair. Lange enjoyed his time with Rawlings at Cross Creek, and she, in turn, visited Lange after he and his family moved to Indiana. Silverthorne believed that Herrick had feelings for Rawlings, but he was significantly older and not of interest to her. Rawlings habitually wrote to Lange in words he considered "vitriolic, acid and cutting," followed by apologies that evinced her "real affection" for him (Silverthorne 115). The differences in how Rawlings and Glasgow displayed their respective temperaments comes across in their letters to and about their lovers. Glasgow's letters about Frank Paradise are indirect and passive-aggressive. Any more passionate letters about Gerald B— or Henry Anderson were either destroyed or written in coded language. Rawlings, on the other hand, alternately spewed venom at and embraced affectionately her lovers, telling friends enough details about her affairs to corroborate them easily. Both women felt intensely, but they handled those emotions differently.

Glasgow's final and most easily verifiable relationship was with fellow Richmondite and politician Henry Anderson. Rawlings may have learned about this relationship from Glasgow herself when they met. Many of her interviews with friends of Glasgow and Anderson focused on pinning down the facts about their relationship, beyond what she had read in Glasgow's autobiography. Called "Harold S—" in both Glasgow's autobiography and in their letters to one another, in which he referred to her as "Varda," Henry Anderson came from common stock, a self-made man who had worked his way through law school. At the beginning of their relationship, Glasgow wrote that she had felt an "unconquerable isolation," that the present was marked by "utter desolation," not the "loneliness of the spirit in freedom" that she actually preferred (*WW* 221). After entering into a relationship with Anderson, she "ceased to fear loneliness" but also "ceased to love it" (*WW* 226). She wrote of this time: "I was not myself; my very identity was altering; after a brief period of restlessness, my creative faculty sank into a trance" (*WW* 226).

The initial stages of Glasgow's relationship with Anderson brought to Rawlings's mind the beginning of her own relationship with Norton Baskin. Rawlings worried that her relationship was "something of a gamble" and most assuredly impeded her "creative faculty" and work ethic by distracting her and taking up her time. The difference was that she was happy with Baskin in spite of his impact on her work. Glasgow admitted to being happy in the relationship with Anderson for only "seventeen months out of twenty-one years" (*WW* 227). During that time, they exchanged an appreciable number of love letters, including Anderson's attempts at overly formal love poetry. Baskin also took his turn at writing during his WWII correspondence with Rawlings, including a story from his youth that Rawlings pronounced "'embarrassingly' bad" (Silverthorne 231). By the time Anderson left Glasgow to serve with the Red Cross in WWI, they were engaged; when he returned, they were no longer speaking. Anderson became romantically involved with Queen Marie of Romania during his service, and had stopped writing to Glasgow (Godbold 121). He remained infatuated with Marie after returning to

Richmond, and kept a portrait of her in his home, eventually giving it to Marie's daughter Ileana when she visited him. Queen Marie of Romania had many affairs throughout her marriage to King Ferdinand I, especially when he was abroad. Anderson is not even listed in her purported attachments, though several images of the two together were published by the American Red Cross at the time. Glasgow pieced together the details of the affair from the few letters she received and from gossip from those familiar with Anderson's group in Jassy, in northeastern Romania. In her autobiography, she catalogued the evidence of the affair, first with a letter from Anderson describing his interactions with the queen and telling her that he had been asked "to come tonight for a private talk over work" (*WW* 231). Next, she heard of the Red Cross giving "more than a liberal share" of its funds to Romania and of Anderson's attempted rescue of the queen "from both the Germans and the Bolsheviks." Much later, Glasgow read a biography of "a Balkan Queen" that included a scene in which "as she said farewell to a Southern Colonel, he had fallen on his knees before her and kissed the hem of her skirt" (*WW* 232); Anderson was a colonel with the Red Cross. On his return to Richmond, Anderson met Glasgow in his uniform because he thought she would want to see him looking majestic. Glasgow wrote in her autobiography that he spoke only of Queen Marie, and she commented, "I felt no interest in queens, especially in this queen, who seemed to be, as Goethe remarked of the assassination of Julius Caesar, not in good taste" (*WW* 235). Glasgow experienced intense pain and loss over Anderson. No religion or philosophy could help her out of it, and instead she let herself be utterly consumed by her past, swallowing a handful of sleeping tablets and letting dreams overtake her. When she awoke, nauseated and still alive, she railed against life and then unwillingly submitted to a physician's care. Anderson continued to write to her, but his letters became contentious, and Glasgow wrote sardonically of receiving two letters from him on the same day, one decrying the condition of the starving peasants in Romania and another describing a lavish ball given to honor Queen Marie (*WW* 242). Glasgow included this enigmatic comment in the typescript of her autobiography: "If I have told too much of these years, I can only insist that I have not told the one incredible fact which alone might explain the inconsistencies, and reduce the illogical to the laws of logic"

(*WW* 312). This "one incredible fact" remains unknown, but could have been that "shocking" incident to which Rawlings alluded in a letter to Norton Baskin following an interview with Anne Virginia Bennett, when she wrote: "If I use the incident in the biography—and how can I not?—it will create a scandal to rock all Virginia, and will make my book too lurid for my own taste" (*PM* 691). Rawlings never mentioned the incident again, and died two months after writing that letter. It is not mentioned in Glasgow's subsequent biographies.

Rawlings was more fortunate with her final love story. She met Norton Baskin in 1933, the year of her divorce. Baskin managed a hotel in Cross Creek beginning that year, and met Rawlings at her home when she hosted a gathering of some locals. In 1938 they began writing to each other romantically. Rawlings's correspondence with Baskin was published in its entirety in a collection called *The Private Marjorie*, edited by Rodger Tarr. Baskin's charm initially made Rawlings suspicious of him. After all, Chuck Rawlings had been quite the charmer. Rawlings's first meeting with Baskin included witty repartee as Rawlings presented him with a recently published article that described Baskin, the new hotel manager, "passing water" at every table during a luncheon with the local Episcopal church (Silverthorne 96). Having just met Baskin, Rawlings unabashedly remarked, "How in the world did you manage that?" (Silverthorne 96). Baskin's equally witty retort secured their friendship: "You have to save up" (Silverthorne 96). The first recorded correspondence from Rawlings to Baskin was a telegram wired to him in August of 1938 from the Jacksonville hospital, where Rawlings was being treated for chronic diverticulosis. The telegram told Baskin when he could visit, and was signed, "MUCH LOVE" (*PM* 35). The two were married in 1941. Their correspondence was drastically different from her exchanges with Charles Rawlings before their marriage, but it was nevertheless filled with similar anxieties and attacks. Rawlings vacillated between fighting the idea of marrying Baskin and nervously feeling out his interest in marrying her.

Rawlings was remarkably candid with Baskin in their letters, much more so than Glasgow and Anderson were in the formal and sometimes overly dramatic letters they exchanged. Rawlings and Baskin shared a bawdy sense of humor, and used their letters to adopt comedic personas and exaggerate stories from their daily lives. This humor was earthier and lower-brow than that of Ellen Glasgow. To Anderson, Glasgow was "Varda." When writing with a pseudonym to Baskin, Rawlings took on the name of her "valuable but evil-tempered" Jersey cow, Dora Rolley (Silverthorne 155). The letters also show Baskin's adroit handling of Rawlings's emotional volatility. He helped her to see the danger of her alcohol consumption and its effect on her personality, explaining that Rawlings "used liquor as a prescription for whatever affected her" (Silverthorne 298). Baskin also calmed her down during emotional storms and guided her through resolutions of conflict with her friends and family members. Rawlings was grateful for Baskin's even temper and constancy. Their marriage was a healthy and happy one from beginning to end. As a hotelier, Baskin needed independence as much as Rawlings did, and the two were able to enjoy their time together and their time apart in equal measure. He understood her need for time alone at Cross Creek, Crescent Beach, or Van Hornesville to work on her manuscripts. Rawlings did not adjust as well when Baskin traveled overseas to serve with the American Field Service in WWII. She could barely write at all, and found herself anxious over his absence and his safety. She was well into her forties when she married Baskin, thus reducing their chances of having a child together, but the two discussed children and came close to adopting Rawlings's nephew. They both wanted a son. Glasgow never had this type of companionship with her lovers. She had the added hardship of living in a Southern town with strict views of how men and women should behave with one another, views that made nearly all normal romantic relationships illicit from their inception.

Rawlings confided to Glasgow her anxieties over her second marriage, thinking that Glasgow herself had faced similar hurdles. The two established their friendship shortly before Rawlings's marriage to Baskin and the completion of *Cross Creek*. Rawlings and Glasgow discussed men during their initial meeting in Richmond. In a letter written after that first meeting, Rawlings recalled for Glasgow the former's "great relief of being free of an oppressive and almost entirely hideous marriage," which they had discussed, and Rawlings's "eight years of being entirely alone . . . in the large rambling farmhouse" during which time "there were many months at a time when there was not even anyone in the tenant house at the far side of [Rawlings's] grove" (Bigelow and Monti 215). This time for Rawlings was "punctuated by emotional entanglements" (Bigelow and Monti 215). The letter left some uncertainty as to whether Glasgow had done any confiding in Rawlings. The latter's notes on Glasgow's love life give the impression that Rawlings knew very little of Glasgow's romantic experiences as she began her work on Glasgow's biography. However, she believed that the two women understood one another because of scenes in Glasgow's novels that made Rawlings think that Glasgow understood the "pain" of emotional entanglements (Bigelow and Monti 215). Rawlings admitted in the letter mentioned above that her marriage to Baskin, "a man whom I had known for eight years and who had been my dear close friend for nearly four, was something of a gamble, and there are few to whom I could or would admit this" (Bigelow and Monti 215). Rawlings was most concerned about the need, one Glasgow shared, for long periods of isolation, "above all, the peculiar mental independence of the creative worker," which Rawlings worried was "not the best of bases for a successful marriage" (Bigelow and Monti 215–216). She admitted to Glasgow that this particular issue would not be as disastrous with Baskin as it had been with her first husband because Baskin was also "accustomed to independence," not to mention "generous," "tolerant," and "tender" (Bigelow and Monti 216). Her tempestuous relationship with Chuck Rawlings, which had bordered on violence, did not remotely resemble the "deep and quiet" love that Rawlings felt with Baskin. She told Glasgow that "being with him is like coming into harbor after long storms" (Bigelow and Monti 216). Rawlings, however, still felt torn between her desire for an "isolated rural life" and his career, which required a "more or less sophisticated and urban life" (Bigelow and Monti 216).

Baskin purchased the St. Augustine hotel Castle Warden, where he and Rawlings built their life together and where Rawlings met many other writers and prominent figures on their travels through Florida. Later, he sold the hotel and began managing the restaurants and bar at Marineland, an equally demanding job that also led to run-ins with celebrities, like Ernest Hemingway, who visited with his then-wife Martha Gellhorn and ended up coming back to Rawlings's Crescent Beach cottage and staying late into the night (Silverthorne 186–187). Baskin and

Rawlings were both financially successful, though Rawlings tried to maintain her own separate finances, especially when it came to rendering assistance to her ne'er-do-well brother, Arthur. Glasgow lacked Rawlings's financial independence, and relied heavily on a trust fund set up by her own brother Arthur.

While researching Ellen Glasgow's life in Richmond, Rawlings wrote letters home to Baskin and took notes on index cards during interviews. All of these interviews with Glasgow's friends, family members, and colleagues included some line of questioning about her alleged engagement to Henry Anderson or the identity of the mysterious Gerald B— from Glasgow's autobiography. Rawlings added her own speculations in her notes.

Rawlings collected some of Anderson's writings to get a better idea of his background. His relationship with Glasgow was not a secret. Anderson wrote to his mother during WWI to let her know that he was pleased she had visited "E," presumably Ellen Glasgow, because he felt it would do them both good.[1] He implied that Glasgow was close to his mother during the engagement, and that they were both concerned for him during WWI. Rawlings also appreciated Henry Anderson's political views. In an address to the graduating class of Washington and Lee University at their commencement ceremony, titled "An American Citizen," Anderson implored graduates to put their country and community ahead of their self-interest.[2] On paper, he was a noble match for Glasgow, intelligent and socially conscious.

Rawlings took extensive notes from the sections of *The Woman Within* that described Anderson. She noted how Glasgow wondered "How I who worship reason could have remained, for almost 20 years, an unwilling prisoner of unreason" (*WW* 213). This line spoke directly to Rawlings's own experiences in a failed first marriage, even though the Anderson relationship more closely paralleled, in the two women's timelines, Rawlings's relationship with Baskin. Glasgow did not meet Anderson until "just before her forty-third birthday" (Goodman 140). Their relationship spanned the latter part of her life, and they experienced the same estrangement during WWI that Rawlings experienced from Baskin during WWII. The First World War was especially hard for Glasgow because she lost the company of both Anderson and her secretary and longtime companion, Anne Virginia Bennett, who served as an army nurse in France (Godbold 121). Rawlings documented from Glasgow's autobiography the drastic shift from Glasgow's overdose of sleeping tablets in July 1918 after she had accepted that her relationship with Anderson had ended, and she felt that "Sleep or death did not matter," to Anderson's last words, with which he called Glasgow "the greatest thing" (*WW* 238).

Rawlings spent a lot of her time in Richmond with Anderson, trying to draw out his side of the story about how he and Glasgow met and what their relationship was like. Anderson remembered sitting with Glasgow at a luncheon in 1916 when she asked for a copy of a speech he had written. They ended up walking home together and becoming "intellectual friends" who shared many of the same views. Anderson tried to convince Glasgow to write comic fiction, because "the world needed laughter" and her books "were too tragic," but Glasgow countered by saying, "But life ends that way." Anderson thought Glasgow was too "autocratic," "like all the Glasgows." She wanted things done her way, but Anderson told Rawlings that he very seldom fulfilled those demands. While he claimed that he did not find Glasgow beautiful or even pretty, Anderson admitted that she "had lovely eyes" and "dressed beautifully." Her charm, to him, lay in her mind and "brilliant conversation." Her deafness frequently led Glasgow to talk over others during dinner parties, making the event "drag on." Anderson complimented Glasgow's "fastidiousness" and charity, recalling many instances of her preparing food baskets for the poor.[3] In all of these descriptions, Anderson avoided the central question regarding the nature of his relationship with Glasgow.

After Anderson and Rawlings haltingly told one another what each knew of Glasgow's prior relationships in order to determine what the other knew or did not know, Anderson explained to Rawlings that Glasgow "had strict principles" and "believed in restraint, in tradition," supporting the supposition by some scholars that Glasgow may have never consummated any of her romantic relationships. However, Anderson was driven into a coughing fit when Rawlings asked him whether "her restraint was responsible for her never marrying."[4] His reaction could have been part of his attempt to keep their engagement a secret, or it could have resulted from his desire not to discuss the physical nature of his relationship with Glasgow out of respect for her.

Glasgow and Anderson also shared a professional relationship. He read through and commented on the first chapters of *The Builders* (1919), for which he provided copies of his own speeches as a political candidate. Those speeches also figured heavily in *One Man in His Time* (1922). Parts of his 1916 speech "An American Citizen" were quoted verbatim in *The Builders*. Carrie Duke told Rawlings that Glasgow helped Anderson with his speeches, which Rawlings thought suggested that she helped Anderson more than he helped her, regardless of his claims to the contrary.[5] They both benefited from each other's respective skill sets in writing and rhetoric. Anderson told Rawlings that he had not wanted to appear too directly in Glasgow's novel because he did not want it to seem as if Glasgow were "propagandizing" for him." His copy of *The Builders* included the inscription, "To Henry W. Anderson, with whose help and inspiration this book was written. From Ellen Glasgow, Richmond, Virginia, November the first, 1919."[6]

Without admitting to their engagement, Anderson told Rawlings that marriage was out of the question for the two of them because they were both too "individualistic" and "could never have gotten along." He also thought that Glasgow was carried away by her emotions too easily. He contradicted himself, Rawlings noted, in telling her at one point that he never showed Glasgow the impatience he frequently felt with her because of her sensitivity, yet at another point telling her that he found fault with her writing only tragedy. When Rawlings asked him directly whether he and Glasgow had been engaged, Anderson diverted the question with an adage he claimed to have learned at his mother's knee "never to talk about a woman." Frustrated by his response, Rawlings said that she thought such lessons were learned by men from their fathers to which Anderson replied that his father had been very busy.[7]

According to friends, Henry Anderson and Ellen Glasgow's brother Arthur had very similar personalities and had once been quite close, but they had had a falling-out when Anderson was given a position over Arthur during their service in the Balkans. For a time following the First World War, Arthur would not come down to dinner during his visits home if he knew Anderson would be there. They later reconciled and worked together after Ellen Glasgow's death in establishing One West Main as a memorial.

After interviewing Anderson, Rawlings wrote her impressions of him and of his sincerity. She called Anderson "over-suave, callous, hard, egocentric, and wary."[8] James Branch Cabell told Rawlings that Anderson was definitely "covering up," and that "he knew perfectly well what you wanted." Cabell remembered Anderson calling Ellen "Miss Glasgow" in a way he felt to be cold.[9] Anderson had not cared for those of Glasgow's books that the author herself preferred. He felt that her "humor or wit or effervescence," the qualities he most admired in Glasgow, did not appear in her writing. Her humor seemed, in Anderson's opinion, to turn to "cynicism" in her last years. What Anderson did love about Glasgow's books was that they were written in "good English" with a rare level of "meticulousness."[10] Margaret Cabell, who was actually introduced to James Branch Cabell by Rawlings after the death of Cabell's first wife, told Rawlings the gossip that she heard surrounding Anderson and Glasgow, namely that Glasgow turned Anderson down initially because he had "no apparent background," and then was subsequently turned down by Anderson after "he proved himself brilliant and made money." The Cabells told Rawlings that Anderson had gone to Glasgow's house for supper "every Sunday night until the end."[11]

Henry Anderson, like many Richmondites of the time, had traditional views about men and women, despite his progressive political stance as a Southern Republican in the 1910s. In his last letter to Rawlings, Anderson defended himself against her expressed "view that it is necessary to stand up for the woman as against the man in controversial cases in actual life." He noted that women had currently achieved "all the rights of women" and were "claiming all the rights of men." He found this to be unfair, and was determined that "they can not have both." Anderson believed that women were "happier where the dominance of the man in the relationship is recognized, at least to the extent of his obligations." Too much progress, in Anderson's opinion, was detracting from the happiness that should be the "ultimate objective of life." In this final letter, he described what could have been the actual rift in his relationship with Glasgow when he stated that he did not like "weak men" nor "women who are too aggressive."[12] In an amusing letter sent to Anderson by Rawlings following her interview with Maude Williams, who had introduced Glasgow and Anderson, she responded to such sentiments by including flowers with a note saying that "for many, many years I have sent flowers to men whom I loved, liked, admired or to whom I had reason to be grateful. You may take your choice of my reason for thus be-flowering you."[13] Glasgow and Anderson could never have experienced the partnership that Rawlings shared with Norton Baskin as an equal.

Rawlings met repeatedly with Anderson in an attempt to learn the true nature of his relationship with Glasgow. At their second interview, Anderson opened by telling Rawlings that he had not slept the night before because he "was worrying" about their discussion. He claimed that talking about his relationship with Glasgow at this point "would violate all the principles of my life." He then explained to Rawlings how Glasgow and he had possessed two separate sides, "one, the emotional, which is the feminine and the affirmative, the other, the mind of the intellectual, which always says 'Be careful. Be careful.'" Anderson came across as narrow and contradictory during this discussion, claiming to have destroyed all Glasgow's letters, something Rawlings knew then to be untrue. He also did not credit Glasgow for her intellectual contributions to their relationship, whereas he later expounded upon their complementary views of "visionary socialism." Rawlings asked him directly about their alleged engagement. Anderson repeated his diversionary tactics from the prior interview, this time by saying, "If I told you that, I should have to tell you why it was broken off. (Hastily) That is if there ever was. . . ." He then repeatedly referred to Glasgow as "a personal person."[14] Rawlings annotated these remarks with a comment Anderson had made earlier in their interview that he "like[d] to avoid disagreeable things" and considered himself "an escapist." She connected these sentiments to Glasgow's depiction of Anderson in *One Man in His Time*, in which she observed "that instinct for evasive idealism which the generations had bred." Anderson implored Rawlings to include him in her biography of Glasgow "as little as possible."[15]

Anderson continued to keep silent about the details of his relationship with Glasgow, but he permitted Rawlings a private interview with Maude Williams at his home, excusing himself due to ill health so that the two women could discuss matters alone. Anderson gave implicit permission to Williams to discuss any matters about his relationship with Glasgow that she chose, saying, "Now I want you to tell Mrs. Rawlings everything you know about Ellen, only she mustn't print it." As soon as he was out of sight, Williams whispered to Rawlings, "Ellen was simply WILD about Henry Anderson."[16] She introduced the two of them at a luncheon she had held for the sole purpose of their meeting. Williams did not feel that Glasgow had had a normal girlhood or young womanhood because she had not had beaux at the right time, potentially because of an unhappy home life. Mrs. Scrivenor, one of Glasgow's childhood friends, confirmed this report, telling Rawlings that Glasgow had gone to some college events with her brothers, and that a "chrysanthemum and college ribbons, etc., meant everything to a girl," but "Glasgow did not have it."[17] When Glasgow met Anderson, Williams was of the impression that he was her first serious relationship.

Williams recalled fondly how Glasgow "never made me feel uneducated or dumb or anything. She made everybody feel good about themselves." This does not align with other reports about Glasgow, who often came across as distracted or disinterested in others due to her deafness. What does make sense is Williams's recollection of Glasgow's "capacity for suffering." She told Rawlings that she felt that Glasgow would "suffer with [her]."[18] Williams placed herself fifth in Glasgow's list of closest confidantes, after Glasgow's sisters Cary and Rebe, Roberta Wellford, a close friend of Glasgow and Cary, and Carrie Duke. (Williams did not include Anne Virginia Bennett in the list, possibly because of her position as an employee.)

Williams admired the way in which Henry Anderson had left home with twenty dollars and worked his way through college. Actually, Anderson had not been able to afford college at that time, and instead took a law course to earn an LL.B., later having the more prestigious LL.D. conferred upon him, as well as a Phi Beta Kappa key. Williams's only real criticism of Anderson was that he had been "a perfect fool" about Queen Marie, whose "glamor" had gone to his head.[19] Williams believed that Glasgow and Anderson had been engaged and that he had been Queen Marie's lover, but that she had simply "worked him to a turn" in exchange for preferential treatment; Red Cross supplies were delivered in excess to Romania during the war. Williams described Anderson as being "mad about" Queen Marie, and then "very much in love" with Glasgow, giving his feelings for Glasgow a more formal and less-passionate tint. Williams thought that Glasgow impressed Anderson with her success and intelligence, but that she lacked experience with men, having not so much as danced with one while getting through childhood and adolescence in an overcrowded and unhappy home. Anderson, for his part, liked the independence that their relationship afforded him.

Following their romance, Glasgow, according to Williams, realized by degrees that they were still intellectually congenial, even though she was bitter toward him. Williams believed that Glasgow had already purchased clothes for their wedding when Anderson broke off the engagement. Rawlings wondered whether Glasgow decided to hold onto the friendship "partly because there was a terrible scarcity of men" after the First World War. Rawlings also wrote by hand on these typed notes that Williams thought Anderson "too cautious ever to have fathered *anyone.*"[20] Rawlings suspected that he had fathered a child with Queen Marie, which could have explained Princess Ileana's visit to him, but Williams discounted that possibility.

Rawlings continued investigating the relationship by gaining the confidence of Glasgow's closest companion, Bennett, who took up Glasgow's side of the story, even underreporting Glasgow's reactions to the end of her relationship with Anderson. Bennett reportedly tore up both of Glasgow's pictures of Anderson after her death, one in which he was wearing his military decorations. Rebe, Glasgow's younger sister, took the jewelry Anderson had given to Glasgow and sent it to Baltimore to be sold. Such actions made Rawlings wonder whether the women had covered up other relationships that Rawlings had not discovered. According to Bennett, Anderson gave Glasgow "several watches" and jeweled pins. Glasgow gave him a much less-personal gift of silver serving dishes. Bennett confessed that, following Glasgow's orders, she had destroyed all of Glasgow's letters to and from Anderson, except for a small batch that Glasgow had designated for her literary executors, because she "wrote letters recklessly."[21] Anderson promised Bennett that he would have Glasgow's letters to him destroyed "unread" when he died, which contradicted his assertion to Rawlings that such letters had already been destroyed. Rawlings could tell that Anderson was holding back something in their discussions. Bennett felt sorry for Anderson at Glasgow's funeral, where the other women shunned him. She recounted his generous request that Bennett live with him and Glasgow should they marry. Bennett, however, did not support the engagement of Anderson and Glasgow, reportedly telling Anderson "that she wouldn't spend one night under his roof" and that she would "want and expect [Glasgow] to divorce [Anderson] after 24 hours."[22]

Bennett shared with Rawlings letters sent to her by Glasgow during Glasgow's relationship with Anderson that suggested a physical affair. In one letter, Glasgow described the orchids Anderson had sent her during one of her trips abroad, and his meeting her at the dock when she returned from the trip with "gardenias and a box of roses and delphinium."[23] The two reportedly left the dock for the hotel alone while another acquaintance, Dan Longwell, waited for Carrie Duke to go through customs. Glasgow wrote, "Everything went well. Tooth trouble."[24] Whether the two were physically intimate or not, they managed to escape the constant chaperoning suggested by other letters. Rawlings also had a letter Glasgow sent to Rebe telling her that Anderson had sent Bennett a "gorgeous basket of red roses and white heather" when she was bedridden with bronchitis (*PC* 79). He was kind to both women during and after his relationship with Glasgow.

Many of her note cards from interviews described Rawlings's attempts to find out more about the mysterious, less easily identified love interests in Glasgow's autobiography, namely the infamous Gerald B—. Roberta Wellford told Rawlings that Glasgow was "desperately in love" with a local gentleman named Mr. Mumford as a child, throwing a tantrum when he married that was only "assuaged" by his gift of a "small gold ring" that Wellford kept after Glasgow's death. She also confided in Rawlings that Glasgow was interested in James Branch Cabell after first meeting him at the College of William and Mary.[25] Cabell preferred women who would take care of him. In one interview, Rawlings wrote that Carrie Duke suspected Glasgow was referring to Frank Paradise in the autobiography, and she does, but not as Gerald B—. He is mentioned as her first fiancé, the one with whom there was no passion (*WW* 178). Glasgow was quoted as saying that she was engaged "to a minister who later had 13 children" and was glad to have escaped such a fate.[26] This was an exaggeration of Paradise's "six children from two marriages," but it helped to make her point about preferring her life to the constant childbearing of her mother's time (Goodman 104). Rawlings theorized that Gerald B— was Dr. Holbrook Curtis, one of Glasgow's physicians in New York. She knew that Curtis had two daughters instead of two sons, but thought that Glasgow was trying to disguise his identity as much as possible in her autobiography. He was also married. While Glasgow claimed that Gerald B— did not have her intellectual aspirations, Curtis had his own ear clinic where he treated many famous opera singers, and was one of the founders of the National Academy of Arts and Letters (Dunster et al. 909). Rawlings learned from Carrie Duke and others that Glasgow saw Curtis daily during her time in New York when he was treating her, giving her ample time to form a secret relationship.

Rawlings copied Glasgow's notes on falling in love with Gerald B— from the autobiography, including Glasgow's "deep conviction" that she was "unfitted for marriage"; Rawlings noted here, "mid-twenties?" (*WW* 178). In trying to figure out exactly when this life-changing relationship began, Rawlings wrote, "Winter after own return from abroad— Rebe and Carrie say 26 almost 27? Carrie says about 1903."[27] Glasgow stayed in an older apartment house called The Florence, downtown off 5th Avenue, during those years.[28] Rawlings was put off by Gerald B—'s lines about his married life, questioning in her notes whether his claim that he was not currently living with his wife was not a usual "'out' for a lover???"[29] She was also skeptical about Glasgow's description of her time with Gerald B— in Switzerland because someone would have been traveling with her, possibly Rebe. She made a note to check on Glasgow's news of Gerald's death from the Paris edition of the *New York Herald*, which would have disqualified Curtis as a candidate, if accurately portrayed—Curtis did not pass away until 1920. Carrie Duke did not believe that Gerald B— was actually involved with Wall Street, and insisted to Rawlings that she did not know his real name.

Rawlings took notes on affairs not included in the autobiography but disclosed by Glasgow's friends in interviews. One of the men, Mulhern, was mentioned briefly in Glasgow's autobiography as a man who had shown interest in her, but had asked about her deafness and caused Glasgow to retreat and shy away from him. Bennett told Rawlings that

Mulhern had owned the apartment house in New York where Glasgow stayed with Bennett and Carrie Duke after her sister Cary's death in 1911. Bennett believed that there was "only a physical attraction" between the two because Mulhern was "big & vital."[30] However, Duke claimed that the relationship "went on a long time."[31] Roberta Wellford also described Mulhern as "a large, vital man, and immaculate."[32] She went on to say that he had no background, presumably meaning that he did not come from a well-established family, but visited the New York apartment many times. Wellford was surprised that Glasgow never married, "if only to have the experience of it," and said that it would be "reasonable to expect" Glasgow to have had an all-out affair "just to know what it was all about."[33] However, she was uncertain whether Glasgow had experienced a physical affair, remarking that she was "always having violent love-affairs" that "never went very far."[34] All of Glasgow's purported affairs, except for her relationship with Henry Anderson, occurred in New York. Wellford told Rawlings that Glasgow felt "free to do things in New York she would never have done in Richmond" and that "only two or three of us knew about the men in New York and she knew we would never mention it at home. She was always discreet in Richmond."[35] Glasgow did not come across as prudish in any of these New York engagements, and responded to Herschel Brickell, when asked how she knew "all these things that a maiden lady isn't supposed to know," with "Oh, I've been 'aboot'!"[36] Glasgow knew when to allow herself certain liberties and when to act with discretion to maintain her position in society.

In her private notes on these affairs, Rawlings repeatedly wondered whether Glasgow had considered herself beautiful and whether she was "surer of her works than of herself."[37] For a woman to become so successful as a writer meant sacrificing many of the expected norms, like marriage and motherhood, especially in a time during which even her most convivial partner, Anderson, told Glasgow that women were typically happier in relationships when they allowed men to play a dominant role. Rawlings could commiserate with Glasgow's uncertainty. Prior to the success of her first novel, Rawlings had deferred to the literary advice of her husband Chuck, even when his recommendations drove her to drink. Glasgow was discouraged from publishing by everyone except for her sister and brother-in-law, and found herself working against a culture that preferred wives and mothers to women writers.

At the same time, Glasgow lived during the heyday of Freudian psychoanalysis, which led some of her closest friends to question whether her psychoses could be linked to a repression of sexuality. One of Glasgow's physicians, Dr. William Porter, told Rawlings that Glasgow "all but defeated research work in Richmond medical circles," and that he did not think she was ever "sexually fulfilled." Dr. Porter believed that Glasgow's personification and love of animals was an "aberrant emotional outlet."[38] He also doubted Irita Van Doren's belief that Glasgow's affair with the married man earlier in her life had "made her very happy." Rawlings was inclined to agree with Van Doren, finding Dr. Porter's theories "too stereotyped," and that it was "too easy to attribute all to sexual frustration."[39] Rebe also adamantly insisted that Glasgow "did not have a love affair of any kind in her youth."[40] She explained to Rawlings that she believed "people attribute such a love affair to Ellen because they believe her unhappiness must have come from one, without considering that her ill health and introspective genius could also lead to unhappiness."[41] Rebe simultaneously attempted to protect Glasgow's memory and support the view, taken years later by Pamela Matthews, that scholars (and Rawlings to an extent, at least in her interviews) focused too closely on Glasgow's relationships with men rather than women. To Rebe, that focus was misplaced, because it took away from a better understanding of Glasgow's psychological complexity; to Matthews, a preoccupation with Glasgow's romantic relationships with men detracted from a study of her more critical relationships with women.

While it is true that focusing too intently on this author's romantic relationships shifts attention away from the more important contributions of her professional and charitable work, the acknowledgment of Glasgow's desires was understandably important to Rawlings. Neither writer had children. Both broke traditional norms, notably with Rawlings's divorce in 1933 and second marriage, and with Glasgow's decision never to marry. Rawlings wrote about her romantic challenges in a poem titled "Sacred and Profane Love" (1945), which she sent to her friend the Reverend Bertram C. Cooper:

> Men's lips have not lain on my mouth
> With the unearthly grace
> Of wind, importunate from the south,
> Brushing across my face.
>
> I have not found embrace of men
> So strong, so fierce, so sweet,
> As surf, drawing, again, again,
> Vast hands from head to feet.
>
> I dare not breed a mortal child
> Lest, called by some far tune,
> He meet half-brothers running wild,
> Bastards of the moon. (Tarr and Kinser 312)

The poem speaks to the views of both Rawlings and Glasgow that there is more to be had in this life than the embrace of a lover. The freedom felt by Rawlings in the natural world, by Glasgow as she explored European ruins, and by both women as they composed literary masterpieces overshadowed, by far, their mortal desires, fulfilled or unfulfilled.

7

"A Woman of To-Morrow"

On one side all the womanhood within her quivered with desire; on the other, a man's ambitions struggled to survive. It was the new woman warring against the old—the twentieth century rebelling against the nineteenth.

"A Woman of To-Morrow," by Ellen Glasgow

IN HER FIRST PUBLISHED work of fiction, Ellen Glasgow, aged twenty-two, imagined the life of Patricia Yorke, the first woman to be considered for the position of Associate Justice of the Supreme Court. The story, "A Woman of To-Morrow" (1895), exemplified the conflict experienced by so many ambitious women who find that their rise to success will require sacrifices greater than those of their male counterparts. Written well before the Nineteenth Amendment granted women the right to vote, this story sees such changes as inevitable, and grieves for those women who would sacrifice parts of themselves to ensure that those changes would be made. Yorke's rise to fame comes at a price. She lives with regret for the lover she left behind to pursue her law career. However, her impulsive decision to return home and find him shows her the condition of the "tired woman in a soiled gown, with a child upon her shrunken breast—a woman who had borne many burdens and whose strength had not been sufficient unto her need," and Yorke leaves thanking God for the decision that kept her from a similar fate (Raper 14). Ellen Glasgow achieved the life that she imagined for Patricia Yorke by breaking into a publishing world that rejected her until she was able to prove herself with an anonymously published first novel. Years later, she discovered a novel by another woman who had broken barriers of her own. Marjorie Kinnan Rawlings braved the landscape and wildlife of Florida, mostly on her own, while writing *The Yearling*, a novel that rekindled Glasgow's desire to reconnect with the primal forces of nature, fierce and unforgiving. The struggles both women overcame to become successful writers instilled in Glasgow and Rawlings a compassion for women that extended to other marginalized groups.

Rawlings did not suffer from the same blatant sexism that Glasgow experienced early in her career, but she empathized with Glasgow's experiences when studying her life. Glasgow, armed with fifty dollars from her sister Cary and her first full manuscript, *Sharp Realities*, set out to meet with a literary advisor in New York at the age of eighteen (Goodman 41). Such a pursuit took tremendous courage. Glasgow, who had never even attended school, did not have any experiences to prepare her for this meeting. Her naiveté proved costly when the so-called literary advisor questioned her about where she was staying and whether she would come back later when the building was empty (*WW* 96). When she did so, he assaulted her physically and tried to force her to kiss him. She was able to escape by promising that she would come again. Glasgow wrote, "I was bruised, I was disgusted, I was trembling with anger" (*WW* 97). She resolved never to write again, and sent for the manuscript, throwing it in the fire without unwrapping it.

Glasgow continued writing in spite of her declaration, but went about publishing her next novel more carefully, obtaining letters of introduction to reputable publishers. Their response was barely an improvement. Price Collier with Macmillan's took her out for lunch to tell her that he "could tell, without reading it, that there was not a chance of Macmillan's accepting the book" (*WW* 108). Collier then insulted Glasgow by advising her to "stop writing, and go back to the South and have some babies" (*WW* 108). This time, Glasgow's tenacity took hold, and she used other connections to have the book reviewed by the University Publishing Company, where it was entrusted to a younger publisher named Mr.

Patton. Patton regarded her skeptically at first, but ended up finishing *The Descendant* in a single sitting, and told Glasgow not to worry: "That book shall be published if I have to build a publishing house in order to publish it" (*WW* 112). He compared her to Victor Hugo. Patton published the novel with Harper & Brothers after convincing Glasgow to release the first edition anonymously, so it would not be dismissed as women's literature. His advice helped establish her career.

Susan Goodman explained in her biography of Glasgow just how complicated reader reception was for women in 1897. After Harper's released Glasgow's name and identity three months following the publication of *The Descendant*, Glasgow immediately adopted an overly feminine persona that flew in the face of reviewers who had used words like "audaciously virile" to describe the novel following its release (Goodman 60). Goodman gave a perfect description of Glasgow's performance at this time: "The contrast between her 'feminine' facade and 'masculine' mind apparently caused this woman with a penchant for scent, lace-trimmed negligees, and high-heeled shoes more amusement than anguish" (Goodman 60–61). Glasgow was a woman who longed for Victorian style and a glamorous wardrobe, while also demanding equitable treatment in her writing career.

By the end of her career, Glasgow had resolved many of her narrative conflicts regarding women in her posthumously published sequel to *In This Our Life*, titled *Beyond Defeat*. Helen Levy explains that through the character of Kate Oliver, Glasgow was able to "transcend the victimization that threatens her strongest female protagonists" and create "a home presided over by a wise woman who overcomes aging and loss to form a haven in nature that welcomes refugees from the urban wasteland" (Scura 225). This novel, written with encouragement from Marjorie Kinnan Rawlings, may very well be modeling the character of Kate on Rawlings, whom Glasgow had come to admire. Contrasting the beneficent Kate Oliver on her farm with the stoic Dorinda Oakley from *Barren Ground* or the determined Patricia Yorke in "A Woman of To-Morrow," it is clear that Glasgow has, indeed, traveled beyond defeat in her writing of women to locate a space in which a woman's story may come to fruition, in spite of her life's suffering. That space, so like the one that Rawlings inhabited in her actual life, has a woman giving birth to a safe haven for all those who have been defeated by their life's circumstances. Cross Creek, and Rawlings herself, were such havens for all who knew them.

For all of her experiences with hunting and preference for a rural lifestyle, Rawlings expressed a similar preference for what could be considered the traditionally feminine. She responded to letters she received from serviceman about her descriptions of meals in her novels by publishing her own cookbook, *Cross Creek Cookery*. In her own attempt at memoir when she was younger, *Blood of My Blood*, Rawlings constantly demands the best fashions. Her biographer described Rawlings as shopping in New York for the perfect furnishings to go in her Crescent Beach cottage (Silverthorne 176). Where Glasgow experienced extreme prejudice from misogynistic publishers, Rawlings met with the opposite reaction. When she appeared in tears at the *New Republic*'s office in New York after having her purse containing her "last nickel stolen," Signe Toksvig—coincidentally, a close friend of Ellen Glasgow's—"kissed [her] and insisted on loaning [her] a ten dollar bill," explaining to Rawlings, "Some day you may have a chance to do the same thing for some other young soul just starting out and in trouble" (*BB* 149). Before composing her first full-length manuscript, Rawlings established a career in journalism, albeit working on predominantly gendered columns for the YWCA and "Live Women in Live Louisville." She also composed a series of "Songs of the Housewife" for the *Times-Union* in Rochester. These endeavors helped Rawlings become financially independent, but were also largely based on writing meant to appeal exclusively to a female audience.

Only after she moved to Florida was Rawlings able to find subject matter that lent life to her writing. She was suddenly writing for herself, to meet her own expectations for her writing career. As Bigelow and Monti point out in their edited collection of Rawlings's letters, "After more than ten years of discouragement from sending out story after story with nothing but rejection slips to show, she was understandably thrilled to have her first Florida piece accepted by one of the country's most prestigious literary magazines," *Scribner's* (Bigelow and Monti 36). Not only did Rawlings publish her stories on Florida Crackers as quickly as she could write them, but she was also assigned Maxwell Perkins as her editor. Perkins, who was the editor for Fitzgerald, Hemingway, and Wolfe, remained Rawlings's editor and friend throughout her career. She is the only woman author named in the historical landmark on Perkins's former residence. Rawlings's stories and novels focused almost exclusively on male protagonists in traditionally masculine survival scenarios in the scrub, complete with illegal moonshining activities, hunting, and the rigors of farming in an inhospitable environment. She spoke frankly about sex, but did not include detailed sexual scenes in her writing. She held her own among her male colleagues, and maintained close friendships with many male authors of her day, including James Branch Cabell, Ernest Hemingway, F. Scott Fitzgerald, Robert Herrick, and Robert Frost, as well as with many women writers, like Edith Pope, Margaret Mitchell, and Marcia Davenport.

In spite of her similar literary success, Glasgow had to contend with a readership and critics that too easily stereotyped her as a woman writer in reviews of her work. In a newspaper article Rawlings discovered by Burton Rascoe, he described Glasgow's home decor, physical appearance, fashion choices, foot size, and stereotypically feminine characteristics, including her complete ignorance of financial matters and how that helped her to obtain lucrative contracts.[1] Rawlings would have been appalled, or perhaps simply amused, by such a reception.

Dorothea Mann, in one of the pieces Rawlings selected for her biography of Glasgow, admitted that Glasgow had an advantage as a woman writer from the South because the South considered "writing and teaching" to be respectable professions for women (15). In the impoverished South following the Civil War, it was considered more ladylike to do without and live on modest means than to enter the marketplace with an occupation; Glasgow deplored this mindset. Mann described women rising before dawn to scrub steps when no one could see them laboring, and then suffering hunger, just so they would be able to subsist on a meager income without taking on more visible work to bring in more money (15). Women supported one another by sending their children to learn at home schools run by independent women in the community or by buying books written by other women. Glasgow felt this was unfair to the children who did not always benefit academically from such arrangements, and published her first novel anonymously to have her work judged with impunity.

A large portion of the criticism Rawlings chose for her book on Glasgow categorized the latter's portrayals of gender as feminist, noting the ways in which she allowed her female characters to develop outside traditional gender roles in her narratives. In a booklet titled "Ellen Glasgow" (1928), Dorothea Lawrance Mann argued that Glasgow was interested in the whole feminist movement, not just suffrage, because she felt that women were "always in revolt," but it was unusual for them to unite together to create change (2). Mann named Glasgow not only a woman in revolt, but also the most prominent woman "and only Southern woman" in the previous twenty years to have stood up for women's intellectual freedom by critiquing the sentimental Southern tradition that harbored her (3). Mann also pointed out that Glasgow was ahead of her time in explaining how the real effort of plantation life fell to the women "who cared for the slaves" while the men "sat idly sipping on juleps" before or after a hunt (7). This care encompassed the moral and religious education of slaves, as well as their physical well-being. In fact, Glasgow portrayed men harshly in novels like *The Battle Ground* as, themselves, children needing care from the women around them. Mann wrote of Glasgow, "She has delivered women from the tyranny of love by showing them how silly it is that they should ask so much less of life than men and give so much more" (10). Glasgow resisted the romantic plots adopted by so many of her fellow Virginia women writers.

Glasgow's novels frequently used women characters to expose the harmful gender norms of her day or to offer alternative ways of living as women. In "Ellen Glasgow" (1928), Mann cited *Virginia* (1913) as an example of Glasgow's critique of womanly self-sacrifice and exaggerated feminine ideals, arguing that Glasgow herself was more like Dorinda from *Barren Ground* (1925), a character who demanded from life the same terms as a man and relegated love to a subordinate position in her life. Other novels Mann discussed in her review included *The Builders* (1919), which depicted a woman, Angelica, as a destructive force in the lives of men, and *The Romantic Comedians* (1926), in which Glasgow asserted that a woman who has not cultivated her mind is bound to be "a beautiful and virtuous bore" and ultimately fail, as the mind is all that lasts (24). Mann also praised Glasgow's ability to write from the male perspective as psychologically fascinating, pointing to Glasgow's caustic descriptions of older men's fascination with the young girl "without corsets and without conversation" (25). Emily Clark praised Glasgow in "Ellen Glasgow" (1929) for being comparable to Jane Austen as "unillusioned," rather than disillusioned, by representing men objectively without glamorization or a necessary romance plot (44). Even when she did write about relationships between men and women, Glasgow purposefully rejected formulaic plot lines, empowering her women characters to seek fulfillment through their labors, rather than through their relationships. Glasgow's best-known novel, *Barren Ground*, exemplifies this by offering a complete reversal of the typical "fallen woman" narrative seen in works by writers like Thomas Hardy. Dorinda Oakley overcomes her tragic undoing by Jason Greylock to become the most successful dairy farmer in Virginia, even though most readers see the crux of the plot in Dorinda's inability to overcome her feelings of betrayal and loss at Greylock's hands. The bitterness that remains with Dorinda throughout her professional success strengthens her resolve, but also reveals the challenges that exist when a woman brought up to desire romantic fulfillment recognizes the limitations of that lifestyle and chooses to take a different path. The loneliness and isolation Dorinda experiences are palpable.

Rawlings represented women harshly in most of her writing, aligning herself more closely with her male characters. One exception was Ase Linden's wife, Nellie, in *The Sojourner* (1953), who was modeled after Rawlings's maternal grandmother, Fanny. Rawlings wrote about the real Fanny in "Fanny—You Fool!" (1942), describing her as both phenomenal in the kitchen and an erstwhile prankster around the farm. Despite Nellie's positive portrayal in *The Sojourner*, critics like Veronica Makowsky point out that she is unable to comprehend the anti-materialistic view of her husband Ase. Makowsky argues: "Nellie is unable to view time and life as a whole, so though she is generous with her food and energy, she, too, ultimately settles for the prevailing attitude of division and possessiveness" (251). Nellie may be seen, therefore, as sympathetic, but still limited as a woman. The other female character in that novel,

Ase's mother Amelia, is arguably the most detestable woman portrayed in any of Rawlings's works, and is responsible for the death of her own granddaughter.

Glasgow's ex-fiancé, Henry Anderson, in fact took Rawlings to task over her portrayals of women. He was convinced Rawlings had some prejudice against her own sex because of the disagreeable Ma Baxter from *The Yearling* and Amelia Linden from *The Sojourner*.[2] More recently, there have also been defenses of Rawlings's treatment of women in her writing. Christopher Rieger uses the frequent comparisons between women and the natural landscape of Florida to argue that *South Moon Under* uses fences to "symbolize the modern society that Rawlings seeks to escape . . . their encroachment into the virtually uninhabited scrub region of north central Florida entails, in her view, the threat of subjugation of nature and women alike" (200). While her female characters do not reflect on their lives intellectually, they do portray the organic, natural realm that Rawlings privileged in her narratives. Stories like "Gal Young Un" and "Jacob's Ladder" compare women, and their male counterparts, to animals surviving in the wild.

Glasgow and Rawlings lived through a time of great change for women politically. By the time women's suffrage passed at the national level, Glasgow had already established her career, and Rawlings had just completed her degree at the University of Wisconsin and taken her first position as a journalist in New York. Glasgow was an ardent supporter of women's suffrage. In a handwritten statement Rawlings collected that had been sent by Glasgow to Mary Johnston, Glasgow wrote: "Suffrage for women is an inevitable fact in the social development of the race, and sentiment is as powerless to stay its coming as it is to stem the advancing tide of evolution."[3] In her 1913 essay "Feminism," Glasgow explained her views:

If, as man has so confidently asserted in the past, woman exists, not as an active agent of life, but merely as the passive guardian of the life force, then, indeed, is her revolt doomed to fail and her struggle to bear fruit in her sorrow. If her fight is a fight against law, if it is nature's purpose that woman shall sit and watch, then, as surely as night follows day, she will continue to sit and watch until the end of time. (Raper 35)

Glasgow asserted that such passivity is "acquired," and not inherent—as many believed—and would therefore "disappear in the higher development of the race" (Raper 35). Her essay, which mostly discussed the representation of women in literature, stood up for women's rights. She also supported women's suffrage financially. The reason Glasgow sometimes took a backstage approach to these matters was that she was, first and foremost, an intellectual and professional writer who found that the movements required for change resulted in a type of radicalism that could itself be problematic. As Monique Frazee points out in "Ellen Glasgow as Feminist": "Radicalism has to work for immediate efficiency, with hits and blows and violence in order to burst open recalcitrant doors. Ellen Glasgow hated violence; she chose more subdued means of action: moderate, disciplined, gentle; yet, under her velvet glove, one feels the iron hand of conviction, the cutting edge of her wit and satire" (Frazee 187). Most of her work for women's equality was tempered by Glasgow's distaste for excessive conflict. In her autobiography, Glasgow wrote, "I was always a feminist, for I liked intellectual revolt as much as I disliked physical violence. On the whole, I think women have lost something precious, but have gained, immeasurably, by the passing of the old order" (*WW* 163–164). This declaration occurs in the chapter of her autobiography on her first love interest, Gerald B—, and may be further evidence of Glasgow having had less of a physical relationship with her lovers than an intellectual companionship with them.

Rawlings came of age when the women's suffrage movement was close to completion. She took up the banner of women in the workplace after writing in "[The Old Order Hath Changed]" (1918) for the university's literary magazine, "suffrage has at last become almost a certainty" (Tarr and Kinser 137). The article, written during WWI, when many positions had become available to women in the workplace, detailed the numerous opportunities for women and encouraged their ambitions. Rawlings implored young women to seek out these positions, writing, "Success should be waiting with open arms for the determined young woman who studies law, medicine, agriculture, pharmacology; or who takes a commerce course, with an eye to big things" (Tarr and Kinser 138). As a university graduate, Rawlings witnessed the rise of women in both higher education and professional positions.

Following college, Rawlings supported women's issues by working with the Young Women's Christian Association (YWCA) in New York, promoting their efforts to advance women's work lives and philanthropy in a variety of areas. One of the first initiatives she covered, in "The Blue Triangle Follows the Switchboard" (1919), was the YWCA's housing for women telephone operators of the Signal Corps in France during WWI in units that "were located only twelve miles behind the firing line, and were subjected to all the dangers of those within range of the sweeping Teuton guns" (Tarr and Kinser 154). The YWCA secured an international presence during WWI by creating *Foyers des Alliées*, which Rawlings described in "Women as Constructionists" (1919). These foyers offered women working in the war effort "a friendly, intimate refuge from the monotony and strain of war and of hard labor; a welcoming place that belonged exclusively to the girls and women of the factory; a place where they might come at noon for rest, recreation and wholesome food from the cafeteria; where at night they might gather to sing, dance, talk and forget their fatigue and their individual sorrows for a time" (Tarr and Kinser 158). Some of the larger foyers offered educational courses. The YWCA kept the foyers running during the national reconstruction in France following the war at the behest of the French people. Rawlings also wrote a detailed character sketch for the YWCA of Elizabeth Boies, a woman sent into the Foreign Service by the YWCA and known for establishing recreational facilities for girls from local factories in Russia. Rawlings's article, "Through Three Revolutions" (1919), catalogued the unique challenges that Boies and the YWCA faced during a time of political upheaval in Russia (Tarr and Kinser 160). Back at home, Rawlings wrote "Here is Fun for Girls" (1919), about ways in which the YWCA capitalized on the enthusiasm for service evinced by girls during the war with organizational strategies and camps to continue that service in new ways after the war (Tarr and Kinser 178). Her work for the YWCA reinforced Rawlings's own ideas about women in the workplace and allowed her to keep her finger on the pulse of an advancing society of women in *Blood of My Blood*, she later recalled in *Cross Creek* that her family "had colored help in [their] Washington days"; she did this if only to point out that they did not have that sort of help after moving to Wisconsin, which was why Rawlings's younger brother was so unfamiliar with the challenges of hiring workers from a formerly enslaved class (186). Glasgow's family, on the other hand, always employed a retinue of black servants. One of the reasons for maintaining a number of servants was that the former culture of slavery led many former slave owners to continue employing former slaves and their descendants in their homes following emancipation. Glasgow's father, Francis, allegedly had sexual affairs with the help, an act that allegedly made Glasgow's mother refuse to keep a personal maid (Goodman 21). Rawlings published a story, "Black Secret," around the time of Glasgow's death in 1945, about a child who is just beginning to learn of the prevalence of these types of affairs between white men and black women. She had not yet begun research on Glasgow's life at that time, and may or may not have known about Glasgow's own experiences with the subject. Even if she did not know about Glasgow's personal experiences, however, Rawlings would have been familiar with a character in *Virginia* (1913) who closely resembled Glasgow's father. In that novel, Cyrus Treadwell is an industrialist, like Glasgow's father, who fathers a child by a black servant and then refuses to support it financially when the mother asks him for help. Glasgow kept a regular maid and a cook, and often employed their children for odd jobs around the house. Rawlings also hired help for her grove and to keep house, relying on Martha Mickens to appoint or recommend individuals. Mickens took up the slack when Rawlings was short-handed (Silverthorne 183).

Rawlings's dealings with the black community at Cross Creek were informed by her frankness and lack of experience in employing help. The history of these relationships can be found in the volume *Cross Creek* (1942), a series of autobiographical essays. The Cross Creek community included white and black families living in close proximity to each other, all in impoverished conditions. Rawlings named community members, five white families and two "colored families," at the beginning of the book, and described them all as she would close kin, going so far as to claim that the "Creek folk of color are less suspect than the rest of us" (CC 2). There was a spirit of friendly squabbling among community members, but also one of unity whenever trials faced them individually or collectively. Martha Mickens, an older black woman, was the gossip who held them together by making sure everyone knew what was happening with everyone else. She and her husband worked the groves for years and lived in semi-retirement across the creek from Rawlings. Other, poorer blacks who did not own land lived by a set of laws that resembled slavery. Rawlings claimed to have "bought Georgia of her father for five dollars" after being told by friends that the best way to keep a maid "was to take over a very young Negro girl and train her in [your] ways" (*CC* 77). Georgia was "between ten and twelve" at the time and, to her credit, refused to learn what Rawlings wanted from her, preferring to chase butterflies (*CC* 78–79). Rawlings could not afford a grown woman, and hired Patsy next from her grandmother. Rawlings agreed "to train her, clothe her, care for her, and to pay two dollars a week—to the grandmother" (*CC* 79). Her mistake with Patsy was that Rawlings befriended her, rather than training her, and spent most of her time exploring the Florida hammock with her, deciding that the experience "was strangely like having a child" (*CC* 80). Despite their easy companionship, Rawlings lost Patsy when the girl's mother returned and realized that her daughter was old enough to be put to use around her own house (*CC* 81).

These girls were predecessors to the woman who earned her own chapter in *Cross Creek*, 'Geechee. Rawlings did not have much choice in employing 'Geechee, who showed up at her front door after hearing she was looking for help and told Rawlings, "If I don't do to suit you, you can cut my throat" (*CC* 83). Rawlings thought she "looked capable of murder" and tried to scare her off with low wages and hard work, to no avail. The nickname came from the Ogeechee River, known for producing "a special African tribe" that had "kept their identity" through the years (*CC* 84). Her fear of 'Geechee and the woman's one blind eye and tattered clothes dissipated after she saw her at work. Rawlings, cautious at first, realized that she would "never have a greater devotion than [she] had from this woman" (*CC* 85). The relationship described between 'Geechee and Rawlings resembles the fictional relationship described in Glasgow's *Barren Ground* between Dorinda Oakley and Fluvanna, the servant who begins working for the Oakleys after Dorinda's father dies. Fluvanna becomes invaluable to Dorinda as she takes over the farm.

Dorinda's mother describes Fluvanna: "I never saw a darkey that had as much vim . . . she belongs to the new order too. I always thought it spoiled them to learn to read and write till I hired her. She's got all the sense Aunt Mehitable had, and she's picked up some education besides. I declare, she talks better than a lot of white people I know" (269). The relationship that develops reveals how much two women running a farm depend upon one another for survival, even when one is technically serving the other. In the isolated community of Cross Creek, those boundaries between landowner and servant also became blurred. Rawlings went against her better judgment on 'Geechee's behalf to help get her man released from prison, where he was being held for manslaughter. 'Geechee admitted to having spent time in jail herself, and Rawlings decided that 'Geechee's belief in the man meant he could be rehabilitated with some work. She hosted their wedding after he arrived—four days following his release, because he wanted to "carouse" in Jacksonville first. After he threatened Rawlings following a litany of unreasonable complaints on receipt of his first paycheck, which he had not earned through his own labors but through 'Geechee's, Leroy was let go. 'Geechee saw him off, embarrassed by his behavior. Rawlings would have kept her on had 'Geechee not been taken by alcoholism. In those days of Prohibition, Rawlings imbibed the same moonshine as everyone else at Cross Creek, and discovered 'Geechee siphoning off more than her fair share. She repeatedly ended up in drunken stupors, leaving "on vacation" when she felt humiliated by her drunkenness (93). Afterwards, 'Geechee visited Rawlings annually. Cross Creek demanded a familiarity among people that defied race and class, even when those distinctions were obvious in segregated juke joints and places of worship. Rawlings lived with her servants through times of suffering and joy, and treated them less formally than Glasgow treated her hired help.

In spite of her living conditions, Rawlings took time to try to understand the race question fully. She confessed that she did not understand "the Negro"; however, she also called the following "platitudes" "reasonably accurate": "The Negro is just a child. The Negro is carefree and gay. The Negro is religious in an amusing way. The Negro is a congenital liar. There is no dependence to be put in the best of them" (CC 180). Such statements disturb modern-day readers of *Cross Creek*, but Rawlings tried to explain her views. She believed that subjecting a culture to "civilization," first in slavery and then as pseudo-participants in society who received money instead of rations, resulted in an adaptation to injustice through childishness and dishonesty (CC 180–181). Rawlings pointed out, "one is master, and the other, for all of Lincoln, still a slave" (CC 181). Her sentiments on race precede a section in *Cross Creek* on Rawlings's most challenging employees, Kate and Raymond, who let her house fall into complete disrepair when she was away, drinking her liquor, eating all the chickens, stealing money and clothing, failing to milk the cow or feed the dogs, and finally being discovered together with another gentleman "sweetheart" in their bed when Rawlings showed up with her brother to tell them to leave. Rawlings later wrote that she would have worked on reforming them had her brother not been there, because she understood what led them into their behaviors, and they could be corrected. Rawlings appreciated the serious economic and cultural reasons behind racial problems and wanted to work on improving them.

In time, Rawlings grew into a vocal advocate for the African American community. When she joined the Pledge for Peace Committee of the Writers War Board, her sketch was rejected as too controversial for describing a soldier's response to being asked about "fraternizing with Negroes" as, "Well, Lady, I'm from the South myself, but all I can say is, if a man's good enough to die for his country, he's good enough to live with" (Silverthorne 231). By November of 1943, Rawlings had experienced a critical shift in her thoughts on race, writing to a friend, "I have forced myself to take the final mental leap about the Negroes. There is no question but that we must go all out for 'full equality,' meaningless though the phrase may be. Anything else is the height of hypocrisy" (Silverthorne 231). From that point, she fought against segregation wherever she saw it. She accepted a speaking invitation to the all-black Fisk University, turning back her honorarium to a scholarship fund and staying "at the home of the university president, Charles S. Johnson ... a public gesture of support for racial integration" (Silverthorne 287). Rawlings also fought for one of the local Cross Creek workers, Adrenna, when the school bus refused to pick up her daughter Betty Jean because "it was a 'white' school bus," even though "the nearest 'colored' bus was twelve miles away" (Silverthorne 323). Rawlings initially lost her fight with the county, and wrote a stirring account of the story for the *New York Herald Tribune* that resulted in a bus being allocated for Betty Jean (Silverthorne 324). Members of the St. Augustine community called her a "nigger lover" after she wrote a letter to the editor of the local newspaper to protest the use of force and inappropriate language in the removal of a children's nurse who worked for the renowned Henry Seidel Canby, head of the Book-of-the-Month Club, when she inadvertently used a beach near their residence that had been designated as a "'white' beach" (Silverthorne 328). The maid was described as a "quiet and well-educated woman" in her fifties from the West Indies. In these and many other incidents, Rawlings voiced her outrage on behalf of people targeted because of their race.

While Glasgow had a close relationship with her long-term black employees, none came close to Rawlings's working friendship with Idella Parker. Parker worked for Rawlings for a decade. Rawlings thought she treated Parker like a "white person," but Parker felt that she was abused by the incessant demands and mood swings of her employer. Parker's *Idella Parker: From Reddick to Cross Creek* gives her perspective on Rawlings, as well as on the experiences in her own life that brought the two of them together. Parker did not initially want to work at Cross Creek because it was located in a region near Island Grove that was known to be unfriendly to blacks. When her mother packed her trunk in preparation for Parker's departure from home, she told her daughter, "if they come after you out there, you get that trunk and you RUN!" (Parker 84). Once she was at the Creek, Parker fell in love with the grove and its surroundings, and admired Rawlings, who lent her books from her library, while Parker worked "to protect Mrs. Rawlings from being interrupted while she was working" (91). When Parker needed a blood transfusion following an operation for appendicitis, an inebriated Rawlings showed up at the hospital and insisted on donating her blood, despite the fact that Parker's mother objected, worrying that the blood was "nothing but whiskey" (125). After that time, Rawlings, according to Parker, began to have more regular "bouts of depression, frustration and anger . . . all the while accompanied by heavy drinking" (125). Parker decided to leave Rawlings and move to New York. Parker explained Rawlings's dealings with race in this way: "Was she a racist? Not consciously, I think. She was a product of the times she lived in" (146). Glasgow lacked this degree of intimacy with any of her black servants, partly because of the reserve with which Richmond urbanites treated their staff in a rigid class system. Rawlings never had the luxury of such reserve because she frequently needed to work alongside the people she hired, regardless of skin color.

Ellen Glasgow chose not to romanticize the Southern experience of race in her writing, despite the predominance of such idealized portrayals by other Virginia writers. While Dorinda's relationship with Fluvanna in *Barren Ground* may superficially seem condescending, Matthews argues that Glasgow ultimately "distances herself from Dorinda and in fact *criticizes* Dorinda for condescending to Fluvanna" (*EGWT* 161). Matthews concludes that "the nurturing tradition of female community formed by the two women must be a substitute for the tradition of oppression Dorinda and Pedlar's Mill have 'inherited'" (*EGWT* 161). In later works, Glasgow gave her black characters complex lives and emotions, from the young black law student, Parry Clay, wrongly accused of murder in *In This Our Life* (1941), to the portrayal of George Birdsong's lover, Memoria, in *The Sheltered Life* (1932). The film version of *In This Our Life*, which came out at the beginning of WWII, was controversial enough not to be approved for foreign release by the wartime Office of Censorship for its truthful representation of racial discrimination in the American court system. In the novel, a black man's word is not weighted equally with a white person's testimony in a court of law. That particular novel was also lauded for its handling of physical and mental disabilities, especially the focus on disability identity. One critic has claimed that "Glasgow's thoroughgoing examination of disabled identity and her interrogation of ablebodiness make her final novel atypical in the canon of American modernism" (Kornasky 76). Indeed, *In This Our Life*, Glasgow's Pulitzer Prize-winning final novel, makes striking remarks about what it means to be an Other in a society through several suppressed identity groups.

Ellen Glasgow, who lived with black servants her entire life, developed a paternalistic attitude toward them. She felt responsible for the black men and women who had served her family in times of slavery, and for their children. As Rawlings got to know Glasgow's former fiancé, Henry Anderson, she came to understand this perspective. As a Republican in the Reconstruction South, Anderson was challenged by a white majority that opposed voting rights and integration of any sort. His attempts at compromise come across as exceedingly well balanced in "The Solid South" (1927), in which he agrees that leadership in the South must remain white because of the preponderance of white land ownership, educational advancements, and whites' role in developing the civilization into which "Negroes" were enslaved. Anderson then turns the argument around and argues that those leaders should, in return, be held accountable for providing "Negroes" with the educational and religious development needed to raise themselves up, and the ability to self-govern the institutions they were developing for themselves to promote the cultural change that could lead to a more equitable system.[6] In other words, the white leadership should have an obligation to build up the opportunities and social fabric for former slaves and their families, so they might grow into their own responsible self-governing group. Glasgow agreed with these progressive views.

Rawlings collected instances of Glasgow's charitable acts for the black community in Richmond while working on her biography. In her booklet "Ellen Glasgow" (1928), Mann described how Glasgow grew up visiting "Negro" cabins around her home, feeling both protective of and sorry for the black people of her community (12). Mann complimented Glasgow on approaching "Negro" speech and character more closely than any other white writer of her time, something she was able to do because of her regular interactions with that community (12). Glasgow did not forget these obligations in her will, leaving each of her servants $100 and granting her principal servant, James Anderson, a stipend from her $100,000 trust fund of fifty dollars per month for the remainder of his life.[7] James felt equally protective of Glasgow, telling one interviewer when asked whether he had any dependents, "Yes suh, seven chillen and Miss Ellen Glasgow."[8] Rawlings copied that quotation in her own notes. Glasgow provided annually to the "Afro-American Old Folks Home" over the Christmas holidays. As she explained in a letter to Rebe, "Everybody thinks of the children, but these old colored people are so pathetic and so neglected. They are not in the Community Fund" (PC 78). Glasgow took gifts of candy, nuts, fruit, and a coin purse and served the residents Christmas dinner prepared by James. When her father was still alive, Glasgow paid for whiskey and a plum pudding to be given each Christmas to their house servants from her own revenue

(Godbold 79). She attended to the grave of Lizzie Jones, her childhood nanny who featured prominently in the early chapters of Glasgow's autobiography, having a grave marker made for it and visiting it regularly in the Evergreen Cemetery. Rawlings had similarly complex attitudes about race, first expressing her "outrage at the treatment of blacks and, second, stereotyp[ing] them as children who cannot shoulder responsibility and work on their own initiative" (Jones 223). Unfortunately, Glasgow's legacy for her servants did not prevail in the handling of the Glasgow House memorial, which was briefly transferred from the Association for the Preservation of Virginia Antiquities to the American Association of University Women and back again because, according to Roberta Wellford, people were afraid that the Negro university women would attend teas at the house and could not be excluded.[9]

Even their dissatisfaction with servants reveals how attached Glasgow and Rawlings were to the black community. When Glasgow wrote to Rebe in 1939 about "servant trouble," she described her frustration with a newly trained serving woman, Catherine, who took exception to something Bennett said to her and left immediately without completing the morning's work (*PC* 189). While it saved Glasgow from having to pay her the three months of half-wages required when someone was let go suddenly by an employer, Glasgow was exasperated over having trained her to wait at a table formally only to watch her pick up and leave after six months. Catherine had a reputation for "running about at night," and married an older man who supported her (*PC* 189). Glasgow concluded her letter to Rebe with, "I will not let my mind worry over the servant problems. Let them come or go, as they will" (*PC* 189). Glasgow also fired servants when they were incompetent. After several letters to Rebe about the "imbecility" of "Patsy," who left her whole house embedded in dirt, Glasgow let her go (*PC* 35). Other letters written by Glasgow to Rebe describe petty theft by new maids and "the last Mary (that is the Mary before the Mary I have now)" going off with Glasgow's best shirtwaist "and heaven knows what else" (*PC* 40). Richmond society members often shared or traded the best servants with one another, leading to Glasgow's more recent "Mary," who had been another family's servant before they had to economize and let her go (*PC* 39). This sharing kept the best servants employed through times of financial instability, and resembled the way in which members of the Cross Creek community recommended servants to one another as children came of age and no longer needed tending, or servants married, moved, and had children themselves. Glasgow kept a sense of humor about her "servant troubles," writing to Rebe, "After the exodus of Patsy, who departed regretfully but cheerfully, (bearing with her, as we discovered afterwards, the majority of the bed linen, including Cary's) and of Freeman (who was angelic) and Maria (who took everything with her that Patsy had left behind, particularly kitchen things) we hoped in our vanity that we should get a life of quiet. But to reckon without Providence is a small fatality compared to reckoning without Domestics" (*PC* 37). The entire system of servitude was fraught with challenges.

Modern readers may take umbrage at the use of the term "Negroes" in the works of both Rawlings and Glasgow, but historical context places both writers at the forefront of racial advancement for their decisions to include characters of color in their works as they did. Emily Clark pointed out in "Ellen Glasgow" (1929), another article highlighted by Rawlings, that Glasgow's capitalization of "Negroes" in *The Deliverance* (1904) was considered overwhelmingly progressive because it asserted the advancement of that race into one whose name was worthy of capitalization, something not yet done by the majority of writers (37). Furthermore, Clark applauded Glasgow for exposing truths about the relationships between white men and women, Negroes, and family members that were not acknowledged by the South at that time, most significantly the "intricate tissue of lies" told to and perpetuated with white women to protect them from white men's daliances with women of color (37). Clark concluded her essay by describing a summer party in Richmond with Glasgow that ended with a chorus of Negroes singing spirituals "fifty years away from Harlem" (48). Such an evening of spirituals was mirrored at Cross Creek as well. Idella Parker included an image of the "staff" entertaining white guests at Cross Creek in her autobiography (97).

Rawlings's relationship with Zora Neale Hurston gave her an opportunity that Glasgow did not have to form a friendship with a woman of color whom she considered an intellectual equal and who was a fellow writer. Contemporary students of literature are familiar with Hurston's work due in large part to Alice Walker's more recent personal efforts to recover her writings and reestablish them as part of the American literary canon, but Hurston was buried in an unmarked grave, having lived her final years in poverty in Florida. Anna Lillios studied the relationship between Hurston and Rawlings and its effect on each of them in *Crossing the Creek: The Literary Friendship of Zora Neale Hurston and Marjorie Kinnan Rawlings*, and found that Hurston was, in many respects, a catalyst for Rawlings's own shifting views about race. Lillios described how Rawlings found herself "dreading" the impromptu visits of Hurston to Cross Creek after they exchanged Christmas cards in 1943 (Lillios 26). Living in a rural Southern community replete with bigotry, Rawlings was conflicted about what to do when it came to entertaining Hurston overnight, and was ashamed of herself for feeling conflicted. She wrote to Baskin that she overcame her own fears and had Hurston's bags moved from the tenant house where her servants had placed them to her guest room, writing to Baskin, "I was amazed to find that my own prejudices were so deep. . . . But I felt that if I ever was to prove my humanitarian and moral beliefs, even if it cost me the lawsuit I must do it then" (Tarr, qtd. in Lillios 28). Lillios included a dream Rawlings had after the incident, in which she found herself attending "a negro football game where 'high whites' were to be . . . going with Negroes as a moral gesture" (Tarr qtd. in Lillios 29). Rawlings realized at that instant that "a fight must be made, human nature being as selfish as it is," and decided that she wanted to be part of that fight (Tarr, qtd. in Lillios 29). Her experiences with Hurston expanded Rawlings's views of the black community beyond her earlier suppositions on Africanism in *Cross Creek* and showed her that she could stand in solidarity with Hurston by supporting changes that would allow women like Hurston to thrive.

Partly because of their similar experiences interacting with, but never quite being members of, the most prestigious social classes, Rawlings found that she and Glasgow were more likely than some other writers to write stories featuring economically disadvantaged characters. Rawlings studied the impoverished Cracker community in the Florida hammock, a barely recognized group of poor whites living semi-migrant lives, as they attempted to eke out their survival from the land, skirting the law with illegal hunting practices and moonshining. Glasgow, on the other hand, took her ancestral heritage and its foundation in "the fertile wilderness between the Blue Ridge and the Alleghenies" (*CM* 165) as a setting for *Vein of Iron* and the "vanishing border beyond the Shenandoah" for *Barren Ground* (*CM* 157). Glasgow was familiar with these territories, but she wrote about them as an outsider looking in, not as an embedded resident like Rawlings was.

Rawlings was nevertheless interested in Glasgow's portrayals of the economically disadvantaged segments of society and those people's attempts to achieve better fortunes in subsequent generations. An article she found on Glasgow by Douglas Southall Freeman, titled "Ellen Glasgow: Idealist" (1935), described Glasgow's defense of social justice, especially for people of color (11–12). This outspokenness played out in her portrayal of the Fincastles in *Vein of Iron* (1935), as they struggled on the land before being forced to migrate to the nearest urban area, Queenborough, a fictionalized location based on Richmond. Glasgow wrote that her purpose for this novel "was to test the resistance of this vein of iron to outward pressure, and to measure the exact degree of its strength" (*CM* 173). To do so, she tested the Fincastles like Job to show how strong they were in the face of limitless adversity, writing the novel from multiple perspectives to indicate their different reactions to their circumstances.

Glasgow channeled the experiences of her less-affluent Scotch-Irish ancestors into her novels, living with them in her mind if not in reality. As Rawlings read through criticism of Glasgow's works, she recognized many of the same immigrant strains that had settled in Florida and become the basis for her own character sketches. In "Ellen Glasgow" (1928), Dorothea Lawrance Mann explained how these tenacious and hardworking immigrants, as depicted by Glasgow, rebuilt the South, despite the fact that they were allied with neither slave nor slave owner (6). Mann used *The Deliverance* (1904) as an example of how Glasgow treated all classes equally by showing how no class had all the virtues or could escape all the vices. Many critics felt that Glasgow's depiction of poor whites in *Barren Ground* (1925) was avant-garde, especially given its critical success and comparison to works by Thomas Hardy. In writing *Barren Ground*, Glasgow did not intend to focus on the "poor white" population or the "shiftless class of sharecropper" (*CM* 156). Instead, she categorized the families of Pedlar's Mill and Old Farm as "land poor," "a social unit which, though it has been consistently ignored alike by Southern literature and tradition, has borne a liberal part in the making of Southern history" (*CM* 156–157). Dorinda Oakley's narrative pivots on the class distinction between her "land poor" family and the wealthier physician's son who betrays her. Roxanne Harde points to examples of class consciousness in Glasgow's collection of gothic short stories, *The Shadowy Third*, as well. Using Foucault's idea that gothic narratives "'essentially focus on the abuse of power,' and their function is to reactivate, through the imaginary, knowledge about power structures," Harde argues that "economic power structures and their abuse" function through the ghost child of the titular story, "The Shadowy Third" (1923), which is about a nurse who sees the ghost child of a woman whose husband, a physician, has hired her to help justify his decision to have his wife institutionalized (193). The ghost child helps prove that the physician had married the woman for her money and killed her child, and it takes revenge by leaving a ghostly skipping rope on the stairs. The domineering doctor falls to his death by tripping on the rope before he can kill his current wife and get remarried, to a former lover. Harde's reading of this scene shows how justice may be enacted through the intervention of a supernatural character. Other stories in this collection could be read in a similar vein.

Rawlings saw poverty close-up for the first time when she moved to Cross Creek and became committed to understanding the Florida Crackers. Initially, she offended members of this community by not understanding their ways. One of her employees, Tim, lived with his wife and baby in her tenant house and worked the grove. When Tim's wife appeared at her door to ask her to read a mailing because she was illiterate, Rawlings, innocently enough, asked how she was "getting on" (*CC* 66). The woman's response about excessive mosquitoes and ants in their pantry made Rawlings realize for the first time that the tenant house "was wide open to the intrusion not only of insects, but of wind and weather" (*CC* 67). Rawlings confessed that she never offered to help improve these conditions because she "took others' discomfort for granted" (*CC* 67). The family left shortly after the scenes Rawlings related in *Cross Creek* (1942), but their memory haunted her, and inspired Florry in *Jacob's Ladder* and Allie in *Golden Apples* (*CC* 68).

Glasgow adopted a political stance against economic disparity by favoring Marxism. Her first novel, *The Descendant*, served as a case study in Marxist thinking. Comparing that novel and its protagonist, Michael Akershem, with Glasgow's "What I Believe" (1933) lays out her theoretical model for correcting class distinctions. In her essay on economic issues, Glasgow wrote:

> I believe that the private ownership of wealth should be curbed; that our natural resources should not be exploited for individual advantage; that every man should be assured of an opportunity to earn a living and a fair return for his labor; that our means of distribution should be readjusted to our increasing needs and the hollow cry of "overproduction" banished from a world in which millions are starving; that the two useless extremes of society, the thriftless rich and the thriftless poor, should be mercifully eliminated by education or eugenics. (Raper 222)

The essay explains complications in Marxist philosophies for the United States, where the "proletariat" may be rightly offended by the label given them, as it is easier to assign than accept classification. While most of Glasgow's charitable acts were focused on the poor black community, she regularly assisted other segments of the impoverished Richmond community as well. There were years when she filled stockings for poor children and provided stockings to poor women. Her contributions, however meager, allowed Glasgow to feel as if she were participating in the betterment of the impoverished population in her own community.

Glasgow supported race and class consciousness in other Southern novels of her day, as well, writing in "The Novel in the South" (1928) that "whenever the Southern writer escaped from beneath the paw of the stuffed lion into the consciousness of a different race or class, he lost both his cloying sentiment and his pose of moral superiority" (Raper 73). In other words, an author writes less-affected and more realistic prose when writing humbly about a disadvantaged populace.

Glasgow's position could not be applied as easily to Rawlings's writing because of the latter's intimate proximity to the Florida subjects of her works. After reading reviews of *South Moon Under* (1933), Rawlings felt "quite cheap, quite the Judas, at having apparently delivered the Cracker into the hands of the Philistines" (*MM* 94). She had not imagined that her representation of the Cracker community would be misconstrued as ugly, as many reviewers declared it to be. She hoped readers outside of Florida would benefit from the values espoused in the Florida wilderness. Where she lived, local residents who wanted to read her book waited for the one copy in the local library to become available.

Rawlings defended the Florida Cracker community against reviews of her works, and tried to mitigate the ways in which her works were sensationalized by editorials. In a response to an article from the *Ocala Evening Star* that criticized the "Cracker Chidlings," vignettes she had published in *Scribner's Magazine*, as misrepresenting the culture of the Cracker community, Rawlings took the author to task, calling the "lack of sympathy" his and not hers (Tarr and Kinser 254). She staunchly defended the Cracker people, specifically a well-loved chaplain of Raiford, moonshiners, and cattlemen, all of whom Rawlings admired. Her article "Florida: A Land of Contrasts" (1944) introduces more formally the poorer white population of Florida that had "drifted down [to Florida] over the years from the south-eastern seaboard of the United States" and comprised mostly "English, Scottish, and Irish, sturdy and honest Anglo-Saxons," similar to the rural class from the mountainous region of Virginia depicted by Glasgow (Tarr and Kinser 304). Rawlings tried to elevate them by comparing their speech to "picturesque Chaucerian and Shakespearean idiom" (Tarr and Kinser 304). She also explained two competing theories for the origin of the term Cracker: "the habit of frontiersmen of cracking long rawhide whips over the backs of their oxen" and the fact that "corn, cracked in a form known as hominy grits, or ground into meal" was "one of the staple foods of the Florida countryman," leading William Bartram to characterize Florida in 1790 as "the land of corn and crackers" (Tarr and Kinser 304). Her historical overview of the people and attempts to relate them back to their European predecessors further humanized a class of people commonly mocked by her educated readership.

Rawlings was able to substantiate Ellen Glasgow's complex economic views and their origin in her research on Glasgow's writing and biographical notes. Glasgow's personal views were more political than Rawlings's, which she described in "What I Believe" (1933). After explaining her decision to write her first novel, *The Descendant* (1897), on the "despised and rejected," Glasgow remembered her late brother-in-law, George Walter McCormack, who had not only encouraged her work as a writer, but also introduced her to the economic theories of John Stuart Mill and Karl Marx (Raper 220). These studies had led Glasgow to believe that economic systems "must be revised or discarded" throughout the ages for the betterment of the social order, and that no system should be treated as sacrosanct. Furthermore, she pointed out that "an American workingman of active intelligence" could easily "change places with an American banker, also of active intelligence, and in a few weeks neither the workingman nor the banker could be sure of the class in which he belonged" (Raper 225). The reason for this confusion, Glasgow claimed, lies in the fact that "the gulf" between those classes is not nearly as insurmountable as it would have been "between an unwashed peasant and a perfumed aristocrat" (Raper 225). The intermingling and lack of distance between classes leads to a different set of conflicts that must be examined. Glasgow was a Republican in the times of Democratic homogeneity in Virginia following the Civil War, a time when the Democratic Party favored poll taxes and segregation and a return to old Southern values. More than simply throwing her support to the Republicans, Glasgow wrote a speech that she never delivered, but circulated through friends in the party. "My Fellow Virginians" (1921) was written when her longtime friend and former fiancé, Henry Anderson, was running as the Republican nominee for governor. At the time, the Republican platform included "poll-tax repeal, election-law reform, right of labor to organize and bargain collectively, better schools and roads, and a business administration" (Raper 55). Glasgow took Democrats to task for their fear of the black vote: "That a small and ineffectual minority such as the negro race in Virginia—without education, without experience in government, without property, and without influence of any sort, should constitute a serious menace to the established rule of the white people—is a proposition that could be advanced only by the Democratic Party in Virginia or by Alice in Wonderland" (Raper 60–61). Glasgow compared their fear of the black vote to her own childhood fear of the imaginary Mr. Wugglemuggle. She also called out the Democratic Party for its hypocritical stance on impoverished women, namely mothers' pensions, telling the story of a New York banquet for exporters at which a gentleman requested that attendees "give three cheers to the poor" of the city "who have not enough clothing" as they sat in the room enjoying as much food and drink as they could ingest (Raper 64). Glasgow imagined that the Democratic Party should similarly rise up to "give three cheers for mothers" (Raper 64). Glasgow used her celebrity status as a writer to speak up for political changes that would benefit the lower classes of Virginia society and overturn the vestiges of an Old South system that maintained class and race boundaries at all costs.

In a song supporting women's suffrage titled "The Call" (1912), Ellen Glasgow charged women to rise up together and inherit their liberty, and the call to action demanded by that liberty. Rawlings answered this call in her own way to address issues of social justice. The two writers used their works as a platform for expressing opinions on racial injustice, poverty, and gender stereotypes. Due to her weaker constitution, Glasgow struggled to be as active a participant as some of the women in her political circles. She composed "The Call" as a way of contributing to the suffragist movement when she lacked the physical stamina to march. Later, she discovered Rawlings to be a sympathetic supporter of a common cause, to raise up the dejected and rejected of society and offer them a place at her table. Glasgow's song is a fitting tribute to the work of both authors:

> Woman called to woman at the daybreak
>   When the bosom of the deep was stirred
> In the gold of dawn and in the silence,
>   Woman called to woman and was heard!
>
> Steadfast as the dawning of the polestar,
>   Secret as the fading of the breath;
> At the gate of Birth we stood together,
>   Still together at the gate of Death.
>
> Queen or slave or bond or free, we battled,
>   Bartered not our faith for love or gold;
> Man we served, but in the hour of anguish
>   Woman called to woman as of old.

Hidden at the heart of earth we waited,
　　Watchful, patient, silent, secret, true;
All the terrors of the chains that bound us
　　Man has seen, but only woman knew!

Woman knew! Yea, still, and woman knoweth!—
　　Thick the shadows of our prison lay—
Yet that knowledge in our hearts we treasure
　　Till the dawning of the perfect day.

Onward now as in the long, dim ages,
　　Onward to the light where Freedom lies;
Woman calls to woman to awaken!
　　Woman calls to woman to arise! (Raper 18–19)

Afterword
"Beyond Defeat"

IN HER GROUNDBREAKING *In Search of Our Mothers' Gardens*, Alice Walker wrote, "I became aware of my need of Zora Neale Hurston's work some time before I knew her work existed" (Walker 83). The more she read, the more Walker appreciated that a great woman had come before her to do the work she longed to do. The downside to this realization came when she tried to read criticism on Hurston and found it to be derisive and inaccurate. Walker described her disheartened reaction: "For if a woman who had given so much of obvious value to all of us (and at such risks: to health, reputation, sanity) could be so casually pilloried and consigned to a sneering oblivion, what chance would someone else—for example, myself—have? I was aware that I had much less gumption than Zora" (Walker 86–87). Fortunately for American literature, Walker did not give up her work. Instead, she pursued Hurston's memory with love and vigor. Hurston's grave in St. Lucie County, Florida, is a testament to Walker's fidelity, as it is now adorned with a headstone she ordered to mark the grave of the woman who so inspired her.

When Rawlings befriended Glasgow, she found inspiration in their paralleled experiences with the writing process and those "wells" of creativity they constantly needed to refill through introspection and periods of rest or distraction. Virginia Woolf felt the same way after reading about the life and literature of Aphra Behn, of whom she wrote, "All women together ought to let flowers fall upon the tomb of Aphra Behn" (Woolf 71). Woolf explained the need to rediscover her predecessors, "For masterpieces are not single and solitary births; they are the outcome of many years of thinking in common, of thinking by the body of the people, so that the experience of the mass is behind the single voice" (Woolf 71). Rather than locating in their foremothers the "anxiety of influence" Harold Bloom describes for male writers of the Romantic and early Modern periods, these women found comfort, solidarity, and a firm foundation in the works of similarly minded women who had come before them. When Marjorie Kinnan Rawlings received that first letter of support from the renowned Ellen Glasgow, she did not respond with condescension or competitiveness. She responded with gratitude. Her work had been recognized by a woman who had blazed a trail before her in the field of Southern literature, taking on the overly idealized Southern romantics and the agrarians alike to establish a realism she felt was necessary for the people of Virginia. Their relationship was not the only one of its kind, but it was one of the great literary friendships in the South, and it needs to be recognized and studied for its influential mark on both women and on their writing.

Glasgow had already established herself as a prolific correspondent with other women writers of her day, many of whom became lifelong friends. Some, like Virginia Woolf, never reciprocated as strongly as Glasgow would have desired, but others, like Mary Johnston, Signe Toksvig, and Radclyffe Hall, were influential in her career and personal life. Pamela Matthews began her study of Glasgow's female friendships with a quotation from Glasgow to Signe Toksvig after a year and a half of correspondence: "There aren't many women one would like, if one were a man, to be married to; but . . . you leave the impression of perfect companionship" (*PC* xiii). That quote became the title of Matthews's *Perfect Companionship: Ellen Glasgow's Selected Correspondence with Women*, which includes the exchange between Rawlings and Glasgow. Matthews makes the argument that these relationships should be included as a measure of Glasgow's accomplishments: "To Glasgow's more public accomplishments—her medals, her awards, and her degrees—perhaps it is time we add her great gifts for perfect companionship fostered through correspondence with women" (*PC* xxix). Too often, critics have focused on Glasgow's arguments with other writers in a way that suggested her intent was to assert her own literary superiority in her relationships. However, those quarrels were mostly with men, like James Branch Cabell, who had their own problems in treating the literary works of women fairly. By releasing these letters, Matthews hoped to demonstrate the ways in which Glasgow endeared herself to other women writers and relied upon their friendship and support throughout her life.

Just as her novels focus more on male protagonists than female, the letters of Marjorie Kinnan Rawlings were mostly written to the men in her life: Norton Baskin, Max Perkins, and her brother Arthur Kinnan. However, Rawlings also enjoyed a strong support system made up of women, like fellow writers Edith Pope and Margaret Mitchell. Her relationship with her mother may have been troubling, but Ida Traphagen Kinnan put aside her own comfort to support her daughter through her education and afterwards. Rawlings later flexed her own maternal muscles in befriending and mentoring Julia Scribner Bigham. One of her earliest run-ins with an editor in New York resulted in a warm embrace and loan from Signe Toksvig, who simply asked that she return the favor to some other young writer one day. At Cross Creek, Rawlings had complex relationships with her servants, who ultimately became like family to her, even if that designation could be considered problematic. In college, Rawlings, who was active in theater, formed a lasting friendship with fellow thespian Beatrice Humiston McNeil, with whom she visited and corresponded for the rest of her life. Dessie Smith Prescott helped educate Rawlings on the outdoors life in Florida, and accompanied her on her post-divorce excursion down the St. Johns River.

Anna Lillios explored, at length, the relationship between Marjorie Kinnan Rawlings and Zora Neale Hurston in *Crossing the Creek: The Literary Friendship of Zora Neale Hurston and Marjorie Kinnan Rawlings*. Lillios discovered that the two women had "shared a deep appreciation of the cultural, mythic, artistic, and human qualities of the communities about which they wrote" (Lillios 3). Her book also demonstrates the ways in which their relationship expanded Rawlings's appreciation for racial concerns and increased her feelings of culpability in altering the racial climate of Florida. Letters included by Lillios between Rawlings and Baskin during her friendship with Hurston reveal a deep-seated conviction regarding her own actions toward Hurston and the black community at large, as well as an admission of the fears and anxieties that reared up when she considered acting more openly on behalf of the black community. What Lillios proves from a relational standpoint is that

Rawlings felt much more inclined to expand and alter her views of a situation if she had an emotional connection with another woman in that situation. In this way, such relationships prove how women writers can connect through their craft, and then use that connection to bridge their differences.

After Glasgow's death, Marjorie Kinnan Rawlings eagerly began work on the biography of her friend, completing *The Sojourner* just before this new project. For Rawlings, it was of the utmost importance to record the story of the woman she respected and loved while she could still consult with Glasgow's closest friends and family members. She stayed in Richmond to conduct interviews, and defended her work to family members, like her Aunt Wilmer, who criticized her for not taking a break to "rest on [her] laurels and just have a good time" (Bigelow and Monti 390). From the onset of their friendship, Rawlings begged Glasgow to finish her autobiography, telling her that the world needed to know her thoughts and the experiences that had accompanied her career. Rawlings was able to read that completed work in its unpublished state while working on her biography of Glasgow. Glasgow's greatest work, in Rawlings's opinion, was a collection of her prefaces, published as *A Certain Measure*, that encouraged Rawlings by speaking to feelings she had believed to be solely her own. Glasgow spoke a truth that Rawlings had shared as a fellow writer. The dream that she related in her first letter to Glasgow after their initial meeting solidified the mystical bond that held the two women together throughout their lives.

For her own part, Ellen Glasgow found her relationship with Rawlings to be so significant that she chose a piece of their correspondence for the concluding scene in her posthumously published autobiography. That letter, published in its entirety in the epilogue to Glasgow's autobiography, led Glasgow to realize that "with faithful friends I had come over the last hill into the endless valley" (*WW* 295). While the letter seems specific to their friendship, Glasgow extrapolated from it her own feelings of connection with many other women in her life, naming Anne Virginia Bennett and Carrie Duke as the two who came most readily to mind. Glasgow's relationship with Rawlings reminded Glasgow of the importance that women's friendships had always played in her life, and gave her hope that the mystical connections she had so frequently experienced with kindred spirits in her own life would continue to be felt by the next generation of women.

While they encountered one another late in their lives and corresponded only a handful of times, meeting only once in the flesh, Glasgow and Rawlings each had a profound impact on the other by unmasking a sympathetic thread shared by both. Their love for the truth and desire to capture the human experience in its rawest form was coupled with their similar struggles to refine their writing processes and live both among their friends and family members and, as necessary, apart from them in the private sphere of their writing lives. Through this shared sympathy, Glasgow and Rawlings bolstered and made an indelible impression on one another that should not be forgotten.

At the funeral of Marjorie Kinnan Rawlings, her attorney and friend, Phil May, concluded the service by reading the end of *Cross Creek*, a fitting tribute to both Rawlings and Glasgow, and to the legacy they left behind:

> Who owns Cross Creek? The red-birds, I think, more than I.... And after I am dead, who am childless, the human ownership of grove and field and hammock is hypothetical. But a long line of red-birds and whippoorwills and blue-jays and ground doves will descend from the present owners of nests in the orange trees, and their claim will be less subject to dispute than that of human heirs. (Silverthorne 8)

Notes

Introduction: Friendship and Sympathy

1. Throughout her career, Glasgow published nineteen novels, a poetry collection titled *The Freeman and Other Poems*, a collection of ghost stories titled *The Shadowy Third and Other Stories*, a collection of critical essays titled *A Certain Measure*, and a posthumously published autobiography titled *The Woman Within*. She also composed a sequel to *In This Our Life* that was published as *Beyond Defeat* by her literary executors in 1966.
2. MKR, letter to EG, May 30, 1940, U.Va.
3. Rawlings published the essay that she presented as a lecture at the Annual Luncheon of the National Council of Teachers of English in New York (1939) in *College English* (1940) and *English Journal* (1940). The printed version, with notes from the informal presentation of the material, may be found in Tarr and Kinser's *The Uncollected Writings of Marjorie Kinnan Rawlings* (2007).

Chapter 1. A Letter and a Dream

1. This personal interview with Anne Virginia Bennett from Feb./Mar. 1953 is in the Marjorie Kinnan Rawlings Papers, Special and Area Studies Collections, George A. Smathers Libraries, University of Florida, Gainesville, Florida. Subsequently, this collection will be identified as MKRP.
2. The correspondence described here was first printed in the *Atlanta Journal* as "An Exchange of Letters" in 1946 and was later recovered and reprinted in a 1982 article by Tonette L. Bond in *The Ellen Glasgow Newsletter*.
3. "An Exchange of Letters," *Atlanta Journal*, April 26, 1946. Copy of original. Between EG and MKR, U.F.
4. In one letter to Max Perkins preceding the publication of *South Moon Under* dated November 18, 1932, Rawlings admits to having bullied Charles Rawlings into reading a few chapters, and then to having gone into a "red fog" when he advises her to omit the profanity and make the novel over into a book for boys (*MM*

73). Throughout the letter, she is torn between the advice of her then-husband Charles, her editor Max Perkins, and her own ideas about the book.

5. Glasgow's correspondence with Max Perkins from 1936 to 1939, during the publication of the Virginia Edition of her novels and the writing of prefaces to those novels that were later collected and published as *A Certain Measure*, may be found in the Marjorie Kinnan Rawlings Papers at U.F.
6. In a 1941 letter to Glasgow found in the Glasgow Papers at U.Va. and reprinted in Godbold's biography of Glasgow, Cabell writes, "With your great zest for life, it is dreadful to think of you as a virgin, but your books offer almost irrefutable testimony to the fact, unless indeed, your Virginian ladihood stepped in and caused you to become reticent" (Godbold 284).
7. This letter, in particular, inspired Rosemary M. Magee's anthology *Friendship and Sympathy: Communities of Southern Women Writers*, which features chapters on Glasgow and Rawlings.
8. Glasgow's correspondences with these women writers, including the letters she exchanged with Marjorie Kinnan Rawlings, may be found in *Perfect Companionship: Ellen Glasgow's Selected Correspondences with Women*, edited by Pamela Matthews.
9. MKR, letter to EG, May 11, 1942, Papers of Ellen Glasgow, Accession #5060, Special Collections, University of Virginia Library, Charlottesville, Virginia. Subsequently, this collection will be identified as U.Va.
10. MKR, letter to EG, Jan. 17, 1942, U.Va.
11. MKR, letter to EG, Oct. 7, 1943, U.Va.
12. James Branch Cabell dedicated *Something About Eve* (1927) to Ellen Glasgow and *There Were Two Pirates* (1946) to Marjorie Kinnan Rawlings.
13. MKR, letter to EG, Oct. 7, 1943, U.Va.
14. MKR, letter to EG, May 11, 1942, U.Va.
15. MKR, letter to EG, May 30, 1940, U.Va.
16. Ibid.
17. Ibid.
18. EG, letter to AVB, [1936], U.F.
19. MKR, letter to EG, May 15, 1945, U.Va.
20. Glasgow attempted suicide by taking sleeping pills after learning about Henry Anderson's affair with Queen Marie of Romania. Prior to leaving for service, Henry Anderson had become engaged to Glasgow. They never resumed their relationship (*WW* 238).
21. MKR, letter to EG, May 11, 1942, U.Va.
22. Ibid.
23. Ibid.
24. MKR, letter to Clifford Lyons, Feb. 10, 1953. Note appended to letter by Clifford Lyons on Feb. 22, 1988, U.F.

25. MKR, letter to Clifford and Gladys Lyons, July 8, 1953, U.F.
26. Trust fund sources,[June], 1931, U.F.
27. Questions to be asked in interviews for EG biography, note cards, U.F.
28. Memoir [EG's], notes from, U.F.
29. MKR, interview of Irita Van Doren for EG biography, U.F.
30. Questions to be asked in interviews for EG biography, note cards, U.F.
31. MKR, interview of Anne Virginia Bennett for EG biography, U.F.
32. MKR, interview of Irita Van Doren for EG biography, U.F.
33. MKR, interview of Mrs. Trigg for EG biography, U.F.
34. Ibid.
35. MKR, interview of Irita Van Doren for EG biography, U.F.
36. Ibid.
37. MKR, interview of Maude Williams for EG biography, U.F.
38. Ibid.
39. Ibid.
40. MKR, interview of Irita Van Doren for EG biography, U.F.
41. Ibid.
42. Ibid.
43. Ibid.
44. MKR, interview of Dr. Alexander Brown for EG biography, U.F.
45. Ibid.
46. Emma (Gray) Trigg, letter to MKR, June 8, 1953. Thanking her for the mangoes and *The Sojourner*, U.F.
47. MKR, interview of Anne Virginia Bennett for EG biography, U.F.
48. Ibid.
49. MKR, interview of Roberta Wellford for EG biography, U.F.
50. MKR, interview of Maude Williams for EG biography, U.F.
51. Anne Virginia Bennett, letter to MKR, May 7, 1953, U.F.
52. Memoir [EG's], notes from, U.F.
53. MKR, interview of Irita Van Doren for EG biography, U.F.
54. Memoir [EG's], notes from, U.F.
55. MKR, interview of James Branch Cabell for EG biography, U.F.
56. Ibid.
57. Ibid.
58. MKR, interview of Irita Van Doren for EG biography, U.F.
59. EG, letter to James Branch Cabell, Sept. 20, 1927. Commenting on his new book, dedicated to her (*Something about Eve*), U.F.
60. EG, letter to James Branch Cabell, Aug. 22, 1939. Describing the scenery of Castine and how much she writes, U.F.
61. EG, letter to James Branch Cabell, July 3, 1941. Discussing title of his book of "literary criticism," U.F.

62. MKR, interview of Dr. Alexander Brown for EG biography, U.F.
63. Ibid.
64. MKR, interview of Mrs. Scrivenor for EG biography, U.F.
65. MKR, interview of Irita Van Doren for EG biography, U.F.
66. MKR, interview of Dr. Alexander Brown for EG biography, U.F.
67. MKR, interview of Anne Virginia Bennett for EG biography, U.F.

Chapter 2. A Certain Measure of Achievement

1. MKR, letter to EG, April 25, 1939, U.Va.
2. Ibid.
3. MKR, letter to EG, May 30, 1940, U.Va.
4. MKR, letter to EG, May 11, 1942, U.Va.
5. Copies of scrapbook of book reviews: *Sojourner*, 1952–1954, U.F.
6. Ibid.
7. MKR, interview of Miss Francis Williams for EG biography, U.F.
8. An interview with EG by Robert Van Gelder. Typed excerpt from the *New York Times Book Review*, Oct. 18, 1942, U.F.
9. Ibid.
10. Copies of scrapbook of book reviews: *South Moon Under*, 1933–1934, U.F.
11. Copies of scrapbook of book reviews: *The Yearling*, 1938–1948, U.F.
12. Ibid.
13. Copies of scrapbook of book reviews: *South Moon Under*, 1933–1934, U.F.
14. Ibid.
15. Ibid.
16. Ibid.
17. Ibid.
18. Copies of scrapbook of book reviews: *Golden Apples*, 1935–1944, U.F.
19. Ibid.
20. Copies of scrapbook of book reviews: *The Yearling*, 1938–1948, U.F.
21. Ibid.
22. Copies of scrapbook of book reviews: *Cross Creek*, 1941–1944, U.F.
23. Copies of scrapbook of book reviews: *Sojourner*, 1952–1954, U.F.
24. Egly, William H.: Bibliography of EG, U.F.
25. Brooks, Van Wyck. "Appreciation of EG." Address given at the annual meeting of the American Academy of Art and Letters, May 17, 1946. U.F.
26. Ibid.
27. Mims, Edwin. "EG: Social Historian of Virginia." Correspondence about this speech—Arthur Glasgow and E. Randolph Williams, U.F.
28. Copies of scrapbook of book reviews: *The Yearling*, 1938–1948, U.F.
29. Ibid.

30. Brooks, Van Wyck. "Appreciation of EG." Address given at the annual meeting of the American Academy of Art and Letters, May 17, 1946. U.F.
31. Mims, Edwin. "EG: Social Historian of Virginia." Correspondence about this speech—Arthur Glasgow and E. Randolph Williams, U.F.
32. Radclyffe Hall, letter to EG, April 18, 1936, U.F. It is interesting to note that in a 1943 letter to Glasgow, Hall requests a copy of *Vein of Iron*, claiming not to have read it because of her vision problems in 1935 (*PM* 221). This could call into question the letter transcriptions provided to Rawlings by Anne Virginia Bennett, which do include several misspellings, including, most notably, Radclyffe Hall's name, which Bennett spells "Radcliffe."
33. Carrington C. Tutwiler, "EG; the writer as Reader." Delivered in Glasgow home. (Letter to Arthur Glasgow, letter from Arthur Glasgow, U.F.)
34. An interview with EG by Robert Van Gelder. Typed excerpt from the *New York Times Book Review*, Oct. 18, 1942, U.F.
35. Copies of scrapbook of book reviews: *Sojourner*: 1952–1954, U.F.
36. Copies of scrapbook of book reviews: *Cross Creek*, 1941–1944, U.F.
37. Ibid.
38. Brooks, Van Wyck. "Appreciation of EG." Address given at the annual meeting of the American Academy of Art and Letters, May 17, 1946. U.F.
39. Mims, Edwin. "EG: Social Historian of Virginia." Correspondence about this speech—Arthur Glasgow and E. Randolph Williams, U.F.
40. Copies of scrapbook of book reviews: *Cross Creek*, 1941–1944, U.F.
41. Ibid.
42. Brooks, Van Wyck. "Appreciation of EG." Address given at the annual meeting of the American Academy of Art and Letters, May 17, 1946. U.F.
43. An interview with EG by Robert Van Gelder. Typed excerpt from the *New York Times Book Review*, Oct. 18, 1942, U.F.
44. Ibid.
45. It should be noted that Glasgow believed her poetry to be "certainly strong besides being good verse," as stated in a letter to Walter Hines Page prior to the publication of *The Freeman and Other Poems* (1902) (Rouse 36).

Chapter 3. Blood of My Blood

1. Arthur Glasgow, letter to MKR, Feb. 16, 1953, U.F.
2. It should be noted that the suit of clothes received belonged to Glasgow's brother, Frank, who had just committed suicide (Goodman 113).
3. Glasgow, Francis T. [EG's father.] Notes for MKR's biography of EG, U.F.
4. Ibid.
5. MKR, interview of Roberta Wellford for EG biography, U.F.
6. MKR, interview of Carrie Duke for EG biography, U.F.

7. Arthur Glasgow, letter to MKR, April 15, 1953, U.F.
8. The missing closing parenthesis is MKR's (*PC* 40n).
9. MKR, interview of Rebe Glasgow Tutwiler for EG biography, U.F.
10. MKR, letter to Arthur Glasgow, Dec. 3, 1952, U.F.
11. Ibid.
12. Ibid.
13. EG, letter to Arthur Glasgow, April 5, 1932, U.F.
14. Arthur Glasgow, letter to EG, April 6, 1939, U.F.
15. Arthur Glasgow, letter to EG, Sept. 24, 1940, U.F.
16. Arthur Glasgow, letter to EG, June 13, 1925, U.F.
17. Arthur Glasgow, letter to Rebe Glasgow Tutwiler, Jan. 8, 1946, U.F.
18. Glasgow, Arthur. "Making Democracy and the World Mutually Safe." Pamphlet, June 1943, U.F.
19. Glasgow, Arthur. "Unrestricted Suffrage and its Consequences, Pamphlet, June 1948, U.F.
20. Ibid.
21. MKR, interview of Rebe Glasgow Tutwiler for EG biography, U.F.
22. Ibid.
23. MKR, interview of Arthur Glasgow for EG biography, U.F.
24. EG, letter to Arthur Glasgow, Dec. 27, 1921, U.F.
25. MKR, interview of Arthur Glasgow for EG biography, U.F.
26. Ibid.
27. EG, letter to AG, Feb. 18, 1936, U.F.
28. While Glasgow most likely knew of the legal struggles faced by Rawlings, given the national press on the case, she and Rawlings never discussed the suit in their correspondence. The Invasion of Privacy trial did not occur until 1946, the year after Glasgow's death, though the initial libel suit was filed in 1943.

Chapter 4. Women Who Will—Do

1. Van Gelder, Robert. "An Interview with Miss Ellen Glasgow." *The New York Times Book Review*. October 18, 1942 U.F.
2. Ibid.
3. MKR, letter to EG, Oct. 7, 1943, U.Va.
4. Ibid.
5. Selby, John. "Work and Friends Make Life Interesting for Miss Glasgow." *Richmond Times-Dispatch*. March 20, 1938, U.F.
6. Van Gelder, Robert. "An Interview with Miss Ellen Glasgow." *The New York Times Book Review*. October 18, 1942 U.F.
7. Ibid.
8. Ibid.

9. MKR, letter to EG, May 11, 1942, U.Va.
10. Ibid.
11. Ibid.
12. Ibid.
13. Nicholson, Donald J. "Notes on the Breeding of the Ground Dove in Florida." Reprinted from the Wilson Bulletin, June 1937. With a note on the cover for MKR signed by EG, U.F.
14. Ibid.
15. Ibid.
16. Benét, Stephen Vincent and Rosemary Benét. "Miss Ellen: Rebel Against Regimentation." New York Herald Tribune Books, Nov. 17, 1940. Typed excerpt, U.F.
17. "Birds Need Help, Public is Advised." Article from the SPCA in a local news publication, unnamed, submitted to MKR by Margaret Dashiell, along with Richmond Reverie, U.F.
18. "The Thousand Dollar Dog." Typed excerpt and poem. Probably from the Richmond Times Dispatch, May 6, 1952, U.F.
19. Ibid.
20. Society for Prevention of Cruelty to Animals, EG's Message, 1934 or 1935. Copy. U.F.
21. Ibid.
22. Ibid.
23. MKR, interview of Margaret Dashiell for EG biography, U.F.
24. Ibid.
25. Ibid.
26. EG, letter to Rebe Glasgow Tutwiler, Spring 1939. U.F.
27. EG, letter to Rebe Glasgow Tutwiler, May 26, 1939. U.F.
28. Ibid.
29. "The Thousand Dollar Dog." Typed excerpt and poem. Probably from the Richmond Times Dispatch, May 6, 1952, U.F.
30. Ibid.
31. Ibid.
32. MKR, interview of Irita Van Doren for EG biography, U.F.
33. Ibid.
34. MKR, interview of Anne Virginia Bennett for EG biography, U.F.
35. MKR, interview of Margaret Dashiell for EG biography, U.F.
36. EG, letter to Rebe Glasgow Tutwiler, July 2, 1907. U.F.
37. Acknowledgment to EG for $25 given to Bide-a-Wee Pet Animal Cemetery, U.F.
38. MKR, interview of Margaret Dashiell for EG biography, U.F.
39. Ibid.
40. MKR, interview of Dr. William Porter for EG biography, U.F
41. Ibid.

42. Ibid.
43. MKR, interview of Irita Van Doren for EG biography, U.F
44. MKR, interview of Frances Williams for EG biography, U.F
45. Ibid.
46. MKR, interview of Roberta Wellford for EG biography, U.F
47. Ibid.
48. Ibid.
49. Society for Prevention of Cruelty to Animals, EG's Report, U.F.
50. Ibid.
51. EG, letter to Rebe Glasgow Tutwiler, undated. Filed as having been written in 1945, U.F.
52. EG, letter to Rebe Glasgow Tutwiler, February 18, 1924, U.F.
53. Rascoe, Burton. "Ellen Glasgow Deplores Real Estaters and Dry Spies." Copy of a clipping that does not show newspaper or date, U.F.
54. Ibid.
55. Ibid.
56. MKR, interview of Frances Williams for EG biography, U.F
57. Selby, John. "Work and Friends Make Life Interesting for Miss Glasgow." *Richmond Times-Dispatch*. March 20, 1938, U.F.
58. Rascoe, Burton. "Ellen Glasgow Deplores Real Estaters and Dry Spies." Copy of a clipping that does not show newspaper or date, U.F.
59. MKR, interview of Henry Anderson for EG biography, U.F, U.F.
60. Ibid.
61. Ibid.
62. Henry Anderson, letter to Randolph Williams. Typed copy. Salonica, April 20, 1919, U.F.
63. Ibid.
64. Henry Anderson, letter to his mother. Typed copy. Bucharest, August 2, 1919, U.F.
65. Henry Anderson. Address in the opening state campaign, when nominee of the Republican Party for governor of Virginia. Excerpts, Sept. 5, 1921, U.F.
66. Margaret Dashiell, ALS to MKR. Enclosing a print and a clipping of Archer House that has been said to be the house of "One Man in His Time." Article included with clipping from 1953. Written by the editor of the *Richmond Times Dispatch*, U.F. "The Little Things" by James Stephens courtesy of the Society of Authors as the Literary Representative of the Estate of James Stephens.
67. "Having left Cities Behind Me" by Marjorie Kinnan Rawlings, copyright © by Marjorie Kinnan Rawlings, copyright renewed © 1963 by Norton Baskin. First appeared in Scribner's Magazine. Used by permission of Brandt & Hochman Literary Agents, Inc. Any copying or distribution of this text is expressly forbidden. All rights reserved.

Chapter 5. In Search of Truth, Not Sensation

1. "What America is Reading." From the *New York Herald Tribune Books*, Feb. 2, 1936, U.F.
2. McCole, John C. "Lucifer at Large," Longmans, 1937. (Three lives quotations,) U.F.
3. Freeman, Douglas Southall: "Ellen Glasgow: Idealist." From *The Saturday Review*, August 31, 1935, U.F.
4. MKR, interview of Irita Van Doren for EG biography, U.F
5. Ibid.
6. In a letter to EG following her Pulitzer Prize, MKR wrote, "I have no intention of congratulating you on the receipt of the Pulitzer Prize, but am seriously considering writing the committee to congratulate them on at last giving recognition where it is due." MKR, letter to EG, May 11, 1942, U.Va.

Chapter 6. The Sheltered Life

1. Henry Anderson, letter to his mother from Bucharest, Aug. 2, 1919, U.F.
2. Henry Anderson, "An American Citizen," excerpts from a speech before the Literary Societies and graduating class of Washington and Lee University, June 1916, U.F.
3. MKR, interview of Henry Anderson for EG biography, U.F.
4. Ibid.
5. Ibid.
6. Ibid.
7. Ibid.
8. Ibid.
9. Ibid.
10. Ibid.
11. Ibid.
12. Henry Anderson, letter to MKR, Jan. 6, 1953, U.F.
13. MKR, letter to Henry Anderson, March 5, 1953, U.F.
14. MKR, interview of Henry Anderson for EG biography, U.F.
15. Ibid.
16. MKR, interview of Maude Williams for EG biography, U.F.
17. MKR, interview of Mrs. Scrivenor for EG biography, U.F.
18. MKR, interview of Maude Williams for EG biography, U.F.
19. Ibid.
20. Ibid.
21. MKR, interview of Anne Virginia Bennett for EG biography, U.F.
22. Ibid.
23. EG, letter to Anne Virginia Bennett, Sept. 14, 1927, U.F.
24. Ibid.
25. MKR, interview of Roberta Wellford for EG biography, U.F.
26. MKR, interview of Irita Van Doren for EG biography, U.F.

27. MKR, notes from EG's memoir, U.F.
28. Ibid.
29. Ibid.
30. MKR, interview of Anne Virginia Bennett for EG biography, U.F.
31. Ibid.
32. MKR, interview of Roberta Wellford for EG biography, U.F.
33. Ibid.
34. Ibid.
35. Ibid.
36. Ibid.
37. MKR, notes from EG's memoir, U.F.
38. MKR, interview of Dr. William Porter for EG biography, U.F.
39. Ibid.
40. Rebe Glasgow Tutwiler, letter to MKR, Nov. 14, 1953, U.F.
41. Ibid.

Chapter 7. "A Woman of To-Morrow"

1. Rascoe, Burton. "Ellen Glasgow Deplores Real Estaters and Dry Spies." Copy of a clipping that does not show newspaper or date, U.F.
2. Henry Anderson, letter to MKR, Dec. 29, 1952, U.F.
3. Statement by Ellen Glasgow on monogrammed stationary of Mary Johnson, typed copy, on Women's Suffrage, U.F.
4. Radclyffe Hall, letter to EG, April 18, 1936, U.F. Refer to note 107 for details of this letter.
5. Ibid.
6. Henry Anderson, "The Solid South," excerpts from speech before the Institute of Public Affairs at the University of Virginia, Aug. 19, 1927, U.F.
7. Many bequests, Dec. 3, 1945, U.F.
8. MKR, interview of James Anderson (EG's cook) for EG biography, U.F.
9. MKR, interview of Roberta Wellford for EG biography, U.F.

Works Cited

Bellman, Samuel I. *Marjorie Kinnan Rawlings*. Twayne Publishers, 1974.
Bigelow, Gordon E. *Frontier Eden: The Literary Career of Marjorie Kinnan Rawlings*. University Press of Florida, 1966.
Bigelow, Gordon E., and Laura V. Monti, editors. *Selected Letters of Marjorie Kinnan Rawlings*. University Press of Florida, 1988.
Bond, Tonette L. "'A Thrilling Sense of Friendship and Sympathy': The Correspondence of Ellen Glasgow and Marjorie Kinnan Rawlings." *The Ellen Glasgow Newsletter*, no. 16, March 1982, pp. 2–5.
Cabell, James Branch. "The Last Cry of Romance." *Ellen Glasgow*, edited by Dorothea Lawrance Mann, Doubleday, Doran, & Company, 1928, pp. 26–31.
Collins, Joseph. "Realism in a Southern Novel." *Ellen Glasgow*, edited by Dorothea Lawrance Mann, Doubleday, Doran, & Company, 1928, pp. 32–38.
Dunster, Edward Swift, et al. "Obituary: H. Holbrook Curtis, M.D." *International Record of Medicine and General Practice Clinics*, vol. 111, May 1920, p. 909.
"Ellen Glasgow House." *National Park Service U.S. Department of the Interior*, www.nps.gov/nr/travel/richmond/Ellen_Glasgow.html. Accessed 3 August 2015.
Ewing, Majl. "The Civilized Uses of Irony: Ellen Glasgow." *English Studies in Honor of James Southall Wilson*, edited by Fredson Bowers, University of Virginia Press, 1951, pp. 81–91. University of Virginia Studies 4.
Frazee, Monique Parent. "Ellen Glasgow as Feminist." *Ellen Glasgow: Centennial Essays*, edited by Thomas M. Inge, University Press of Virginia, 1976, pp. 167–187.
Freeman, Douglas. "Ellen Glasgow: Idealist." *Saturday Review of Literature*, vol. 12, August 1935, pp. 11–12.
Glasgow, Ellen. *Barren Ground*. Harcourt Brace & Company, 1925.
———. *Beyond Defeat*. University Press of Virginia, 1966.
———. *A Certain Measure: An Interpretation of Prose Fiction*. Harcourt, Brace and Company, 1938.
———. *The Descendant*. Harper & Brothers Publishers, 1899.
———. *The Freeman and Other Poems*. Doubleday, Page & Co., 1902.
———. *In This Our Life*. Harper & Brothers Publishers, 1941.
———. *The Romantic Comedians*. Doubleday, Page, & Company, 1926.

———. *The Sheltered Life*. Harcourt Brace & Company, 1932.
———. *Vein of Iron*. Harcourt Brace & Company, 1935.
———. *Virginia*. Penguin Books, 1989.
———. *The Woman Within*. UP of Virginia, 1954.
Godbold, E. Stanly., Jr. *Ellen Glasgow and the Woman Within*. Louisiana State University Press, 1972.
Goodman, Susan. *Ellen Glasgow: A Biography*. Johns Hopkins University Press, 1998.
Graham-Bertolini, Alison. "Marjorie Kinnan Rawlings and the Reckoning of Ideology." *Southern Quarterly*, vol. 43, no. 1, Fall 2005, pp 49–62.
Harde, Roxanne. "'At rest now': Child Ghosts and Social Justice in Nineteenth-Century Women's Writing." *Transnational Gothic: Literary and Social Exchanges in the Long Nineteenth Century*, edited by Monika Elbert and Bridget M. Marshall, Ashgate Publishing Company, 2013, pp. 189–200.
Hudson, W. H. *Green Mansions*. Alfred A. Knopf, 1925.
HW Anderson 1916 Foster Collection, Visual Resources Collection, Virginia Historical Society, Richmond, Virginia.
Jones, Carolyn M. "Race and the Rural in Marjorie Kinnan Rawlings's *Cross Creek*." *The Mississippi Quarterly*, vol. 57, no. 2, Spring 2004, pp. 215–230.
Kornasky, Linda. "Disabling Modernism: Ellen Glasgow's *In This Our Life*." *The Ellen Glasgow Journal of Southern Women Writers*, vol. 4, January 2011, pp. 73–100.
Leuschner, Eric. "A Certain Art of the Novel: Ellen Glasgow and the Construction of Celebrity." *Southern Studies: An Interdisciplinary Journal of the South*, vol. 17, no. 2, Fall/Winter 2010, pp. 51–68.
Lillios, Anna. *Crossing the Creek: The Literary Friendship of Zora Neale Hurston and Marjorie Kinnan Rawlings*. University Press of Florida, 2010.
MacDonald, Edgar E. "An Essay in Bibliography." *Ellen Glasgow: Centennial Essays*, edited by M. Thomas Inge, University of Press of Virginia, 1976.
———. "A Retrospective Henry Anderson and Marjorie Kinnan Rawlings." *Ellen Glasgow Newsletter*, vol. 12, no. 1, March 1980, pp. 4–6.
Magee, Rosemary M., editor. *Friendship and Sympathy: Communities of Southern Women Writers*. University Press of Mississippi, 1992.
Makowsky, Veronica. "The Changing American Hero and the 'Eternal Bitch' in Marjorie Kinnan Rawlings's *The Sojourner*." *The Mississippi Quarterly*, vol. 57, no. 2, Spring 2004, pp.247–253.
Mann, Dorothea Lawrance. *Ellen Glasgow*. Doubleday, Doran, & Company, 1928.
Marjorie Kinnan Rawlings Papers, Special and Area Studies Collections, George A. Smathers Libraries, University of Florida, Gainesville, Florida.
Matthews, Pamela. *Ellen Glasgow and a Woman's Traditions*. University Press of Virginia, 1994.
———, editor. *Perfect Companionship: Ellen Glasgow's Selected Correspondence with Women*. University of Virginia Press, 2005.

McCole, John D. *Lucifer at Large*. Longmans, Green & Co., 1937.
Papers of Ellen Glasgow, Accession #5060, Special Collections, University of Virginia Library, Charlottesville, Virginia.
Parker, Idella, Bud Crussell, and Liz Crussell. *Idella Parker: From Reddick to Cross Creek*. University Press of Florida, 1999.
Poole, Leslie Kemp. *Saving Florida: Women's Fight for the Environment in the Twentieth Century*. University Press of Florida, 2015.
Prenshaw, Peggy Whitman. *Composing Selves: Southern Women and Autobiography*. Louisiana State University Press, 2011.
Raper, Julius Rowan, editor. *Ellen Glasgow's Reasonable Doubts: A Collection of Her Writings*. Louisiana State University Press, 1988.
Rawlings, Marjorie Kinnan. *Blood of My Blood*. University Press of Florida, 2002.
———. *Cross Creek*. Charles Scribner's Sons, 1942.
———. *Cross Creek Cookery*. Charles Scribner's Sons, 1942.
———. *Golden Apples*. Charles Scribner's Sons, 1935.
———. *The Secret River*. Charles Scribner's Sons, 1955.
———. *Short Stories by Marjorie Kinnan Rawlings*. Edited by Rodger L. Tarr, University Press of Florida, 1994.
———. *The Sojourner*. Charles Scribner's Sons, 1953.
———. *South Moon Under*. Charles Scribner's Sons, 1933.
———. *The Yearling*. Charles Scribner's Sons, 1938.
Reiger, Christopher. "Don't Fence Me In: Nature and Gender in Marjorie Kinnan Rawlings's *South Moon Under*." *The Mississippi Quarterly*, vol. 57, no. 2, Spring 2004, pp. 199–214.
Ribblett, David L. "From Cross Creek to Richmond: Marjorie Kinnan Rawlings Researches Ellen Glasgow." *Virginia Calvacade*, vol. 36, no. 1, Summer 1986, pp. 4–15.
Rouse, Blair, editor. *Letters of Ellen Glasgow*. Harcourt, Brace and Company, 1958.
Scura, Dorothy M., editor. *Ellen Glasgow: New Perspectives*. University of Tennessee Press, 1995.
Sherman, Stuart P., Sara Haardt, and Emily Clark. *Ellen Glasgow: Critical Essays*. Doubleday, Doran & Company, Inc., 1929.
Silverthorne, Elizabeth. *Marjorie Kinnan Rawlings: Sojourner at Cross Creek*. Overlook Press, 1988.
Tarr, Rodger L., editor. *Max and Marjorie: The Correspondence between Maxwell E. Perkins and Marjorie Kinnan Rawlings*. University Press of Florida, 1999.
———, editor. *The Private Marjorie: The Love Letters of Marjorie Kinnan Rawlings to Norton Baskin*. University Press of Florida, 2004.
———, editor. *Short Stories by Marjorie Kinnan Rawlings*. University Press of Florida, 1994.
Tarr, Rodger L., and Brent E. Kinser, editors. *The Uncollected Writings of Marjorie Kinnan Rawlings*. University Press of Florida, 2007.

Thiébaux, Marcelle. *Ellen Glasgow*. Frederick Ungar Publishing Co., 1982.
Van Vechten, Carl. "A Virginia Lady Dissects a Virginia Gentleman." *Ellen Glasgow*, edited by Dorothea Lawrance Mann, Doubleday, Doran, & Company, 1928, pp. 39–42.
Walker, Alice. *In Search of Our Mother's Gardens*. Harcourt, Inc., 1983.
Woolf, Virginia. *A Room of One's Own*. Harcourt Brace & Company, 1929.

Index

Page numbers in *italics* refer to illustrations.

"Abe Traphagen's Farm" (Rawlings), 129
Adventures of Huckleberry Finn (Twain), 63, 163
American Academy of Arts and Letters, 44
American Association of University Women, 216
"An American Citizen" (Anderson), 185, 187
American Field Service, 21, 108, 183
Anderson, Henry, *103*, 190; and American Red Cross, 180–81, 190; and Arthur Glasgow, 187; and Ellen Glasgow, 17, 35–36, 41, 107, 127, 167, 172, 174, 179–83, 185–92, 194; and politics, 127–28, 185, 187, 223; and Queen Marie, 25, 180–81, 190, 232n20; and race relations, 214–15; and Rawlings, 29, 186–91, 204; and religion, 127; and views of women, 188–89, 204
Anderson, James (cook), 30–31, 35, 116, 215
Association for the Preservation of Virginia Antiquities, 28, 216
The Atlanta Journal, 12
Austen, Jane, 48, 87, 203

Bailey, Pearce, 171
Balzac, Honoré de, 71
Bartram, William, 222
Baskin, Norton, *105*; and Arthur Kinnan, 93–99; and *Blood of My Blood*, 174; and Castle Warden Hotel, 12, 17, 21, 26, 107, 184; and Rawlings, 3, 6, 21, 42, 56, 73, 80, 92–98, 107, 110–11, 115, 117, 149–50, 179–80, 182–85, 189, 218, 228; service in WWII, 21, 25–26, 52, 94, 96, 107–10, 180, 183, 185
Behn, Aphra, 226
"Bells of Heaven" (Hodgson), 114
Bennett, Anne Virginia (secretary-companion), 24, 28–31, 33–36, 38, 41–42, 88, 90, 114–21, 130, 182, 186, 190–94, 216, 229, 235n32
Berg, Norman, 54–55, 132
Bhagavad Gita, 14
Bigham, Julia Scribner, 18, 73, 174, 228
Bloom, Harold, 227
Bogardus, Dominie, 72
Boies, Elizabeth, 206
The Book of Knowledge Annual (McLoughlin, ed.), 66
Book of the Month Club, 46, 59, 213
Boyd, James, 47
Brandt, Carl, 144
Brickell, Herschel, 194
Brooks, Van Wyck, 61–62, 64–65, 108
Brown, Dr. Alexander., Jr., 32, 40–41

Cabell, James Branch, 5, 13, 17–19, 21, 23, 35–40, 42, 46–48, 50, 53–54, 61, 112, 124, 134, 170, 188, 192, 201, 227, 232n6, 232n12
Cabell, Margaret Freeman, 38, 188
Caldwell, Erskine, 57, 140
Canby, Henry Seidel, 133, 213
Caruthers, William Alexander, 135
Cason, Zelma, 93–94, 96, 141
Castine, Maine, 14, 18, 21, 25, 30, 38, 42, 110
Castle Warden Hotel, 12, 17, 21, 23, 26, 51, 107, 117, 184

· 245

Cather, Willa, 37, 54, 62, 133, 207
Children of God (Fisher), 127
Civil War, 16, 61, 71, 75, 135, 138–39, 149, 223
Colcorton (Pope), 23
College of William and Mary, 37, 192
Collier, Price, 198
Cooper, Reverend Bertram C., 195
Cosmopolitan, 144, 150
Crescent Beach, 12, 13, 18, 21–22, 67, 110, 183–84, 200
Cross Creek, 12–13, 21, 24–25, 31, 46, 51, 67, 71, 93, 104, 110–11, 113, 118, 122, 143, 176, 179, 182–83, 200, 209–13, 217–18, 220, 228
Crossing the Creek: The Literary Friendship of Zora Neale Hurston and Marjorie Kinnan Rawlings (Lillios), 60, 92, 218, 228–29
Curtis, Holbrook, 171, 193

Darwin, Charles, 63, 83
Dashiell, Alfred S., 142
Dashiell, Margaret, 115, 117–18
Davenport, Marcia, 201
Dickens, Charles, 121
Dillard, Barney, 154
Douglas, Marjory Stoneman, 125
Dreiser, Theodore, 54, 133
Duke, Carrie Coleman, 28, 34–35, 42, 84, 87, 90, 187, 190, 192–94, 229

Edgeworth, Maria, 87
Egly, William H., 61
"Ellen Glasgow" (Clark), 203, 217
"Ellen Glasgow" (Mann), 202, 215, 219
"Ellen Glasgow: Idealist" (Freeman), 219
Ellen Glasgow and a Woman's Tradition (Matthews), 170, 172, 172–73, 195, 214
Ellen Glasgow Newsletter, 172
European Morals and Rationalism in Europe (Lecky), 77
Everglades National Park, 125
The Everglades: River of Grass (Douglas), 125

Faulkner, William, 56–57, 137, 140, 146
Ferdinand I, King of Romania, 181
The First Gentlemen of America (Cabell), 23

Fisk University, 212
Fitzgerald, F. Scott, 6, 18, 150, 154, 201
Five O'Clock, 74
Flaubert, Gustave, 63, 71
Florida Southern College, 29
Flush (Woolf), 121
Foucault, Michel, 220
Foyers des Alliées, 206
Freeman, Douglas Southall, 35, 56, 112, 127, 140, 219
Freud, Sigmund, 195
Friendship and Sympathy: Communities of Southern Women Writers (Magee), 4–5, 232n7
Frontier Eden (Bigelow), 114
Frost, Robert, 201

Galsworthy, John, 126
Geismar, Maxwell, 55
Gellhorn, Martha, 184
Gerald B—, 169–73, 178–79, 185, 192–93, 205
Glasgow, Anne Gholson (mother), 72, 74–78, 80, 84, 86
Glasgow, Arthur (brother), 22, 27–28, 35, 38, 42, 62, 71, 76, 80, 83–84, 86–91, 96, 100, 120–21, 185, 187
Glasgow, Cary. *See* McCormack, Cary Glasgow
Glasgow, Ellen, *102*; and alcohol, 29–31, 40–41, 106, 116, 122; and animals, 34, 37, 42, 71, 78, 108, 111–23, 130, 195; critical reception, 132–36, 139, 141, 146–47, 154, 162, 165, 199, 201; deafness, 28, 35–36, 40–41, 84, 90–91, 107, 119, 166, 168–70, 186, 190, 193; death, 41–42, 209; and disability studies, 214; and economically disadvantaged, 125–26, 138, 186, 208, 219–24; finances, 27, 37, 91, 185, 201, 208; and food, 29–31; health problems, 15, 21–22, 40–41, 50, 53, 192–93; humor, 40–41, 115, 183, 186, 188; letters to Rawlings, 4, 18–19, 48, 51–52, 54; and Marxism, 221, 223; and mysticism, 14–15, 20, 55, 114, 123, 166, 170, 229; and narrative structure, 159; political views, 127–28, 180, 223–24; and race relations, 30, 75, 112, 202,

208–11, 214–17, 221, 223; and realism, 52, 55, 60, 63, 67, 134–40, 147–48, 157–59, 221, 227; regionalism, 54, 134–38, 140, 146–47, 155, 157–58, 162, 165, 227; and religion, 31–32, 57, 114, 120, 126–27, 170, 181; romantic relationships, 149, 166–74, 178–96, 205; and servants, 216–17; and sexism, 7, 127, 138, 146–49, 188, 194, 198–99, 201–2; sexual assault, 7, 198; sexuality, 14, 33, 112–13, 119, 171–73, 186, 191–95, 205, 207, 227, 232n6; and smoking, 40; and the Southern gothic, 140, 220; suicide attempt, 41, 181, 186, 232n20; travel, 27–28, 86–87, 107, 119–20, 123, 125–26, 166, 170–73, 192–93, 196; and Victorian period, 14, 57, 72, 149, 159, 168, 197, 199; and women's issues, 113, 171, 197–205, 224–25; and women's suffrage, 57, 197, 202, 204–5, 224–25; writing process, 2, 19, 31, 33, 38, 45, 48–49, 51–53, 65–69, 136, 226, 229–30
Glasgow, Ellen, works by:
—autobiography: *The Woman Within*, 3, 10, 19–20, 30, 35, 55, 70, 75–76, 90, 138, 155, 166, 168–70, 181, 185, 205, 208, 229, 231n1
—criticism: *A Certain Measure*, 17, 19, 37–39, 44, 49, 51, 56, 59, 127, 229, 231n1, 232n5
—miscellaneous writings: "Feminism," 204–5; "The Novel in the South," 135, 221; "One Way to Write Novels," 68; "What I Believe," 221–22
—novels: *Barren Ground*, 37, 61–62, 81, 88, 113, 134, 141, 148, 156–57, 159, 178, 199, 202–3, 210–11, 214, 219–20; *The Battle-Ground*, 62, 136, 202; *Beyond Defeat*, 3, 50, 199, 226, 231n1; *The Builders*, 127, 187, 202; *The Deliverance*, 66, 217, 219; *The Descendant*, 7, 55, 83, 146, 155–56, 159, 199, 221, 223; film adaptation, 24, 214, 231n1; *In This Our Life*, 3–4, 19–20, 37, 44, 48, 50–51, 55, 89, 141, 199, 214; *Life and Gabriella*, 45, 158–59; *The Miller of Old Church*, 84, 173; *One Man in His Time*, 187, 189; *The Romantic Comedians*, 63–64, 202; *Sharp Realities*, 198; *The Sheltered Life*, 19, 55, 78, 136, 139, 141, 166–68, 214; *Vein of Iron*, 56, 60, 62, 113, 127, 133, 147, 173, 207, 219; *Virginia*, 74, 78–79, 89, 139, 141, 159, 202, 209; *The Voice of the People*, 37, 148; *Wheel of Life*, 173
—poetry: "The Call," 224; "A Creed," 114; *The Freeman and Other Poems*, 231n1, 235n45; "A Plea," 114
—short stories: *The Shadowy Third*, 34, 220, 231n1; "A Woman of To-Morrow," 197, 199
Glasgow, Emily. *See* Houston, Emily Glasgow
Glasgow, Francis (father), 32, 34, 38, 73, 75–80, 82, 88, 91, 118, 178, 209
Glasgow, Frank (brother), 76–77, 91, 170, 235n2
Glasgow, Margaret (sister-in-law), 121
Glasgow, Rebe. *See* Tutwiler, Rebe Glasgow
Glasgow House. *See* One West Main
Godbold, Stanly, 15–17, 170–71, 232n6
Goethe, Johann Wolfgang von, 181
Gone with the Wind (Mitchell), 146
Goodman, Susan, 17, 76, 135, 146, 171 72, 178, 199
Graham-Bertolini, Alison, 143
Great Depression, 1, 59, 123
Green Mansions (Hudson), 126

Haardt, Sara, 57
Hall, Radclyffe, 18, 62, 207, 227, 235n32
Hanna, A. J., 23, 112, 124
Harde, Roxanne, 220
Hardy, Thomas, 54, 62–63, 121, 141, 145–46, 152, 203, 219
Harold S——. *See* Anderson, Henry
Harper & Brothers, 199
Hemingway, Ernest, 18, 54, 184, 201
Herrick, Robert, 47, 179, 201
Holmes, George Frederick, 7
Houston, Emily Glasgow (sister), 34, 86
Howells, William Dean, 158
Howland, Hewitt Hanson, 171–72
Hugo, Victor, 199
Humane Society, 120, 123
Hurston, Zora Neale, 60, 207, 217–18, 226

Index · 247

"The Idealist" (Freeman), 140
Idella Parker: From Reddick to Cross Creek (Parker), 213
Ileana, Princess of Romania, 181, 191
In Search of Our Mothers' Gardens (Walker), 226
Institute for Fiction, Gold Medal, 54, 133
Island Grove, 213

James, Henry, 63
Jefferson, Thomas, 62
Jerdone Castle, 70, 76
Johnson, Charles S., 212
Johnston, Mary, 32–33, 122, 204, 227
Jones, Lizzie, 216
Jurgen (Cabell), 17

Kinnan, Arthur, Sr. (father), 71–72, 79–83, 93, 175
Kinnan, Arthur, Jr., (brother), 74, 83, 91–100, 185, 212, 228
Kinnan, Asahel Simeon, 72
Kinnan, Barbara (niece), 94, 100
Kinnan, Ida May Traphagen (mother), 71, 73–74, 82–83, 97, 174–76, 228
Kinnan, Jeff (nephew), 97–99
Kinnan, Marjorie Lou (niece), 94
Kinnan, Mary, 72
Kinnan, Wilmer (aunt), 54, 132, 229

Ladies Home Journal, 174
La Follette, Robert M., 72
Lange, Otto, 96, 179
"The Last Cry of Romance" (Cabell), 61, 134
Levy, Helen, 199
Lewis, Sinclair, 54, 133
Lincoln, Abraham, 63
"Little Things" (Stephens), 130
Louisville Courier-Journal, 74, 207
Lucifer at Large (McCole), 59, 133
"Lycidas" (Milton), 42
Lyons, Clifford, 26–27, 232n24, 233n25

MacDonald, Edgar, 17, 26
Macmillan, 7, 198

Makowsky, Veronica, 203
Mann, Dorothea Lawrance, 148–49, 201–2, 215, 219
Marie, Queen of Romania, 25, 180–81, 190–91, 232n20
Marineland, 117, 184
Marjorie Kinnan Rawlings Historic State Park, 46, 124
Marjorie Kinnan Rawlings Rose, 28–29
Marx, Karl, 221, 223
Matthews, Pamela, 14
Maupassant, Guy de, 63
May, Phil, 230
McCormack, Cary Glasgow (sister), 28, 34, 83–85, 170, 190, 194, 198, 217
McCormack, George Walter (brother-in-law), 83, 223
McNeil, Beatrice Humiston, 179, 228
Mencken, H. L., 151
Meredith, George, 60
Mickens, Martha, 111, 209–10
Mill, John Stuart, 83, 223
Milne, Caleb, 109
Mims, Edward, 61–62, 64, 90
Mitchell, Margaret, 146, 201, 228
Modern Language Association, 45, 65, 141
Morley, Frank, 29, 35
Moulton, Louise Chandler, 173
Mulhern, Mr., 193–94
Mumford, Mr., 192
Munford, Lizzie, 41, 70
"My Fellow Virginians" (Anderson), 223

National Academy of Arts and Letters, 193
National Council of Teachers of English, 3, 54, 145, 231n3
National Institute of Social Sciences, Presentation Medal, 45
New Republic, 200
New York City, 1, 5, 7, 9, 12, 21, 40, 50, 54, 74, 81, 83–86, 107, 123, 145, 155–59, 168, 171, 193–94, 198, 200, 204, 206–7, 213, 224, 228
New York Herald Tribune, 45, 112, 133, 141, 152, 172, 193, 213
New York Times Book Review, 56, 65, 108

Nobel Prize, 59, 133
Norwood, Robert, 32
"Notes on the Breeding of the Ground Dove in Florida" (Nicholson), 112

Ocala Evening Star, 128, 151, 222
O'Connor, Flannery, 140
Office of Censorship, 214
O. Henry Prize, 67
One West Main, 28–30, 63, 71, 88, *101*, 122, 159, 187, 216

Page, Thomas Nelson, 62
Page, Walter Hines, 171
Paradise, Frank, 178–79, 192
Parker, Idella, 30, 213, 217
Patton, Mr., 7, 199
Peck, Gregory, 24
Perfect Companionship: Ellen Glasgow's Selected Correspondence with Women (Matthews), 4–6, 170, 227–28, 232n8
Perkins, Maxwell, 3, 6, 14, 16, 18–19, 48, 49–50, 54, 65, 92, 96, 144, 150–53, 155, 160, 163–64, 177, 200–201, 228, 231n4, 232n5
Phi Beta Kappa, 190
Pledge for Peace Committee, 212
Pope, Edith, 18, 23, 33, 115, 201, 228
Porter, William (physician), 118–19, 195
Portrait of the Artist as a Young Man (Joyce), 171
Prenshaw, Peggy, 15
Prescott, Dessie Smith Vinson, 129, 176, 228
The Private Marjorie (Tarr), 97, 182
Proust, Marcel, 63, 169
Pulitzer Prize, 3, 16, 23, 44, 54, 141, 214, 239n6

Queenborough, 21, 60

Rainwater, Catherine, 113
Rascoe, Burton, 122, 201
Rawlings, Charles ("Chuck"), 16, 32, 74, 142, 149, 163, 175–77, 179, 182, 184, 194, 231n4
Rawlings, Marjorie Kinnan, *105*; and alcohol, 29–30, 98, 106, 122, 163, 175, 177, 183, 194, 201, 211, 213; and animals, 110–13, 115,
117–18, 121, 123, 125, 230; and conservation efforts, 112, 123–25, 130–31; cosmic themes, 153; critical reception, 136–37, 151–53, 155, 162, 165, 222; death, 42, 230; dream of Glasgow, 4, 5, 13–18, 19–20, 70, 165, 229; and farming, 161, 163; finances, 185; and Florida Cracker community, 8, 18, 58–60, 67, 122, 126, 128–29, 130–31, 137, 140–41, 143–44, 151–55, 200, 218, 220–22; and food, 29–31, 129–30, 161, 200; and gender, 149–51, 200–201, 203–4, 228; health problems, 13, 15, 22, 42, 50, 182; humor, 109–10, 113, 115, 150, 155, 162, 182–83; hunting, 92–93, 118, 121, 124, 143, 163, 200–201; invasion of privacy trial, 141–42, 236n28; journalism, 72, 83, 142, 200, 204, 207; and juvenilia, 137, 144–45, 162–64; letters to Glasgow, 2, 13–18, 20–21, 23–24, 52–53, 112, 165, 229, 239n6; letters to servicemen, 26, 107, 109–10, 151, 200; and mysticism, 32, 114, 196, 228–29; and Prohibition, 211; and race relations, 128, 207–14, 217–18, 228; and regionalism, 15, 66, 137, 140–41, 144–46, 154–55, 160, 162, 165; and religion, 32, 127; romantic relationships, 149–50, 167, 174–77, 179–80, 182–85, 195–96; and servants, 217, 228; and sexuality, 96, 113, 168, 174–75, 201; and women's issues, 205–7; and women's suffrage, 205; writing process, 31, 48–49, 51–53, 65–67, 136, 184, 226, 230
Rawlings, Marjorie Kinnan, works by:
—book for children: *The Secret River*, 15
—cookbook: *Cross Creek Cookery*, 31, 115, 123, 129, 151, 161, 200
—memoir: *Cross Creek*, 4, 15, 22–23, 46, 49–52, 59, 63–64, 94, 96, 111, 129, 138, 140–41, 143, 161, 176, 183, 209–12, 218, 220, 230
—miscellaneous writings: "The Blue Triangle Follows the Switchboard," 206; "A Family for Jock," *Lassie* screenplay, 163; "Fanny—You Fool!," 203; "Florida: An Affectionate Tribute," 125; "Florida: A Land of Contrasts," 124, 222; "Here is Fun for Girls," 206; "I Sing While I Cook," 129;

Rawlings, Marjorie Kinnan—*continued*
"Live Women in Live Louisville," 200, 207; "[The Old Order Hath Changed]," 205–6; "Regional Literature of the South," 145; "Songs of the Housewife," 72, 200; "Through Three Revolutions," 206; "Trees for Tomorrow," 123; "Women as Constructionists," 206
—novels: biblical references in, 63, 70; *Blood of My Blood*, 8, 70, 73, 82–83, 91, 160, 174–75, 200, 209; film adaptation, 24, 163; *Golden Apples*, 28, 59, 144, 150, 152, 155, 160, 220; *The Sojourner*, 4, 52, 54–56, 59, 63, 70, 81, 94–96, 99–100, 110–11, 129, 141, 145, 159–62, 203–4, 229; *South Moon Under*, 1, 45–46, 57–59, 65, 80, 143–44, 153–55, 163–64, 176, 204, 221, 231n4; *The Yearling*, 2–3, 12, 19, 20, 44–46, 49–51, 55, 57, 59, 61–64, 80, 106, 115, 122, 138, 144, 150, 163–64, 168, 198, 204, 207
—poetry: "Having Left Cities behind Me," 130; "Sacred and Profane Love," 195–96
—short stories: "Black Secret," 209; "Cracker Chidlings," 128–29, 142, 151, 222; "Gal Young Un," 67, 149, 204; "Jacob's Ladder," 143, 168, 204, 220; "Jessamyn Springs," 127; "A Mother in Mannville," 97, 163; "The Pardon," 47
Ribblett, David, 26
Richmond-Times Dispatch, 108, 116, 123
Richmond, Virginia, 12, 16–18, 21–22, 31, 46, 48, 55, 70, 113, 115–16, 122–23, 127, 132, 159, 168, 172, 180–81, 186–88, 194–95, 214, 216–17, 229; Evergreen Cemetery, 216; Hollywood Cemetery, 36, 117, 120; SPCA, 3, 35, 41, 88–89, 94, 106, 112–16, 119
"A River that Flows through Florida History" (Cabell and Hanna), 124
Rives, Amélie, 18
Rochester, New York, 72, 74, 99, 114, 131, 142, 200
"A Room of One's Own" (Woolf), 148

Saturday Evening Post, 140, 141
Saunders, Frances W., 172

Saving Florida: Women's Fight for the Environment in the Twentieth Century (Poole), 123
Sawaya, Francesca, 56
Scribner's Magazine, 8, 47, 130, 142, 151, 200, 222
Scrivenor, Lucy, 40–41, 190
Selby, John, 123
Sherman, Stuart, 64
Signal Corps, 206
Silverthorne, Elizabeth, 179
Sinclair, May, 121
"The Solid South" (Anderson), 215
"Some Literary Woman Myths" (Cabell), 18
Something About Eve (Cabell), 38, 232n12
Southern Writers Conference, 45, 134–35, 141
St. Augustine, 12, 17–18, 21, 23, 25, 53, 124, 184, 213
Steinbeck, John, 63
St. Johns River, 23, 112, 129, 176, 228

Tarpon Springs, Florida, 176
Tate, Allen, 5
There Were Two Pirates (Cabell), 232n12
Thiébaux, Marcelle, 17
Toksvig, Signe, 18, 200, 207, 227–28
Tompkins, Dr., 40, 42
Traphagen, Abram "Abe" (grandfather), 72, 81, 129, 160–62
Traphagen, Francis "Fanny" (grandmother), 72, 81, 160–62, 203
Travers, William Riggin, 172
Treasure Island (Kipling), 163
Tredegar Ironworks, 71, 78, 80, 91, 118
Trigg, Emma, 32
Troubridge, Una, 207
Truman, Harry S., 125
Tutwiler, Carrington, Sr. (brother-in-law), 84, 178
Tutwiler, Carrington, Jr. (nephew), 63, 78, 84
Tutwiler, Rebe Glasgow (sister), 28, 76–78, 83–86, 88–91, 100, 108–9, 113, 115–16, 118–19, 122–23, 126, 171, 178, 190–93, 195, 215–17

University of Florida, 179
University of Virginia, 7–8, 83, 166
University of Wisconsin-Madison, 5, 8, 12, 72, 92, 109, 142, 167, 175, 179, 204, 208, 228
University Publishing Company, 198
U.S. Patent Office, 80, 142

Valentine, Herbert, 172
Van Doren, Irita, 1, 26, 28–31, 35–38, 40, 45, 75, 78, 117, 119, 140, 172, 195
Van Gelder, Robert, 63
Van Hornesville, New York, 12, 145, 160, 183
Van Vechten, Carl, 29, 40, 63
Vinson, Dessie Smith. *See* Prescott, Dessie Smith Vinson
Virginia Military Institute, 91
Vogue, 161–62

Walden (Thoreau), 63
Walker, Alice, 218, 226
Walker, Nancy, 171
Washington and Lee University, 185
Washington, D.C., 12, 70, 142, 208

Wellford, Roberta, 34–35, 39–41, 83–84, 119, 190, 192, 194, 216
Wells, H.G., 29
Welty, Eudora, 140
West, Anthony and Rebecca, 29
Wharton, Edith, 147
White Sulfur Springs, 117–18
Willcox, Louise Collier, 7, 178
Williamsburg, Virginia, 30
Williams, Frances (cousin), 56, 119, 123, 125
Williams, Maude, 29, 34–35, 188–91
Wolfe, Thomas, 201
Woolf, Virginia, 121, 148, 226–27
Wordsworth, Dorothy, 57
World War I, 25, 61, 107, 109–10, 120, 127–28, 180–81, 185, 187, 191, 205–7
World War II, 21, 24, 25–26, 39, 52, 89, 93–94, 96, 106–11, 123, 128, 145, 164, 180, 183, 185, 214
Writers War Board, 212
Wylie, Elinor, 29

YWCA, 74, 200, 206

ASHLEY ANDREWS LEAR is professor of the humanities at Embry-Riddle Aeronautical University. Her work has appeared in the *Journal of Florida Literature*, the *Ellen Glasgow Journal of Southern Women's Literature*, *Writing and the Digital Generation*, and the College English Association's *Forum*. She is a proud trustee of the Marjorie Kinnan Rawlings Society.

www.ingramcontent.com/pod-product-compliance
Lightning Source LLC
Chambersburg PA
CBHW030729150426
42813CB00051B/352